Collins easy learning

Spanish
Verbs

¿Fuiste tú el
que llamó?

*Estoy muy
cansado.*

Published by Collins
An imprint of HarperCollins Publishers
Westerhill Road
Bishopbriggs
Glasgow G64 2QT

Third edition 2016

ISBN 978-0-00-815843-9

10 9 8 7 6 5 4 3 2 1

© HarperCollins Publishers 2005, 2011, 2016

www.collinsdictionary.com
www.collins.co.uk/languagesupport

Typeset by Davidson Publishing Solutions,
Glasgow

Printed in Italy by GRAFICA VENETA S.p.A.

A catalogue record for this book is available
from the British Library.

If you would like to comment on any aspect
of this book, please contact us at the given
address or online.
E-mail: dictionaries@harpercollins.co.uk
◨ www.facebook.com/collinsdictionary
◨ @collinsdict

Acknowledgements

We would like to thank those authors
and publishers who kindly gave permission
for copyright material to be used in the
Collins Corpus. We would also like to
thank Times Newspapers Ltd for providing
valuable data.

MANAGING EDITOR
Maree Airlie

CONTRIBUTORS
Cordelia Lilly
Maggie Seaton
Eduardo Vallejo

FOR THE PUBLISHER
Gerry Breslin
Craig Balfour

Contents

Introduction

The *Easy Learning Spanish Verbs* is designed for both young and adult learners. Whether you are starting to learn Spanish for the very first time, brushing up your language skills or revising for exams, the *Easy Learning Spanish Verbs* and its companion volume, the *Easy Learning Spanish Grammar*, are here to help.

Newcomers can sometimes struggle with the technical terms they come across when they start to explore the grammar of a new language. The *Easy Learning Spanish Verbs* contains a glossary which explains verb grammar terms using simple language and cutting out jargon.

The text is divided into sections to help you become confident in using and understanding Spanish verbs. The first section looks at verb formation. Written in clear language, with numerous examples in real Spanish, this section helps you to understand the rules which are used to form verb tenses.

The next section of text looks at certain common prepositions which are used with a number of verbs. Each combination of verb plus preposition is shown with a simple example of real Spanish to show exactly how it is used.

The **Verb Tables** contain 120 important Spanish verbs (both regular and irregular) which are given in full for various tenses. Examples show how to use these verbs in your own work. If you are unsure how a verb goes in Spanish, you can look up the Verb Index at the back of the book to find either the conjugation of the verb itself, or a cross-reference to a model verb, which will show you the patterns that the verb follows.

The *Easy Learning Spanish Grammar* takes you a step further in your language learning. It supplements the information given in the *Easy Learning Spanish Verbs* by offering even more guidance on the usage and meaning of verbs, as well as looking at the most important aspects of Spanish grammar. Together, or individually, the *Easy Learning* titles offer you all the help you need when learning Spanish.

6 Glossary

Glossary of Verb Grammar Terms

ACTIVE a form of the verb that is used when the subject of the verb is the person or thing doing the action, for example, *I wrote a letter*. Compare with **passive**.

AFFIRMATIVE an affirmative sentence or instruction is one that does not contain a negative word such as *not*. Compare with **negative**.

AGREE (to) in the case of verbs, to have the form which goes with the person or thing carrying out the action.

AUXILIARY VERB a verb such as *be*, *have* or *do* used with a main verb to form tenses.

BASE FORM the form of the verb without any endings added to it, for example, *walk*, *have*, *be*, *go*.

CLAUSE a group of words containing a verb.

CONDITIONAL a verb form used to talk about things that *would* happen or *would* be true under certain conditions, for example, *I would help you if I could*. It is also used to say what you *would* like or need, for example, *Could you give me the bill?*

CONJUGATE (to) to give a verb different endings according to whether you are referring to *I*, *you*, *they* and so on, and according to whether you are referring to the present, past or future, for example, *I have*, *she had*, *they will have*.

CONJUGATION a group of verbs which have the same endings as each other or change according to the same pattern.

CONTINUOUS TENSE a verb tense formed using *to be* and the *-ing* form of the main verb, for example, *They're swimming* (present continuous); *He was eating* (past continuous).

DIRECT OBJECT a noun or pronoun used with verbs to show who or what is acted on by the verb. For example, in *He wrote a letter* and *He wrote me a letter*, *letter* is the direct object. Compare **indirect object**.

DIRECT OBJECT PRONOUN a word such as *me*, *him*, *us* and *them* which is used instead of a noun to stand in for the person or thing most directly affected by the action expressed by the verb. Compare with **indirect object pronoun**.

ENDING a form added to something such as a verb, for example, *go > goes*.

FUTURE a verb tense used to talk about something that *will* happen or *will* be true.

GERUND a verb form in English ending in *-ing*, for example, *eating*, *sleeping*.

IMPERATIVE the form of a verb used when giving orders and instructions, for example, *Shut the door!*; *Sit down!*; *Don't go!*; *Let's eat*.

IMPERFECT one of the verb tenses used to talk about the past in Spanish, especially in descriptions, and to say what *was happening* or *used to happen*, for example, *It was sunny at the weekend; We were living in Spain at the time; I used to walk to school.* Compare with **preterite**.

IMPERSONAL VERB a verb whose subject is *it*, but where the *it* does not refer to any specific thing, for example, *It's raining; It's 10 o'clock.*

INDICATIVE ordinary verb forms that aren't subjunctive, such as the present, preterite or future. Compare with **subjunctive**.

INDIRECT OBJECT a noun or pronoun used with verbs to show who benefits or is harmed by an action. For example, in *I gave the carrot to the rabbit*, *the rabbit* is the indirect object and *the carrot* is the direct object. Compare with **direct object**.

INDIRECT OBJECT PRONOUN a pronoun used with verbs to show who benefits or is harmed by an action. For example, in *I gave him the carrot* and *I gave it to him*, *him* is the indirect object and *the carrot* and *it* are the direct objects. Compare with **direct object pronoun**.

INDIRECT SPEECH the words you use to report what someone has said when you aren't using their actual words, for example, *He said that he was going out.* Also called **reported speech**.

INFINITIVE a form of the verb that hasn't any endings added to it and doesn't relate to any particular tense. In English the infinitive is usually shown with *to*, as in *to speak, to eat.*

INTRANSITIVE VERB a type of verb that does not take a direct object, for example, *to sleep, to rise, to laugh.* Compare with **transitive verb**.

IRREGULAR VERB a verb whose forms do not follow a general pattern. Compare with **regular verb**.

NEGATIVE a question or statement which contains a word such as *not, never* or *nothing*, and is used to say that something is not happening, is not true or is absent, for example, *I never eat meat; Don't you love me?* Compare with **positive**.

OBJECT a noun or pronoun which refers to a person or thing that is affected by the action described by the verb. Compare with **direct object**, **indirect object** and **subject**.

OBJECT PRONOUN one of the set of pronouns including *me, him* and *them*, which are used instead of the noun as the object of a verb or preposition. Compare with **subject pronoun**.

PASSIVE a form of the verb that is used when the subject of the verb is the person or thing that is affected by the action, for example, *We were told* or *It was sold.*

8 Glossary

PAST PARTICIPLE a verb form which is used to form perfect and pluperfect tenses and passives, for example, *watched, swum*. Some past participles are also used as adjectives, for example, *a broken watch*.

PAST PERFECT see pluperfect.

PERFECT a verb form used to talk about what *has* or *hasn't* happened, for example, *I've broken my glasses; We haven't eaten yet.*

PERSON one of three classes: the first person (*I*, *we*), the second person (*you* singular and *you* plural), and the third person (*he, she, it* and *they*).

PERSONAL PRONOUN one of the group of words including *I*, *you* and *they* which are used to refer to you, the people you are talking to, or the people or things you are talking about.

PLUPERFECT one of the verb tenses used to describe something that *had* happened or *had* been true at a point in the past, for example, *I'd forgotten to finish my homework*. Also called **past perfect**.

PLURAL the form of a word which is used to refer to more than one person or thing. Compare with **singular**.

POSITIVE a positive sentence or instruction is one that does not contain a negative word such as *not*. Compare with **negative**.

PREPOSITION is a word such as *at, for, with, into* or *from*, which is usually followed by a noun, pronoun or, in English, a word ending in *-ing*. Prepositions show how people and things relate to the rest of the sentence, for example, *She's at home; a tool for cutting grass; It's from David.*

PRESENT a verb form used to talk about what is true at the moment, what happens regularly, and what is happening now, for example, *I'm a student; I travel to college by train; I'm studying languages.*

PRESENT CONTINUOUS see continuous tense.

PRESENT PARTICIPLE a verb form in English ending in *-ing*, for example, *eating, sleeping*.

PRESENT SIMPLE see simple tense.

PRETERITE a verb form used to talk about actions that were completed in the past in Spanish. It often corresponds to the ordinary past tense in English, for example, *I bought a new bike; Mary went to the shops; I typed two reports yesterday.*

PRONOUN a word which you use instead of a noun, when you do not need or want to name someone or something directly, for example, *it, you, none.*

PROPER NOUN the name of a person, place, organization or thing. Proper nouns are always written with a capital letter, for example, *Kevin, Glasgow, Europe.*

RADICAL-CHANGING VERBS in Spanish, verbs which change their stem or root in certain tenses and in certain persons.

REFLEXIVE PRONOUN a word ending in -self or -selves, such as myself or themselves, which refers back to the subject, for example, He hurt himself; Take care of yourself.

REFLEXIVE VERB a verb where the subject and object are the same, and where the action 'reflects back' on the subject. A reflexive verb is used with a reflexive pronoun such as myself, yourself, herself, for example, I washed myself; He cut himself.

REGULAR VERB a verb whose forms follow a general pattern or the normal rules. Compare with irregular verb.

SIMPLE TENSE a verb tense in which the verb form is made up of one word, rather than being formed from to have and a past participle or to be and an -ing form; for example, She plays tennis; He wrote a book.

SINGULAR the form of a word which is used to refer to one person or thing. Compare with plural.

STEM the main part of a verb to which endings are added.

SUBJECT a noun or pronoun that refers to the person or thing doing the action or being in the state described by the verb, for example, My cat doesn't drink milk. Compare with object.

SUBJECT PRONOUN a word such as I, he, she and they which carries out the action described by the verb. Pronouns stand in for nouns when it is clear who is being talked about, for example, My brother isn't here at the moment. He'll be back in an hour. Compare with object pronoun.

SUBJUNCTIVE a verb form used in certain circumstances to indicate some sort of feeling, or to show doubt about whether something will happen or whether something is true. It is only used occasionally in modern English, for example, If I were you, I wouldn't bother; So be it.

TENSE the form of a verb which shows whether you are referring to the past, present or future.

TRANSITIVE VERB a type of verb that takes a direct object, for example, to spend, to raise, to waste. Compare with intransitive verb.

VERB a 'doing' word which describes what someone or something does, is, or what happens to them, for example, be, sing, live.

Introduction to Verb Formation

Verbs are frequently used with a noun, with somebody's name or, particularly in English, with a pronoun such as *I*, *you* or *she*. They can relate to the present, the past and the future; this is called their <u>tense</u>.

Verbs are either:

<u>regular</u>; their forms follow the normal rules

<u>irregular</u>; their forms do not follow the normal rules

Almost all verbs have a form called the <u>infinitive</u>. This is a base form of the verb (for example, *walk*, *see*, *hear*) that hasn't had any endings added to it and doesn't relate to any particular tense.

In English, the infinitive is usually shown with *to*, as in *to speak*, *to eat*, *to live*. In Spanish, the infinitive is always made up of just one word (never two as in *to speak* in English) and ends in **-ar**, **-er** or **-ir**: for example, **hab<u>lar</u>** (meaning *to speak*), **com<u>er</u>** (meaning *to eat*) and **viv<u>ir</u>** (meaning *to live*). All Spanish verbs belong to one of these three types, which are called <u>conjugations</u>. We will look at each of these three conjugations in turn on the next few pages.

Regular English verbs have other forms apart from the infinitive: a form ending in -*s* (*walks*), a form ending in -*ing* (*walking*), and a form ending in -*ed* (*walked*). Spanish verbs have many more forms than this, which are made up of endings added to a <u>stem</u>. The stem of a verb can usually be worked out from the infinitive.

Spanish verb endings change depending on who or what is doing the action and on when the action takes place. In fact, the ending is very often the only thing that shows you <u>who</u> is doing the action, as the Spanish equivalents of *I*, *you*, *he* and so on (**yo**, **tú**, **él** and so on) are not used very much. So, both **hablo** on its own and **yo hablo** mean *I speak*. Sometimes there is a name or a noun in the sentence to make it clear who is doing the action.

For further explanation of grammatical terms, please see pages 6–9.

José habla español. José speaks Spanish.

El profesor habla español. The teacher speaks Spanish.

Spanish verb forms also change depending on whether you are talking about the present, past or future, so **(yo) hablaré** means *I will speak* while **(yo) hablé** means *I spoke*.

Some verbs in Spanish do not follow the usual patterns. These <u>irregular verbs</u> include some very common and important verbs like **ir** (meaning *to go*), **ser** and **estar** (meaning *to be*) and **hacer** (meaning *to do* or *to make*). Other verbs are only slightly irregular, changing their stems in certain tenses.

The following sections give you all the help you need on how to form the different verb tenses used in Spanish. If you would like even more information on how Spanish verbs are used, the *Easy Learning Spanish Grammar* shows you when and how numerous different verbs are used when writing and speaking modern Spanish.

The present simple tense

Forming the present simple tense of regular -ar verbs

If the infinitive of the Spanish verb ends in **-ar**, it means that the verb belongs to the <u>first conjugation</u>, for example, **hablar**, **lavar**, **llamar**.

To know which form of the verb to use in Spanish, you need to work out what the stem of the verb is and then add the correct ending. The stem of regular **-ar** verbs in the present simple tense is formed by taking the <u>infinitive</u> and chopping off **-ar**.

Infinitive	Stem (without -ar)
hablar (*to speak*)	habl-
lavar (*to wash*)	lav-

Now you know how to find the stem of a verb you can add the correct ending. The one you choose will depend on who or what is doing the action.

Here are the present simple endings for regular **-ar** verbs:

Present simple endings	Present simple of hablar	Meaning: to *speak*
-o	(yo) habl<u>o</u>	I speak
-as	(tú) habl<u>as</u>	you speak
-a	(él/ella) habl<u>a</u>	he/she/it speaks
	(usted) habl<u>a</u>	you speak
-amos	(nosotros/nosotras) habl<u>amos</u>	we speak
-áis	(vosotros/vosotras) habl<u>áis</u>	you speak
-an	(ellos/ellas) habl<u>an</u>	they speak
	(ustedes) habl<u>an</u>	you speak

Trabaj**o** en un banco. I work in a bank.

No habl**o** alemán. I don't speak German.

¿Busc**as** algo? Are you looking for something?

Compr**a** pan cada día. He/She buys bread every day.

Lydia estudi**a** medicina. Lydia studies *or* is studying medicine.

Funcion**a** bien. It works well.

Viaj**amos** mucho. We travel a lot.

¿Record**áis** aquella noche? Do you remember that night?

Ustedes fabric**an** ventanas, ¿no? You make windows, don't you?

Mis profesores me ayud**an** mucho. My teachers help me a lot.

14 Present Simple

Forming the present simple tense of regular -er verbs

If the infinitive of the Spanish verb ends in -er, it means that the verb belongs to the <u>second conjugation</u>, for example, comer, depender.

The stem of regular -er verbs in the present simple tense is formed by taking the <u>infinitive</u> and chopping off -er.

Infinitive	Stem (without -er)
comer (to eat)	com-
depender (to depend)	depend-

Now add the correct ending, depending on who or what is doing the action.

Here are the present simple endings for regular -er verbs:

Present simple endings	Present simple of comer	Meaning: to eat
-o	(yo) como	I eat
-es	(tú) comes	you eat
-e	(él/ella) come	he/she/it eats
	(usted) come	you eat
-emos	(nosotros/nosotras) comemos	we eat
-éis	(vosotros/vosotras) coméis	you eat
-en	(ellos/ellas) comen	they eat
	(ustedes) comen	you eat

Juan come demasiado. Juan eats too much.
Mis padres me deben 15 euros. My parents owe me 15 euros.
Depende. It depends.

For further explanation of grammatical terms, please see pages 6–9.

Forming the present simple tense of regular -ir verbs

If the infinitive of the Spanish verb ends in -ir, it means that the verb belongs to the third conjugation, for example, vivir, recibir.

The stem of regular -ir verbs in the present simple tense is formed by taking the infinitive and chopping off -ir.

Infinitive	Stem (without -ir)
vivir (to live)	viv-
recibir (to receive)	recib-

Now add the correct ending depending on who or what is doing the action.

Here are the present simple endings for regular -ir verbs:

Present simple endings	Present simple of vivir	Meaning: to live
-o	(yo) vivo	I live
-es	(tú) vives	you live
-e	(él/ella) vive	he/she/it lives
	(usted) vive	you live
-imos	(nosotros/nosotras) vivimos	we live
-ís	(vosotros/vosotras) vivís	you live
-en	(ellos/ellas) viven	they live
	(ustedes) viven	you live

Mi padre recibe muchas cartas. My father gets a lot of letters.

Javier y Antonia viven aquí. Javier and Antonia live here.

Ocurre frecuentemente. It happens frequently.

16 Present Simple

Forming the present simple tense of less regular verbs

Many Spanish verbs do not follow the regular patterns shown previously. There are lots of verbs that change their <u>stem</u> in the present tense when the stress is on the stem. This means that all forms are affected in the present simple <u>apart from</u> the nosotros and vosotros forms. Such verbs are often called <u>radical-changing verbs</u>, meaning root-changing verbs.

For example, some verbs containing an -o in the stem change it to -ue in the present simple for all forms <u>apart from</u> the nosotros/nosotras and vosotros/vosotras forms.

	encontrar *to find*	recordar *to remember*	poder *to be able*	dormir *to sleep*
(yo)	encuentro	recuerdo	puedo	duermo
(tú)	encuentras	recuerdas	puedes	duermes
(él/ella/usted)	encuentra	recuerda	puede	duerme
(nosotros/as)	encontramos	recordamos	podemos	dormimos
(vosotros/as)	encontráis	recordáis	podéis	dormís
(ellos/ellas/ustedes)	encuentran	recuerdan	pueden	duermen

Other verbs containing an -e in the stem change it to -ie for all forms <u>apart from</u> the nosotros/nosotras and vosotros/vosotras forms.

	cerrar *to close*	pensar *to think*	entender *to understand*	perder *to lose*	preferir *to prefer*
(yo)	cierro	pienso	entiendo	pierdo	prefiero
(tú)	cierras	piensas	entiendes	pierdes	prefieres
(él/ella/usted)	cierra	piensa	entiende	pierde	prefiere
(nosotros/as)	cerramos	pensamos	entendemos	perdemos	preferimos
(vosotros/as)	cerráis	pensáis	entendéis	perdéis	preferís
(ellos/ellas/ustedes)	cierran	piensan	entienden	pierden	prefieren

For further explanation of grammatical terms, please see pages 6–9.

A few -ir verbs containing -e in the stem change this to -i in the present simple for all forms <u>apart from</u> the **nosotros/nosotras** and **vosotros/ vosotras** forms.

	pedir *to ask (for)*	**servir** *to serve*
(yo)	pido	sirvo
(tú)	pides	sirves
(él/ella/usted)	pide	sirve
(nosotros/as)	pedimos	servimos
(vosotros/as)	pedís	servís
(ellos/ellas/ustedes)	piden	sirven

The present continuous tense

The Spanish present continuous tense is formed from the <u>present tense</u> of estar and the <u>gerund</u> of the verb. The gerund is the form of the verb that ends in -ando (for -ar verbs) or -iendo (for -er and -ir verbs) and is the same as the -*ing* form of the verb in English (for example, *walking, swimming*).

> <u>Estoy</u> traba<u>jando</u>. I'm working.
> No <u>estamos</u> com<u>iendo</u>. We aren't eating.
> ¿<u>Estás</u> escrib<u>iendo</u>? Are you writing?

To form the gerund of an -ar verb, take off the -ar ending of the infinitive and add -ando:

Infinitive	Meaning	Stem (without -ar)	Gerund	Meaning
hablar	to speak	habl-	hab<u>lando</u>	speaking
trabajar	to work	trabaj-	traba<u>jando</u>	working

> Coge al niño, que <u>está llorando</u>. Pick the baby up; he's crying.
> <u>Está intentando</u> perder peso. He's trying to lose weight.

To form the gerund of an -er or -ir verb, take off the -er or -ir ending of the infinitive and add -iendo:

Infinitive	Meaning	Stem (without -er/-ir)	Gerund	Meaning
comer	to eat	com-	com<u>iendo</u>	eating
escribir	to write	escrib-	escrib<u>iendo</u>	writing

> <u>Estoy haciendo</u> los deberes. I'm doing my homework.
> ¿Qué <u>está ocurriendo</u>? What's happening?

For further explanation of grammatical terms, please see pages 6–9.

The imperative

Forming the imperative: instructions not to do something

In orders that tell you <u>NOT</u> to do something and that have no in front of them in Spanish, the imperative forms for tú, usted, nosotros/nosotras, vosotros/vosotras and ustedes are all taken from a verb form called the <u>present subjunctive</u>. It's easy to remember because the endings for -ar and -er verbs are the opposite of what they are in the ordinary present tense.

In regular -ar verbs, you take off the -as, -a, -amos, -áis and -an endings of the present tense and replace them with: -es, -e, -emos, -éis and -en.

-ar verb	trabajar	to work
tú form	¡no trabajes!	Don't work!
usted form	¡no trabaje!	Don't work!
nosotros/as form	¡no trabajemos!	Let's not work!
vosotros/as form	¡no trabajéis!	Don't work!
ustedes form	¡no trabajen!	Don't work!

In regular -er verbs, you take off the -es, -e, -emos, -éis and -en endings of the present tense and replace them with -as, -a, -amos, -áis and -an.

-er verb	comer	to eat
tú form	¡no comas!	Don't eat!
usted form	¡no coma!	Don't eat!
nosotros/as form	¡no comamos!	Let's not eat!
vosotros/as form	¡no comáis!	Don't eat!
ustedes form	¡no coman!	Don't eat!

In regular -ir verbs, you take off the -es, -e, -imos, -ís and -en endings of the present tense and replace them with -as, -a, -amos, -áis and -an.

-ir verb	decidir	*to decide*
tú form	¡no decidas!	Don't decide!
usted form	¡no decida!	Don't decide!
nosotros/as form	¡no decidamos!	Let's not decide!
vosotros/as form	¡no decidáis!	Don't decide!
ustedes form	¡no decidan!	Don't decide!

A number of irregular verbs also have irregular imperative forms. These are shown in the table below.

	dar *to give*	decir *to say*	estar *to be*	hacer *to do/make*	ir *to go*
tú form	¡no des! don't give!	¡no digas! don't say!	¡no estés! don't be!	¡no hagas! don't do/make!	¡no vayas! don't go!
usted form	¡no dé! don't give!	¡no diga! don't say!	¡no esté! don't be!	¡no haga! don't do/make!	¡no vaya! don't go!
nosotros form	¡no demos! let's not give!	¡no digamos! let's not say!	¡no estemos! let's not be!	¡no hagamos! let's not do/make!	¡no vayamos! let's not go!
vosotros form	¡no deis! don't give!	¡no digáis! don't say!	¡no estéis! don't be!	¡no hagáis! don't do/make!	¡no vayáis! don't go!
ustedes form	¡no den! don't give!	¡no digan! don't say!	¡no estén! don't be!	¡no hagan! don't do/make!	¡no vayan! don't go!

	poner *to put*	salir *to leave*	ser *to be*	tener *to have*	venir *to come*
tú form	¡no pongas! don't put!	¡no salgas! don't leave!	¡no seas! don't be!	¡no tengas! don't have!	¡no vengas! don't come!
usted form	¡no ponga! don't put!	¡no salga! don't leave!	¡no sea! don't be!	¡no tenga! don't have!	¡no venga! don't come!
nosotros form	¡no pongamos! let's not put!	¡no salgamos! let's not leave!	¡no seamos! let's not be!	¡no tengamos! let's not have!	¡no vengamos! let's not come!
vosotros form	¡no pongáis! don't put!	¡no salgáis! don't leave!	¡no seáis! don't be!	¡no tengáis! don't have!	¡no vengáis! don't come!
ustedes form	¡no pongan! don't put!	¡no salgan! don't leave!	¡no sean! don't be!	¡no tengan! don't have!	¡no vengan! don't come!

For further explanation of grammatical terms, please see pages 6–9.

Note that if you take the **yo** form of the present tense, take off the -o and add the endings to this instead for instructions <u>NOT TO DO</u> something, some of these irregular forms will be more predictable.

digo	*I say*	>	negative imperative stem	>	dig-
hago	*I do*	>	negative imperative stem	>	hag-
pongo	*I put*	>	negative imperative stem	>	pong-
salgo	*I leave*	>	negative imperative stem	>	salg-
tengo	*I have*	>	negative imperative stem	>	teng-
vengo	*I come*	>	negative imperative stem	>	veng-

Forming the imperative: instructions to do something

In instructions telling you <u>TO DO</u> something, the forms for **usted, nosotros** and **ustedes** are exactly the same as they are in negative instructions (instructions telling you not to do something) except that there isn't a **no**.

	trabajar *to work*	comer *to eat*	decidir *to decide*
usted form	¡Trabaje!	¡Coma!	¡Decida!
nosotros/as form	¡Trabajemos!	¡Comamos!	¡Decidamos!
ustedes form	¡Trabajen!	¡Coman!	¡Decidan!

There are special forms of the imperative for **tú** and **vosotros/vosotras** in positive instructions (instructions telling you to do something). The **tú** form of the imperative is the same as the **tú** form of the ordinary present simple tense, but without the final -s.

trabajar	>	¡Trabaja!
to work		Work!
comer	>	¡Come!
to eat		Eat!
decidir	>	¡Decide!
to decide		Decide!

22 Imperative

The **vosotros/vosotras** form of the imperative is the same as the infinitive, except that you take off the final -r and add -d instead.

trabajar	>	Trabajad!
to work		Work!
comer	>	Comed!
to eat		Eat!
decidir	>	Decidid!
to decide		Decide!

There are a number of imperative forms that are irregular in Spanish. The irregular imperative forms for **usted**, **nosotros/nosotras** and **ustedes** are the same as the irregular negative imperative forms without the **no**. The **tú** and **vosotros/vosotras** forms are different again.

	dar *to give*	decir *to say*	estar *to be*	hacer *to do/make*	ir *to go*
tú form	¡da! give!	¡di! say!	¡está! be!	¡haz! do/make!	¡ve! go!
usted form	¡dé! give!	¡diga! say!	¡esté! be!	¡haga! do/make!	¡vaya! go!
nosotros/as form	¡demos! let's give!	¡digamos! let's say!	¡estemos! let's be!	¡hagamos! let's do/make!	¡vamos! let's go!
vosotros/as form	¡dad! give!	¡decid! say!	¡estad! be!	¡haced! do/make!	¡id! go!
ustedes form	¡den! give!	¡digan! say!	¡estén! be!	¡hagan! do/make!	¡vayan! go!

	poner *to put*	salir *to leave*	ser *to be*	tener *to have*	venir *to come*
tú form	¡pon! put!	¡sal! leave!	¡sé! be!	¡ten! have!	¡ven! come!
usted form	¡ponga! put!	¡salga! leave!	¡sea! be!	¡tenga! have!	¡venga! come!
nosotros/as form	¡pongamos! let's put!	¡salgamos! let's leave!	¡seamos! let's be!	¡tengamos! let's have!	¡vengamos! let's come!
vosotros/as form	¡poned! put!	¡salid! leave!	¡sed! be!	¡tened! have!	¡venid! come!
ustedes form	¡pongan! put!	¡salgan! leave!	¡sean! be!	¡tengan! have!	¡vengan! come!

For further explanation of grammatical terms, please see pages 6–9.

Note that the nosotros/nosotras form for ir in instructions <u>TO DO</u> something is usually vamos; in instructions <u>NOT TO DO</u> something, it is no vayamos.

Position of object pronouns

If you are telling someone <u>NOT TO DO</u> something, any object pronouns go <u>BEFORE</u> the verb.

> ¡No <u>me lo</u> mandes! Don't send it to me!
> ¡No <u>me</u> molestes! Don't disturb me!
> ¡No <u>los</u> castigue! Don't punish them!
> ¡No <u>se la</u> devolvamos! Let's not give it back to him/her/them!
> ¡No <u>les</u> contestéis! Don't answer them!

If you are telling someone <u>TO DO</u> something, any object pronouns join on to the <u>END</u> of the verb. An accent is usually added to make sure that the stress in the imperative verb stays the same.

> ¡Explíca<u>melo</u>! Explain it to me!
> ¡Perdóne<u>me</u>! Excuse me!
> ¡Díga<u>me</u>! Tell me!
> ¡Esperémos<u>la</u>! Let's wait for her/it!

Reflexive verbs

Forming the present tense of reflexive verbs

The present tense of a reflexive verb is formed in the same way as that of a non-reflexive verb except that reflexive pronouns are included before the verb.

The following table shows the reflexive verb **lavarse** in full.

Reflexive forms of lavarse	Meaning
(yo) me lavo	I wash (myself)
(tú) te lavas	you wash (yourself)
(él) se lava	he washes (himself)
(ella) se lava	she washes (herself)
(uno) se lava	one washes (oneself)
se lava	it washes (itself)
(usted) se lava	you wash (yourself)
(nosotros/nosotras) nos lavamos	we wash (ourselves)
(vosotros/vosotras) os laváis	you wash (yourselves)
(ellos) se lavan	they wash (themselves)
(ellas) se lavan	they wash (themselves)
(ustedes) se lavan	you wash (yourselves)

Position of reflexive pronouns

In ordinary tenses such as the present simple, the reflexive pronoun goes <u>BEFORE</u> the verb.

> <u>Me</u> acuesto temprano. I go to bed early.
> ¿Cómo <u>se</u> llama usted? What's your name?

When telling someone <u>NOT TO DO</u> something, you also put the reflexive pronoun <u>BEFORE</u> the verb.

For further explanation of grammatical terms, please see pages 6–9.

No <u>te</u> levantes. Don't get up.
¡No <u>os</u> vayáis! Don't go away!

When telling someone <u>TO DO</u> something, you join the reflexive pronoun onto the end of the verb.

¡Siénten<u>se</u>! Sit down!
¡Cálla<u>te</u>! Be quiet!

When adding reflexive pronouns to the end of the imperative, you drop the final -s of the **nosotros** form and the final -d of the **vosotros** form, before the pronoun.

¡Vámo<u>nos</u>! Let's go!
¡Senta<u>os</u>! Sit down!

You always join the reflexive pronoun onto the end of infinitives and gerunds (the -ando or -iendo forms of the verb) unless the infinitive or gerund follows another verb.

Hay que relajar<u>se</u> de vez en cuando. You have to relax from time to time.
Acostándo<u>se</u> temprano, se descansa mejor.
You feel more rested by going to bed early.

Where the infinitive or gerund follows another verb, you can put the reflexive pronoun either at the end of the infinitive or gerund or before the other verb.

Quiero bañar**me** *or* **Me** quiero bañar. I want to have a bath.
Tienes que vestir**te** *or* **Te** tienes que vestir. You must get dressed.
Está vistiéndo<u>se</u> *or* **Se** está vistiendo. She's getting dressed.
¿Estás duchándo<u>te</u>? *or* ¿**Te** estás duchando? Are you having a shower?

Note that, when adding pronouns to the ends of verb forms, you will often have to add a written accent to preserve the stress.

The future tense

Forming the future tense

To form the future tense of regular -ar, -er and -ir verbs, add the following endings to the <u>infinitive</u> of the verb: -é, -ás, -á, -emos, -éis, -án.

The following table shows the future tense of three regular verbs: hablar (meaning *to speak*), comer (meaning *to eat*) and vivir (meaning *to live*).

(yo)	hablaré	comeré	viviré	I'll speak/eat/live
(tú)	hablarás	comerás	vivirás	you'll speak/eat/live
(él, ella)	hablará	comerá	vivirá	he'll speak/eat/live
				she'll speak/eat/live
(usted)				it'll speak/eat/live
				you'll speak/eat/live
(nosotros/nosotras)	hablaremos	comeremos	viviremos	we'll speak/eat/live
(vosotros/vosotras)	hablaréis	comeréis	viviréis	you'll speak/eat/live
(ellos/ellas/ustedes)	hablarán	comerán	vivirán	they'll/you'll speak/eat/live

<u>Hablaré</u> con ella. I'll speak to her.
<u>Comeremos</u> en casa de José. We'll eat at José's.
No <u>volverá</u>. He won't come back.
¿Lo <u>entenderás</u>? Will you understand it?

Note that in the future tense only the **nosotros/nosotras** form doesn't have an accent.

Verbs with irregular stems in the future tense

There are a few verbs that <u>DO NOT</u> use their infinitives as the stem for the future tense. Here are some of the most common.

Verb	Stem	(yo)	(tú)	(él) (ella) (usted)	(nosotros) (nosotras)	(vosotros) (vosotras)	(ellos) (ellas) (ustedes)
decir *to say*	dir-	diré	dirás	dirá	diremos	diréis	dirán
haber *to have*	habr-	habré	habrás	habrá	habremos	habréis	habrán
hacer *to do/make*	har-	haré	harás	hará	haremos	haréis	harán
poder *to be able*	podr-	podré	podrás	podrá	podremos	podréis	podrán
poner *to put*	pondr-	pondré	pondrás	pondrá	pondremos	pondréis	pondrán
querer *to want*	querr-	querré	querrás	querrá	querremos	querréis	querrán
saber *to know*	sabr-	sabré	sabrás	sabrá	sabremos	sabréis	sabrán
salir *to leave*	saldr-	saldré	saldrás	saldrá	saldremos	saldréis	saldrán
tener *to have*	tendr-	tendré	tendrás	tendrá	tendremos	tendréis	tendrán
venir *to come*	vendr-	vendré	vendrás	vendrá	vendremos	vendréis	vendrán

Lo <u>haré</u> mañana. I'll do it tomorrow.
No <u>podremos</u> hacerlo. We won't be able to do it.
Lo <u>pondré</u> aquí. I'll put it here.
<u>Saldrán</u> por la mañana. They'll leave in the morning.
¿A qué hora <u>vendrás</u>? What time will you come?

28 Future

Reflexive verbs in the future tense

The future tense of reflexive verbs is formed in just the same way as for ordinary verbs, except that you have to remember to give the reflexive pronoun (me, te, se, nos, os, se).

> Me levantaré temprano. I'll get up early.

The conditional

Forming the conditional

To form the conditional of regular -ar, -er, and -ir verbs, add the following endings to the <u>infinitive</u> of the verb: -ía, -ías, -ía, -íamos, -íais, -ían.

The following table shows the conditional tense of three regular verbs: hablar (meaning *to speak*), comer (meaning *to eat*) and vivir (meaning *to live*).

(yo)	hablar<u>ía</u>	comer<u>ía</u>	vivir<u>ía</u>	I would speak/eat/live
(tú)	hablar<u>ías</u>	comer<u>ías</u>	vlvir<u>ías</u>	you would speak/eat/live
				he would speak/eat/live
(él, ella) (usted)	hablar<u>ía</u>	comer<u>ía</u>	vivir<u>ía</u>	she would speak/eat/live it would speak/eat/live you would speak/eat/live
(nosotros/nosotras)	hablar<u>íamos</u>	comer<u>íamos</u>	vivir<u>íamos</u>	we would speak/eat/live
(vosotros/vosotras)	hablar<u>íais</u>	comer<u>íais</u>	vivir<u>íais</u>	you would speak/eat/live
(ellos/ellas/ustedes)	hablar<u>ían</u>	comer<u>ían</u>	vivir<u>ían</u>	they would/you would speak/eat/live

Me <u>gustaría</u> ir a China. I'd like to go to China.
Dije que <u>hablaría</u> con ella. I said that I would speak to her.
<u>Debería</u> llamar a mis padres. I should ring my parents.

Don't forget to put an accent on the í in the conditional.

30 Conditional

Note that the endings in the conditional tense are identical to those of the imperfect tense for -er and -ir verbs. The only difference is that they are added to a different stem.

Verbs with irregular stems in the conditional

To form the conditional of irregular verbs, use the same stem as for the future tense, then add the usual endings for the conditional. The same verbs that are irregular in the future tense are irregular in the conditional.

Verb	Stem	(yo)	(tú)	(él) (ella) (usted)	(nosotros) (nosotras)	(vosotros) (vosotras)	(ellos) (ellas) (ustedes)
decir *to say*	dir-	diría	dirías	diría	diríamos	diríais	dirían
haber *to have*	habr-	habría	habrías	habría	habríamos	habríais	habrían
hacer *to do/make*	har-	haría	harías	haría	haríamos	haríais	harían
poder *to be able*	podr-	podría	podrías	podría	podríamos	podríais	podrían
poner *to put*	pondr-	pondría	pondrías	pondría	pondríamos	pondríais	pondrían
querer *to want*	querr-	querría	querrías	querría	querríamos	querríais	querrían
saber *to know*	sabr-	sabría	sabrías	sabría	sabríamos	sabríais	sabrían
salir *to leave*	saldr-	saldría	saldrías	saldría	saldríamos	saldríais	saldrían
tener *to have*	tendr-	tendría	tendrías	tendría	tendríamos	tendríais	tendrían
venir *to come*	vendr-	vendría	vendrías	vendría	vendríamos	vendríais	vendrían

For further explanation of grammatical terms, please see pages 6–9.

¿Qué <u>harías</u> tú en mi lugar? What would you do if you were me?

¿<u>Podrías</u> ayudarme? Could you help me?

Yo lo <u>pondría</u> aquí. I would put it here.

Reflexive verbs in the conditional

The conditional of reflexive verbs is formed in just the same way as for ordinary verbs, except that you have to remember to give the reflexive pronoun (**me**, **te**, **se**, **nos**, **os**, **se**).

Le dije que <u>me levantaría</u> temprano. I told him I would get up early.

The preterite

Forming the preterite of regular verbs

To form the preterite of any regular -ar verb, you take off the -ar ending to form the stem, and add the endings: -é, -aste, -ó, -amos, -asteis, -aron.

To form the preterite of any regular -er or -ir verb, you also take off the -er or -ir ending to form the stem and add the endings: -í, -iste, -ió, -imos, -isteis, -ieron.

The following table shows the preterite of three regular verbs: hablar (meaning to speak), comer (meaning to eat) and vivir (meaning to live).

(yo)	hablé	comí	viví	I spoke/ate/lived
(tú)	hablaste	comiste	viviste	you spoke/ate/lived
(él, ella) (usted)	habló	comió	vivió	he spoke/ate/lived she spoke/ate/lived it spoke/ate/lived you spoke/ate/lived
(nosotros/nosotras)	hablamos	comimos	vivimos	we spoke/ate/lived
(vosotros/vosotras)	hablasteis	comisteis	vivisteis	you spoke/ate/lived
(ellos/ellas) (ustedes)	hablaron	comieron	vivieron	they spoke/ate/lived you spoke/ate/lived

Bailé con mi hermana. I danced with my sister.
No hablé con ella. I didn't speak to her.
Comimos en un restaurante. We had lunch in a restaurant.
¿Cerraste la ventana? Did you close the window?

Irregular verbs in the preterite

A number of verbs have very irregular forms in the preterite. The table shows some of the most common.

Verb	(yo)	(tú)	(él) (ella) (usted)	(nosotros) (nosotras)	(vosotros) (vosotras)	(ellos) (ellas) (ustedes)
andar *to walk*	anduve	anduviste	anduvo	anduvimos	anduvisteis	anduvieron
conducir *to drive*	conduje	condujiste	condujo	condujimos	condujisteis	condujeron
dar *to give*	di	diste	dio	dimos	disteis	dieron
decir *to say*	dije	dijiste	dijo	dijimos	dijisteis	dljeron
estar *to be*	estuve	estuviste	estuvo	estuvimos	estuvisteis	estuvieron
hacer *to do, to make*	hice	hiciste	hizo	hicimos	hicisteis	hicieron
ir *to go*	fui	fuiste	fue	fuimos	fuisteis	fueron
poder *to be able*	pude	pudiste	pudo	pudimos	pudisteis	pudieron
poner *to put*	puse	pusiste	puso	pusimos	pusisteis	pusieron
querer *to want*	quise	quisiste	quiso	quisimos	quisisteis	quisieron
saber *to know*	supe	supiste	supo	supimos	supisteis	supieron
ser *to be*	fui	fuiste	fue	fuimos	fuisteis	fueron
tener *to have*	tuve	tuviste	tuvo	tuvimos	tuvisteis	tuvieron
traer *to bring*	traje	trajiste	trajo	trajimos	trajisteis	trajeron
venir *to come*	vine	viniste	vino	vinimos	vinisteis	vinieron
ver *to see*	vi	viste	vio	vimos	visteis	vieron

Note that hizo (the él/ella/usted form of hacer) is spelt with a z.

> Fue a Madrid. He went to Madrid.
> Te vi en el parque. I saw you in the park.
> No vinieron. They didn't come.
> ¿Qué hizo? What did she do?
> Se lo di a Teresa. I gave it to Teresa.
> Fue en 1999. It was in 1999.

The preterite forms of ser (meaning to be) are the same as the preterite forms of ir (meaning to go).

Some other verbs are regular EXCEPT FOR the él/ella/usted and ellos/ellas/ustedes forms (third persons singular and plural). In these forms the stem vowel changes.

Verb	(yo)	(tú)	(él) (ella) (usted)	(nosotros) (nosotras)	(vosotros) (vosotras)	(ellos) (ellas) (ustedes)
dormir to sleep	dormí	dormiste	durmió	dormimos	dormisteis	durmieron
morir to die	morí	moriste	murió	morimos	moristeis	murieron
pedir to ask for	pedí	pediste	pidió	pedimos	pedisteis	pidieron
reír to laugh	reí	reíste	rio	reímos	reísteis	rieron
seguir to follow	seguí	seguiste	siguió	seguimos	seguisteis	siguieron
sentir to feel	sentí	sentiste	sintió	sentimos	sentisteis	sintieron

Note that reír also has an accent in all persons apart from the él/ella/usted and ellos/ellas/ustedes (third persons singular and plural) forms.

> Antonio durmió diez horas. Antonio slept for ten hours.
> Murió en 1066. He died in 1066.
> Pidió paella. He asked for paella.
> ¿Los siguió? Did she follow them?
> Sintió un dolor en la pierna. He felt a pain in his leg.
> Nos reímos mucho. We laughed a lot.
> Juan no se rio. Juan didn't laugh.

caer (meaning to fall) and leer (meaning to read) have an accent in all persons apart from the ellos/ellas/ustedes form (third person plural). In addition, the vowel changes to y in the él/ella/usted and ellos/ellas/ustedes forms (third persons singular and plural).

Verb	(yo)	(tú)	(él) (ella) (usted)	(nosotros) (nosotras)	(vosotros) (vosotras)	(ellos) (ellas) (ustedes)
caer to fall	caí	caíste	cayó	caímos	caísteis	cayeron
construir to build	construí	construiste	construyó	construimos	construisteis	construyeron
leer to read	leí	leíste	leyó	leímos	leísteis	leyeron

Note that construir also changes to y in the él/ella/usted and ellos/ellas/ustedes forms (third persons singular and plural), but only has accents in the yo and él/ella/usted forms.

> Se cayó por la ventana. He fell out of the window.
> Ayer leí un artículo muy interesante.
> I read a very interesting article yesterday.
> Construyeron una nueva autopista. They built a new motorway.

Other spelling changes in the preterite

Spanish verbs that end in -zar, -gar and -car in the infinitive change the z to c, the g to gu and the c to qu in the yo form (*first person singular*).

Verb	(yo)	(tú)	(él) (ella) (usted)	(nosotros) (nosotras)	(vosotros) (vosotras)	(ellos) (ellas) (ustedes)
cruzar *to cross*	crucé	cruzaste	cruzó	cruzamos	cruzasteis	cruzaron
empezar *to begin*	empecé	empezaste	empezó	empezamos	empezasteis	empezaron
pagar *to pay for*	pagué	pagaste	pagó	pagamos	pagasteis	pagaron
sacar *to take out*	saqué	sacaste	sacó	sacamos	sacasteis	sacaron

Crucé el río. I crossed the river.
Empecé a hacer mis deberes. I began doing my homework.
No pagué la cuenta. I didn't pay the bill.
Me saqué las llaves del bolsillo. I took my keys out of my pocket.

Note that the change from g to gu and c to qu before e is to keep the sound hard.

Reflexive verbs in the preterite

The preterite of reflexive verbs is formed in just the same way as for ordinary verbs, except that you have to remember to give the reflexive pronoun (me, te, se, nos, os, se).

Me levanté a las siete. I got up at seven.

The imperfect tense

Forming the imperfect tense

To form the imperfect of any regular -ar verb, you take off the -ar ending of the infinitive to form the stem and add the endings: -aba, -abas, -aba,-ábamos, -abais, -aban.

The following table shows the imperfect tense of one regular -ar verb: hablar (meaning to speak).

(yo)	hablaba	I spoke
		I was speaking
		I used to speak
(tú)	hablabas	you spoke
		you were speaking
		you used to speak
(él/ella/usted)	hablaba	he/she/it/you spoke
		he/she/it was speaking, you were speaking
		he/she/it/you used to speak
(nosotros/nosotras)	hablábamos	we spoke
		we were speaking
		we used to speak
(vosotros/vosotras)	hablabais	you spoke
		you were speaking
		you used to speak
(ellos/ellas/ustedes)	hablaban	they/you spoke
		they/you were speaking
		they/you used to speak

Note that in the imperfect tense of -ar verbs, the only accent is on the nosotros/nosotras form.

Hablaba francés e italiano. He spoke French and Italian.

Cuando era joven, mi tío trabajaba mucho.

My uncle worked hard when he was young.

Estudiábamos matemáticas e inglés. We were studying maths and English.

To form the imperfect of any regular -er or -ir verb, you take off the -er or -ir ending of the infinitive to form the stem and add the endings: -ía, -ías, -ía, -íamos, -íais, -ían.

The following table shows the imperfect of two regular verbs: comer (meaning to eat) and vivir (meaning to live).

(yo)	comía	vivía	I ate/lived I was eating/living I used to eat/live
(tú)	comías	vivías	you ate/lived you were eating/living you used to eat/live
(él/ella/usted)	comía	vivía	he/she/it/you ate/lived he/she/it was eating/living, you were eating/living he/she/it /you used to eat/live
(nosotros/nosotras)	comíamos	vivíamos	we ate/lived we were eating/living we used to eat/live
(vosotros/vosotras)	comíais	vivíais	you ate/lived you were eating/living you used to eat/live
(ellos/ellas/ustedes)	comían	vivían	they/you ate/lived they/you were eating/living they/you used to eat/live

Note that in the imperfect tense of -er and -ir verbs, there's an accent on all the endings.

> A veces, comíamos en casa de Pepe. We sometimes used to eat at Pepe's.
> Vivía en un piso en la Avenida de Barcelona.
> She lived in a flat in Avenida de Barcelona.
> Cuando llegó el médico, ya se sentían mejor.
> They were already feeling better when the doctor arrived.

The imperfect endings for -er and -ir verbs are the same as the endings used to form the conditional for all verbs. The only difference is that, in the conditional, the endings are added to the future stem.

Reflexive verbs in the imperfect tense

The imperfect of reflexive verbs is formed in just the same way as for ordinary verbs, except that you have to remember to give the reflexive pronoun (me, te, se, nos, os, se).

> Antes se levantaba temprano. He used to get up early.

The perfect tense

Forming the perfect tense

As in English, the perfect tense in Spanish has two parts to it. These are:

- the <u>present</u> tense of the verb **haber** (meaning *to have*)
- a part of the main verb called the <u>past participle</u>.

Forming the past participle

To form the past participle of regular -**ar** verbs, take off the -**ar** ending of the infinitive and add -**ado**.

> **hablar** (*to speak*) > **hablado** (*spoken*)

To form the past participle of regular -**er** or -**ir** verbs, take off the -**er** or -**ir** ending of the infinitive and add -**ido**.

> **comer** (*to eat*) > **comido** (*eaten*)
> **vivir** (*to live*) > **vivido** (*lived*)

The perfect tense of some regular verbs

The following table shows how you can combine the present tense of **haber** with the past participle of any verb to form the perfect tense.

In this case, the past participles are taken from the following regular verbs:

hablar (meaning *to speak*); **trabajar** (meaning *to work*); **comer** (meaning *to eat*); **vender** (meaning *to sell*); **vivir** (meaning *to live*); **decidir** (meaning *to decide*).

	Present of haber	Past participle	Meaning
(yo)	he	hablado	I have spoken
(tú)	has	trabajado	you have worked
(él/ella/usted)	ha	comido	he/she/it has eaten, you have eaten
(nosotros/nosotras)	hemos	vendido	we have sold
(vosotros/vosotras)	habéis	vivido	you have lived
(ellos/ellas/ustedes)	han	decidido	they/you have decided

Has trabajado mucho. You've worked hard.
No he comido nada. I haven't eaten anything.

Verbs with irregular past participles

Some past participles are irregular. There aren't too many, so try to learn them.

abrir (to open)	>	abierto (opened)
cubrir (to cover)	>	cubierto (covered)
decir (to say)	>	dicho (said)
escribir (to write)	>	escrito (written)
freír (to fry)	>	frito (fried)
hacer (to do, to make)	>	hecho (done, made)
morir (to die)	>	muerto (died)
oír (to hear)	>	oído (heard)
poner (to put)	>	puesto (put)
romper (to break)	>	roto (broken)
ver (to see)	>	visto (seen)
volver (to return)	>	vuelto (returned)

No ha dicho nada. He hasn't said anything.
Hoy he hecho muchas cosas. I've done a lot today.
Han muerto tres personas. Three people have died.
Carlos ha roto el espejo. Carlos has broken the mirror.
Jamás he visto una cosa parecida. I've never seen anything like it.

he/has/ha and so on must <u>NEVER</u> be separated from the past participle.
Any object pronouns go before the form of haber being used, and <u>NOT</u> between
the form of haber and the past participle.

No <u>lo</u> he visto. I haven't seen it.
¿<u>Lo</u> has hecho ya? Have you done it yet?

Reflexive verbs in the perfect tense

The perfect tense of reflexive verbs is formed in the same way as for ordinary
verbs. The reflexive pronouns (me, te, se, nos, os, se) come before he, has, ha,
and so on. The table below shows the perfect tense of lavarse in full.

(Subject pronoun)	Reflexive pronoun	Present tense of haber	Past Participle	Meaning
(yo)	me	he	lavado	I have washed
(tú)	te	has	lavado	you have washed
(él, ella, uno)	se	ha	lavado	he has washed
				she has washed
(usted)				one has washed
				it has washed
				you have washed
(nosotros)	nos	hemos	lavado	we have washed
(nosotras)				we have washed
(vosotros)	os	habéis	lavado	you have washed
(vosotras)				you have washed
(ellos)	se	han	lavado	they have washed
(ellas)				they have washed
(ustedes)				you have washed

The pluperfect or past perfect tense

Forming the pluperfect tense

Like the perfect tense, the pluperfect tense in Spanish has two parts to it:

- the imperfect tense of the verb haber (meaning to have)
- the past participle.

The table below shows how you can combine the imperfect tense of haber with the past participle of any verb to form the pluperfect tense. Here, the past participles are taken from the following regular verbs: hablar (meaning to speak); trabajar (meaning to work); comer (meaning to eat); vender (meaning to sell); vivir (meaning to live); decidir (meaning to decide).

(Subject pronoun)	Imperfect of haber	Past Participle	Meaning
(yo)	había	hablado	I had spoken
(tú)	habías	trabajado	you had worked
(él/ella/usted)	había	comido	he/she/it/you had eaten
(nosotros/nosotras)	habíamos	vendido	we had sold
(vosotros/vosotras)	habíais	vivido	you had lived
(ellos/ellas/ustedes)	habían	decidido	they/you had decided

Había decidido escribirle. I had decided to write to her.
No había trabajado antes. He hadn't worked before.
Había vendido su caballo. She had sold her horse.
Ya habíamos comido. We had already eaten.
Habían hablado con el médico. They had spoken to the doctor.

44 Pluperfect

Remember that some very common verbs have irregular past participles.

abrir (to open)	>	abierto (opened)
cubrir (to cover)	>	cubierto (covered)
decir (to say)	>	dicho (said)
escribir (to write)	>	escrito (written)
freír (to fry)	>	frito (fried)
hacer (to do, to make)	>	hecho (done, made)
morir (to die)	>	muerto (died)
oír (to hear)	>	oído (heard)
poner (to put)	>	puesto (put)
romper (to break)	>	roto (broken)
ver (to see)	>	visto (seen)
volver (to return)	>	vuelto (returned)

No había dicho nada. He hadn't said anything.

Tres personas habían muerto. Three people had died.

había/habías/habían and so on must NEVER be separated from the past participle. Any object pronouns go before the form of haber being used, and NOT between the form of haber and the past participle.

No lo había visto. I hadn't seen it.

Reflexive verbs in the pluperfect tense

The pluperfect tense of reflexive verbs is formed in the same way as for ordinary verbs. The reflexive pronouns (me, te, se, nos, os, se) come before había, habías, había, and so on. The table on the next page shows the pluperfect tense of lavarse in full.

(Subject pronoun)	Reflexive pronoun	Imperfect tense of haber	Past Participle	Meaning
(yo)	me	había	lavado	I had washed
(tú)	te	habías	lavado	you had washed
(él, ella, uno) (usted)	se	había	lavado	he had washed she had washed one had washed it had washed you had washed
(nosotros) (nosotras)	nos	habíamos	lavado	we had washed we had washed
(vosotros) (vosotras)	os	habíais	lavado	you had washed you had washed
(ellos) (ellas) (ustedes)	se	habían	lavado	they had washed they had washed you had washed

The passive

Forming the passive

In English we use the verb *to be* with a <u>past participle</u> (*was painted, were seen, are made*) to form the passive. In Spanish, the passive is formed in exactly the same way, using the verb **ser** (meaning *to be*) and a <u>past participle</u>. When you say who the action is or was done by, you use the preposition **por** (meaning *by*).

> <u>Son fabricados</u> en España. They're made in Spain.
> <u>Fue escrito</u> por JK Rowling. It was written by JK Rowling.
> La casa <u>fue construida</u> en 1956. The house was built in 1956.
> El cuadro <u>fue pintado</u> por mi padre. The picture was painted by my father.
> El colegio va a <u>ser modernizado</u>. The school is going to be modernized.

Note that the ending of the past participle agrees with the subject of the verb **ser** in exactly the same way as an adjective would.

Here is the preterite of the -ar verb **enviar** (meaning *to send*) in its passive form.

(Subject pronoun)	Preterite of ser	Past Participle	Meaning
(yo)	fui	enviado (masculine) enviada (feminine)	I was sent
(tú)	fuiste	enviado (masculine) enviada (feminine)	you were sent
(él)	fue	enviado	he was sent
(ella)		enviada	she was sent
(usted)		enviado (masculine) enviada (feminine)	you were sent

(Subject pronoun)	Preterite of ser	Past Participle	Meaning
(nosotros)	fuimos	enviados	we were sent
(nosotras)		enviadas	we were sent
(vosotros)	fuisteis	enviados	you were sent
(vosotras)		enviadas	you were sent
(ellos)	fueron	enviados	they were sent
(ellas)		enviadas	they were sent
(ustedes)		enviados (masculine)	you were sent
		enviadas (feminine)	you were sent

You can form other tenses in the passive by changing the tense of the verb **ser**.

| **Future:** | serán enviados | they will be sent |
| **Perfect:** | han sido enviados | they have been sent |

Irregular past participles are the same as they are in the perfect tense. These are shown for many common verbs in the **Verb Tables** at the back of the book.

The gerund

Forming the gerund of regular verbs

To form the gerund of regular -ar verbs, take off the -ar ending of the infinitive to form the stem, and add -ando.

Infinitive	Stem	Gerund
hablar	habl-	hablando
trabajar	trabaj-	trabajando

To form the gerund of regular -er and -ir verbs, take off the -er and -ir ending of the infinitive to form the stem, and add -iendo.

Infinitive	Stem	Gerund
comer	com-	comiendo
vivir	viv-	viviendo

Position of pronouns with the gerund

Object pronouns and reflexive pronouns are attached to the end of the gerund or alternatively put before estar in continuous tenses.

> Estoy hablándote or Te estoy hablando. I'm talking to you.
> Está vistiéndose or Se está vistiendo. He's getting dressed.
> Estaban mostrándoselo or Se lo estaban mostrando.
> They were showing it to him/her/them/you.

Note that you will always have to add an accent to keep the stress in the same place when adding pronouns to the end of a gerund.

For further explanation of grammatical terms, please see pages 6–9.

The subjunctive

Forming the present subjunctive

To form the present subjunctive of most verbs, take off the -o ending of the yo form of the <u>present simple</u>, and add a fixed set of endings.

For -ar verbs, the endings are: -e, -es, -e, -emos, -éis, -en.

For both -er and -ir verbs, the endings are: -a, -as, -a, -amos, -áis, -an.

The following table shows the present subjunctive of three regular verbs: hablar (meaning to speak), comer (meaning to eat) and vivir (meaning to live).

Infinitive	(yo)	(tú)	(él) (ella) (usted)	(nosotros) (nosotras)	(vosotros) (Vosotras)	(ellos) (ellas) (ustedes)
hablar to speak	hable	hables	hable	hablemos	habléis	hablen
comer to eat	coma	comas	coma	comamos	comáis	coman
vivir to live	viva	vivas	viva	vivamos	viváis	vivan

Quiero que <u>comas</u> algo. I want you to eat something.

Me sorprende que no <u>hable</u> inglés. I'm surprised he doesn't speak English.

No es verdad que <u>trabajen</u> aquí. It isn't true that they work here.

Some verbs have very irregular yo forms in the ordinary present tense and these irregular forms are reflected in the stem for the present subjunctive.

Infinitive	(yo)	(tú)	(él) (ella) (usted)	(nosotros) (nosotras)	(vosotros) (vosotras)	(ellos) (ellas) (ustedes)
decir *to say*	diga	digas	diga	digamos	digáis	digan
hacer *to do/make*	haga	hagas	haga	hagamos	hagáis	hagan
poner *to put*	ponga	pongas	ponga	pongamos	pongáis	pongan
salir *to leave*	salga	salgas	salga	salgamos	salgáis	salgan
tener *to have*	tenga	tengas	tenga	tengamos	tengáis	tengan
venir *to come*	venga	vengas	venga	vengamos	vengáis	vengan

Voy a limpiar la casa antes de que <u>vengan</u>.
I'm going to clean the house before they come.

Note that only the **vosotros** form has an accent.

The present subjunctive endings are the opposite of what you'd expect, as **-ar** verbs have endings starting with **-e**, and **-er** and **-ir** verbs have endings starting with **-a**.

Forming the present subjunctive of radical changing verbs

Verbs that change their stems (<u>radical-changing verbs</u>) in the ordinary present usually change them in the same way in the present subjunctive.

Infinitive	(yo)	(tú)	(él) (ella) (usted)	(nosotros) (nosotras)	(vosotros) (vosotras)	(ellos) (ellas) (ustedes)
pensar to think	piense	pienses	piense	pensemos	penséis	piensen
entender to understand	entienda	entiendas	entienda	entendamos	entendáis	entiendan
poder to be able	pueda	puedas	pueda	podamos	podáis	puedan
querer to want	quiera	quieras	quiera	queramos	queráis	quieran
volver to return	vuelva	vuelvas	vuelva	volvamos	volváis	vuelvan

No hace falta que **vuelvas**. There's no need for you to come back.
Me alegro de que **puedas** venir. I'm pleased you can come.

Sometimes the stem of the **nosotros** and **vosotros** forms isn't the same as it is in the ordinary present tense.

Infinitive	(yo)	(tú)	(él) (ella) (usted)	(nosotros) (nosotras)	(vosotros) (vosotras)	(ellos) (ellas) (ustedes)
dormir to sleep	duerma	duermas	duerma	durmamos	durmáis	duerman
morir to die	muera	mueras	muera	muramos	muráis	mueran
pedir to ask for	pida	pidas	pida	pidamos	pidáis	pidan
seguir to follow	siga	sigas	siga	sigamos	sigáis	sigan
sentir to feel	sienta	sientas	sienta	sintamos	sintáis	sientan

Queremos hacerlo antes de que nos <u>muramos</u>.
We want to do it before we die.
Vendré a veros cuando os <u>sintáis</u> mejor.
I'll come and see you when you feel better.

Forming the imperfect subjunctive

For all verbs, there are <u>two</u> imperfect subjunctive forms that are exactly the same in meaning.

The stem for both imperfect subjunctive forms is the same: you take off the -aron or -ieron ending of the ellos form of the preterite and add a fixed set of endings to what is left.

For -ar verbs, the endings are: -ara, -aras, -ara, -áramos, -arais, -aran or -ase, -ases, -ase, -ásemos, -aseis, -asen. The first form is more common.

For -er and -ir verbs, the endings are: -iera, -ieras, -iera, -iéramos, -ierais, -ieran or -iese, -ieses, -iese, -iésemos, -ieseis, -iesen. The first form is more common.

The following table shows the subjunctive of three regular verbs: hablar (meaning to speak), comer (meaning to eat) and vivir (meaning to live).

Infinitive	(yo)	(tú)	(él) (ella) (usted)	(nosotros) (nosotras)	(vosotros) (vosotras)	(ellos) (ellas) (ustedes)
hablar	hablara	hablaras	hablara	habláramos	hablarais	hablaran
to speak	hablase	hablases	hablase	hablásemos	hablaseis	hablasen
comer	comiera	comieras	comiera	comiéramos	comierais	comieran
to eat	comiese	comieses	comiese	comiésemos	comieseis	comiesen
vivir	viviera	vivieras	viviera	viviéramos	vivierais	vivieran
to live	viviese	vivieses	viviese	viviésemos	vivieseis	viviesen

Many verbs have irregular preterite forms which are reflected in the stem for the imperfect subjunctive. For example:

Infinitive	(yo)	(tú)	(él) (ella) (usted)	(nosotros) (nosotras)	(vosotros) (vosotras)	(ellos) (ellas) (ustedes)
dar	diera	dieras	diera	diéramos	dierais	dieran
to give	diese	dieses	diese	diésemos	dieseis	diesen
estar	estuviera	estuvieras	estuviera	estuviéramos	estuvierais	estuvieran
to be	estuviese	estuvieses	estuviese	estuviésemos	estuvieseis	estuviesen
hacer	hiciera	hicieras	hiciera	hiciéramos	hicierais	hicieran
to do/make	hiciese	hicieses	hiciese	hiciésemos	hicieseis	hiciesen
poner	pusiera	pusieras	pusiera	pusiéramos	pusierais	pusieran
to put	pusiese	pusieses	pusiese	pusiésemos	pusieseis	pusiesen
tener	tuviera	tuvieras	tuviera	tuviéramos	tuvierais	tuvieran
to have	tuviese	tuvieses	tuviese	tuviésemos	tuvieseis	tuviesen
venir	viniera	vinieras	viniera	viniéramos	vinierais	vinieran
to come	viniese	vinieses	viniese	viniésemos	vinieseis	viniesen

Forming the imperfect subjunctive of some irregular -ir verbs

In some irregular -ir verbs – the ones that don't have an i in the ellos form of the preterite – -era, -eras, -era, -éramos, -erais, -eran or -ese, -eses, -ese, -ésemos, -eseis, -esen are added to the preterite stem instead of -iera and -iese and so on.

Infinitive	(yo)	(tú)	(él) (ella) (usted)	(nosotros) (nosotras)	(vosotros) (vosotras)	(ellos) (ellas) (ustedes)
decir	dijera	dijeras	dijera	dijéramos	dijerais	dijeran
to say	dijese	dijeses	dijese	dijésemos	dijeseis	dijesen
ir	fuera	fueras	fuera	fuéramos	fuerais	fueran
to go	fuese	fueses	fuese	fuésemos	fueseis	fuesen
ser	fuera	fueras	fuera	fuéramos	fuerais	fueran
to be	fuese	fueses	fuese	fuésemos	fueseis	fuesen

Accents

When pronouns are added to the end of gerunds (the -ando/-iendo form of the verb), infinitives (the form of the verb ending in –ar, -er or –ir) or positive imperatives (instructions to do something), you often have to add an accent to show that the stress remains the same.

You should always add an accent to a gerund when attaching one or more pronouns:

> **Estoy afeitándome.** I'm shaving.
> **Está limpiándotelo.** He's cleaning it for you.
> **Estaba diciéndoselo.** I was telling her.

You should only add an accent to an infinitive when adding two pronouns:

> **Quiero limpiártelo.** I want to clean it for you.
> **¿Podrías hacérmelo?** Could you do it for me?
> **Habría que decírselo.** Somebody should tell her.

Don't add an accent when adding only one pronoun to an infinitive:

> **Tengo que bañarme.** I must have a bath.
> **Debo conseguirlo.** I must get it.

In positive imperatives (instructions to do something) an accent is usually required when attaching one or more pronouns:

> **Tómalo.** Take it.
> **Póngame un kilo de azúcar.** One kilo of sugar, please.
> **Cárguelo a mi cuenta.** Put it on my account.
> **¡Levantémonos!** Let's get up!
> **¡Digámoselo!** Let's tell him!

For further explanation of grammatical terms, please see pages 6–9.

Subídmelo a casa. Bring it up to my house.

Decídmelo claro. Tell me clearly.

Confírmenmelo en cuanto puedan. Confirm it as soon as you can.

However, you wouldn't add an accent when adding just one pronoun to either a vosotros imperative in -ar or -er verbs or to a one-syllable imperative:

Acompañadle. Go with him.

Dadle las gracias. Say thank you to him.

Pensadlo bien. Think it over.

¡Despertaos! Wake up!

Hazlo como te he dicho. Do it the way I told you.

Verb Combinations

Verbs followed by the infinitive with no preposition

Some Spanish verbs and groups of verbs can be followed by an infinitive with no preposition:

- poder (meaning *to be able to, can, may*), saber (meaning *to know how to, can*), querer (meaning *to want*) and deber (meaning *to have to, must*)

    No <u>puede venir</u>. He can't come.
    ¿<u>Sabes esquiar</u>? Can you ski?
    <u>Quiere estudiar</u> medicina. He wants to study medicine.
    <u>Debes hacerlo</u>. You must do it.

- verbs like gustar (meaning *to like*), encantar (meaning *to love*) and apetecer (meaning *to fancy*), where the infinitive is the subject of the verb

    <u>Me gusta estudiar</u>. I like studying.
    <u>Nos encanta bailar</u>. We love dancing.
    ¿<u>Te apetece ir</u> al cine? Do you fancy going to the cinema?

- verbs that relate to seeing or hearing, such as ver (meaning *to see*) and oír (meaning *to hear*)

    Nos <u>ha visto llegar</u>. He saw us arrive.
    Te <u>he oído cantar</u>. I heard you singing.

- the verbs hacer (meaning *to make*) and dejar (meaning *to let*)

    ¡No me <u>hagas reír</u>! Don't make me laugh!
    Mis padres no me <u>dejan salir</u> por la noche.
    My parents don't let me go out at night.

- the following common verbs

decidir to decide
Han <u>decidido comprarse</u> una casa. They've decided to buy a house.

desear to wish, want
No <u>desea tener</u> más hijos. She doesn't want to have any more children.

esperar to hope
<u>Espero poder</u> ir. I hope I can go.

evitar to avoid
<u>Evita gastar</u> demasiado dinero. He avoids spending too much money.

necesitar to need
<u>Necesito salir</u> un momento. I need to go out for a moment.

olvidar to forget
<u>Olvidó dejar</u> su dirección. She forgot to leave her address.

pensar to think
<u>Pienso hacer</u> una paella. I'm thinking of making a paella.

preferir to prefer
<u>Prefiero ir</u> mañana. I'd prefer to go tomorrow.

recordar to remember
<u>Recuerdo haberlo</u> visto. I remember seeing it.

sentir to be sorry, to regret
<u>Siento molestarte</u>. I'm sorry to bother you.

58 Verb Combinations

Some of these verbs combine with infinitives to make set phrases with a special meaning:

querer decir to mean
¿Qué quiere decir eso? What does that mean?

dejar caer to drop
Dejó caer la bandeja. She dropped the tray.

Verbs followed by the preposition a and the infinitive

The following verbs are the most common ones that can be followed by a and the infinitive:

- verbs relating to movement such as ir (meaning *to go*) and venir (meaning *to come*)

    Se va a comprar un caballo. He's going to buy a horse.
    Viene a vernos. He's coming to see us.

- the following common verbs

    aprender a hacer algo to learn to do something
    Me gustaría aprender a nadar. I'd like to learn to swim.

    comenzar a hacer algo to begin to do something
    Comenzó a llover. It began to rain.

    decidirse a hacer algo to decide to do something
    Ojalá se decida a visitarnos I hope she decides to visit us.

    empezar a hacer algo to begin/start to do something
    Ha empezado a nevar. It's started to snow.

    llegar a hacer algo to manage to do something
    No llegó a terminarlo. She didn't manage to finish it.

    llegar a ser algo to become something
    Llegó a ser primer ministro. He became prime minister.

    probar a hacer algo to try doing something
    He probado a hacerlo yo sola pero no he podido.
    I tried doing it on my own but I wasn't able to.

volver a hacer algo to do something again
No vuelvas a hacerlo nunca más. Don't ever do it again.

The following verbs can be followed by a and a person's name or else by a and a noun or pronoun referring to a person, and then by another a and an infinitive.

ayudar a alguien a hacer algo to help somebody to do something
¿Le podrías ayudar a Antonia a fregar los platos?
Could you help Antonia to do the dishes?

enseñar a alguien a hacer algo to teach somebody to do something
Le enseñó a su hermano a nadar. He taught his brother to swim.

invitar a alguien a hacer algo to invite somebody to do something
Los he invitado a tomar unas copas en casa.
I've invited them to come for drinks.

Verbs followed by the preposition de and the infinitive

The following verbs are the most common ones that can be followed by de and the infinitive:

aburrirse de hacer algo to get bored with doing something
Me aburría de no poder salir de casa.
I was getting bored with not being able to leave the house.

acabar de hacer algo to have just done something
Acabo de comprar un móvil. I've just bought a mobile.
Acababan de llegar cuando... They had just arrived when...

acordarse de haber hecho/de hacer algo
to remember having done/to do something
Acuérdate de cerrar la puerta con llave. Remember to lock the door.

alegrarse de hacer algo to be glad to do something
Me alegro de verte. I'm glad to see you.

dejar de hacer algo to stop doing something
¿Quieres dejar de hablar? Will you stop talking?

tener ganas de hacer algo to want to do something
Tengo ganas de volver a España. I want to go back to Spain.

tratar de hacer algo to try to do something
Traté de no pensar en ello. I tried not to think about it.

Verbs followed by the preposition con and the infinitive

The following verbs are the most common ones that can be followed by **con** and the infinitive:

amenazar <u>con</u> hacer algo to threaten to do someting
Amenazó <u>con</u> denunciarlos. He threatened to report them.

soñar <u>con</u> hacer algo to dream about doing something
Sueño <u>con</u> vivir en España. I dream about living in Spain.

Verbs followed by the preposition en and the infinitive

The verb **quedar** is the most common one that can be followed by **en** and the infinitive:

quedar <u>en</u> hacer algo to agree to do something
Habíamos quedado <u>en</u> encontrarnos a las ocho.
We had agreed to meet at eight.

Verbs followed by a and an object

a is often the equivalent of the English word *to* when it is used with an indirect object after verbs like enviar (meaning *to send*), dar (meaning *to give*) and decir (meaning *to say*).

dar algo a alguien to give something to somebody
Se lo di a Teresa. I gave it to Teresa.

decir algo a alguien to say something to somebody
Le dijo una mentira a su profesora. She told her teacher a lie.

enviar algo a alguien to send something to somebody
Tendrías que enviárselo a mi padre. You should send it to my father.

escribir algo a alguien to write something to somebody
¿Le has escrito un correo a tu prima? Have you sent an email to your cousin?

mostrar algo a alguien to show something to somebody
Quería mostrárselo al médico. I wanted to show it to the doctor.

Here are some verbs taking a in Spanish that have a different construction in English.

asistir a algo to attend something, to go to something
No asistieron a la ceremonia. They didn't go to the ceremony.

dirigirse a (un lugar) to head for (a place)
Se dirigió a la terminal del aeropuerto. He headed for the airport terminal.

dirigirse a alguien to address somebody
El Rey se dirigió a la nación. The King addressed the nation.

jugar a algo to play something (sports/games)
Están jugando al fútbol. They're playing football.

llegar a (un lugar) to arrive at (a place)
¿A qué hora llegaste a casa? What time did you get home?

oler a algo to smell of something
Este perfume huele a jazmín. This perfume smells of jasmine.

parecerse a alguien/algo to look like somebody/something
Te pareces mucho a tu madre. You look very much like your mother.

subir(se) a un autobús/un coche to get on a bus/into a car
¡De prisa, sube al coche! Get into the car, quick!
No (se) subió al tren. He didn't get on the train.

subir(se) a un árbol to climb a tree
Se cayó al subirse a un árbol. He fell while climbing a tree.

tener miedo a alguien to be afraid of somebody
Nunca tuvieron miedo a su padre. They were never afraid of their father.

Verbs followed by de and an object

Here are some verbs taking de in Spanish that have a different construction in English:

acordarse de algo/alguien to remember something/somebody
¿Te acuerdas de mí? Do you remember me?

alegrarse de algo to be glad about something
Me alegro de tu ascenso. I'm glad about your promotion.

bajarse de un autobús/un coche to get off a bus/out of a car
Se bajó del coche. He got out of the car.

darse cuenta de algo to realize something
Perdona, no me daba cuenta de que eras vegetariano.
Sorry, I didn't realize you were a vegetarian.

depender de algo/alguien to depend on something/somebody
No depende de mí. It doesn't depend on me.

despedirse de alguien to say goodbye to somebody
Se fue sin despedirse de nosotros. He left without saying goodbye to us.

preocuparse de algo/alguien to worry about something/somebody
Se preocupa mucho de su apariencia.
He worries a lot about his appearance.

quejarse de algo to complain about something
Se quejaba de la falta de información.
He was complaining about the lack of information.

reírse de algo/alguien to laugh at something/somebody
¿De qué te ríes? What are you laughing at?

salir de (un cuarto/un edificio) to leave (a room/a building)
¿A qué hora sales de la oficina? What time do you leave the office?

tener miedo de algo to be afraid of something
Tiene miedo de la oscuridad. He's afraid of the dark.

trabajar de (camarero/secretario) to work as (a waiter/secretary)
Trabajo de camarero. I work as a waiter.

tratarse de algo/alguien
to be a question of something/to be about something/somebody
¿De qué se trata? What's it about?

Verbs followed by con and an object

Here are some verbs taking con in Spanish that sometimes have a different construction in English:

comparar algo/a alguien con algo/alguien
to compare something/somebody to/with something/somebody
Siempre me comparan con mi hermana.
I'm always being compared to my sister.

contar con alguien/algo to rely on somebody/something
Cuento contigo. I'm relying on you.

encontrarse con alguien to meet somebody (by chance)
Me encontré con ella al entrar en el banco.
I met her as I was going into the bank.

enfadarse con alguien to get annoyed with somebody
No te enfades con él, lo ha hecho sin intención.
Don't be annoyed with him, he didn't mean to do it.

estar de acuerdo con alguien/algo to agree with somebody/something
Estoy totalmente de acuerdo contigo. I totally agree with you.

hablar con alguien to talk to somebody
¿Puedo hablar con usted un momento? May I talk to you for a moment?

soñar con alguien/algo to dream about somebody/something
Ayer soñé con él. I dreamed about him yesterday.

Verbs followed by en and an object

Here are some verbs taking en in Spanish that sometimes have a different construction in English:

entrar en (un edificio/un cuarto) to enter, go into (a building/a room)
Entré en la casa. I went into the house.

pensar en algo/alguien to think about something/somebody
No quiero pensar en eso. I don't want to think about that.

trabajar en (una oficina/una fábrica) to work in (an office/a factory)
Trabaja en un banco. She works in a bank.

Verbs followed by por and an object

Here are some verbs taking por in Spanish that have a different construction in English:

interesarse por algo/alguien to be interested in something/somebody or to ask about something/somebody

Me interesaba mucho por la arqueología.

I was very interested in archaeology.

Llamó para interesarse por su salud. He called to ask after her health.

preguntar por alguien to ask for/about somebody

Si preguntan por mí, no digas nada.

Don't say anything if they ask about me.

preocuparse por algo/alguien to worry about something/somebody

Se preocupa mucho por su apariencia.

He worries a lot about his appearance.

Verbs taking a direct object in Spanish but not in English

In English there are a few verbs that are followed by *at*, *for* or *to* which, in Spanish, are not followed by any preposition other than the personal **a** where required.

mirar algo/a alguien to look at something/somebody
Mira esta foto. Look at this photo.

escuchar algo/a alguien to listen to something/somebody
Me gusta escuchar música. I like listening to music.

buscar algo/a alguien to look for something/somebody
Estoy buscando las gafas. I'm looking for my glasses.
Estoy buscando a mi hermano. I'm looking for my brother.

pedir algo to ask for something
Pidió una taza de té. He asked for a cup of tea.

esperar algo/a alguien to wait for something/somebody
Estamos esperando el tren. We're waiting for the train.
Estoy esperando a mi hermana. I'm waiting for my sister.

pagar algo to pay for something
Ya he pagado el billete. I've already paid for my ticket.

Verbs followed by personal a

Spanish speakers use **a** in a way that has no equivalent in English. They use it before nouns referring to specific people and pets when these are the direct object of a verb:

>¿Conoces a Maite? Do you know Maite?
>Quiere a Pablo. She loves Pablo.
>No vi a Juan. I didn't see Juan.
>Quiero invitar a Teresa a cenar. I want to invite Teresa to supper.
>Llama a un médico. Call a doctor.

Personal **a** is also used before certain pronouns referring to people (but NOT object pronouns):

>No conozco a nadie. I don't know anybody.
>¿Viste a alguien? Did you see anyone?
>¿A quién llamaste? Who did you call?

Personal **a** is NOT normally used after **tener** (meaning *to have*):

>Tengo dos hermanas. I've got two sisters.
>Tiene un perro. He's got a dog.

VERB TABLES

Introduction

The **Verb Tables** in the following section contain 120 tables of Spanish verbs (some regular and some irregular) in alphabetical order. Each table shows you the following forms: **Present, Present Perfect, Preterite, Imperfect, Future, Conditional, Present Subjunctive, Imperfect Subjunctive, Imperative** and the **Past Participle** and **Gerund**. For more information on these tenses and how they are formed you should look at the section on Verb Formation in the main text on pages 10–55. If you want to find out in more detail how verbs are used in different contexts, the *Easy Learning Spanish Grammar* will give you additional information.

In order to help you use the verbs shown in the **Verb Tables** correctly, there are also a number of example phrases at the bottom of each page to show the verb as it is used in context.

In Spanish there are both **regular** verbs (their forms follow the normal rules) and **irregular** verbs (their forms do not follow the normal rules). The regular verbs in these tables that you can use as models for other regular verbs are:

hablar (regular **-ar** verb, Verb Table 118–119)
comer (regular **-er** verb, Verb Table 52–53)
vivir (regular **-ir** verb, Verb Table 234–235)

The irregular verbs are shown in full.

The **Verb Index** at the end of this section contains over 1200 verbs, each of which is cross-referred to one of the verbs given in the Verb Tables.
The table shows the patterns that the verb listed in the index follows.

abolir (to abolish)

	PRESENT		PRESENT PERFECT
(yo)			he abolido
(tú)			has abolido
(él/ella/usted)			ha abolido
(nosotros/as)	abolimos		hemos abolido
(vosotros/as)	abolís		habéis abolido
(ellos/ellas/ ustedes)			han abolido

Present tense only used in persons shown

	PRETERITE	IMPERFECT
(yo)	abolí	abolía
(tú)	aboliste	abolías
(él/ella/usted)	abolió	abolía
(nosotros/as)	abolimos	abolíamos
(vosotros/as)	abolisteis	abolíais
(ellos/ellas/ ustedes)	abolieron	abolían

GERUND	PAST PARTICIPLE
aboliendo	abolido

EXAMPLE PHRASES

Hay que **abolirlo**. It ought to be abolished.

¿Por qué no **abolimos** esta ley? Why don't we abolish this law?

Han abolido la pena de muerte. They have abolished the death penalty.

Abolieron la esclavitud. They abolished slavery.

Remember that subject pronouns are not used very often in Spanish.

abolir

	FUTURE	CONDITIONAL
(yo)	aboliré	aboliría
(tú)	abolirás	abolirías
(él/ella/usted)	abolirá	aboliría
(nosotros/as)	aboliremos	aboliríamos
(vosotros/as)	aboliréis	aboliríais
(ellos/ellas/ustedes)	abolirán	abolirían

	PRESENT SUBJUNCTIVE	IMPERFECT SUBJUNCTIVE
(yo)	*not used*	aboliera or aboliese
(tú)		abolieras or abolieses
(él/ella/usted)		aboliera or aboliese
(nosotros/as)		aboliéramos or aboliésemos
(vosotros/as)		abolierais or abolieseis
(ellos/ellas/ustedes)		abolieran or aboliesen

IMPERATIVE
abolid

EXAMPLE PHRASES

Sólo unidos **aboliremos** la injusticia. We will only abolish injustice if we stand together.

Prometieron que **abolirían** la censura. They promised they'd abolish censorship.

Si lo **abolieran**, se producirían disturbios. There would be riots if it were abolished.

Remember that subject pronouns are not used very often in Spanish.

abrir (to open)

	PRESENT		PRESENT PERFECT
(yo)	abro		he abierto
(tú)	abres		has abierto
(él/ella/usted)	abre		ha abierto
(nosotros/as)	abrimos		hemos abierto
(vosotros/as)	abrís		habéis abierto
(ellos/ellas/ustedes)	abren		han abierto

	PRETERITE		IMPERFECT
(yo)	abrí		abría
(tú)	abriste		abrías
(él/ella/usted)	abrió		abría
(nosotros/as)	abrimos		abríamos
(vosotros/as)	abristeis		abríais
(ellos/ellas/ustedes)	abrieron		abrían

GERUND	PAST PARTICIPLE
abriendo	abierto

EXAMPLE PHRASES

Hoy **se abre** el plazo de matrícula. Registration begins today.

Han abierto un restaurante cerca de aquí. They've opened a new restaurant near here.

¿Quién **abrió** la ventana? Who opened the window?

La llave **abría** el armario. The key opened the cupboard.

Remember that subject pronouns are not used very often in Spanish.

abrir

	FUTURE	CONDITIONAL
(yo)	abriré	abriría
(tú)	abrirás	abrirías
(él/ella/usted)	abrirá	abriría
(nosotros/as)	abriremos	abriríamos
(vosotros/as)	abriréis	abriríais
(ellos/ellas/ ustedes)	abrirán	abrirían

	PRESENT SUBJUNCTIVE	IMPERFECT SUBJUNCTIVE
(yo)	abra	abriera or abriese
(tú)	abras	abrieras or abrieses
(él/ella/usted)	abra	abriera or abriese
(nosotros/as)	abramos	abriéramos or abriésemos
(vosotros/as)	abráis	abrierais or abrieseis
(ellos/ellas/ ustedes)	abran	abrieran or abriesen

IMPERATIVE
abre / abrid

Use the present subjunctive in all cases other than these **tú** and **vosotros** affirmative forms.

EXAMPLE PHRASES

Abrirán todas las puertas de la catedral. They'll open all the doors of the cathedral.

Me dijo que hoy **abrirían** sólo por la tarde. He told me that they'd only be open in the evening.

No creo que **abran** un nuevo supermercado por aquí. I don't think they'll open a new supermarket here.

No **abras** ese grifo. Don't turn on that tap.

Remember that subject pronouns are not used very often in Spanish.

Verb tables

actuar (to act)

	PRESENT		PRESENT PERFECT
(yo)	actúo		he actuado
(tú)	actúas		has actuado
(él/ella/usted)	actúa		ha actuado
(nosotros/as)	actuamos		hemos actuado
(vosotros/as)	actuáis		habéis actuado
(ellos/ellas/ ustedes)	actúan		han actuado

	PRETERITE		IMPERFECT
(yo)	actué		actuaba
(tú)	actuaste		actuabas
(él/ella/usted)	actuó		actuaba
(nosotros/as)	actuamos		actuábamos
(vosotros/as)	actuasteis		actuabais
(ellos/ellas/ ustedes)	actuaron		actuaban

GERUND	PAST PARTICIPLE
actuando	actuado

EXAMPLE PHRASES

Actúa de una forma muy rara. He's acting very strangely.

Ha actuado siguiendo un impulso. He acted on impulse.

Actuó en varias películas. He was in several films.

Actuaba como si no supiera nada. She was behaving as if she didn't know anything about it.

Remember that subject pronouns are not used very often in Spanish.

actuar

	FUTURE	CONDITIONAL
(yo)	actuaré	actuaría
(tú)	actuarás	actuarías
(él/ella/usted)	actuará	actuaría
(nosotros/as)	actuaremos	actuaríamos
(vosotros/as)	actuaréis	actuaríais
(ellos/ellas/ ustedes)	actuarán	actuarían

	PRESENT SUBJUNCTIVE	IMPERFECT SUBJUNCTIVE
(yo)	actúe	actuara or actuase
(tú)	actúes	actuaras or actuases
(él/ella/usted)	actúe	actuara or actuase
(nosotros/as)	actuemos	actuáramos or actuásemos
(vosotros/as)	actuéis	actuarais or actuaseis
(ellos/ellas/ ustedes)	actúen	actuaran or actuasen

IMPERATIVE
actúa / actuad

Use the present subjunctive in all cases other than these **tú** and **vosotros** affirmative forms.

EXAMPLE PHRASES

¿Quién **actuará** en su próxima película? Who will be in his next film?

Yo nunca **actuaría** así. I'd never behave like that.

Si **actuara** de forma más lógica, sería más fácil atraparle. It would be easier to catch him if he behaved in a more logical way.

Actuad como mejor os parezca. Do as you think best.

Remember that subject pronouns are not used very often in Spanish.

adquirir (to acquire)

	PRESENT		PRESENT PERFECT
(yo)	adquiero		he adquirido
(tú)	adquieres		has adquirido
(él/ella/usted)	adquiere		ha adquirido
(nosotros/as)	adquirimos		hemos adquirido
(vosotros/as)	adquirís		habéis adquirido
(ellos/ellas/ ustedes)	adquieren		han adquirido

	PRETERITE		IMPERFECT
(yo)	adquirí		adquiría
(tú)	adquiriste		adquirías
(él/ella/usted)	adquirió		adquiría
(nosotros/as)	adquirimos		adquiríamos
(vosotros/as)	adquiristeis		adquiríais
(ellos/ellas/ ustedes)	adquirieron		adquirían

GERUND	PAST PARTICIPLE
adquiriendo	adquirido

EXAMPLE PHRASES

Adquiere cada vez mayor importancia. It's becoming more and more important.

Está adquiriendo una reputación que no merece. It's getting a reputation it doesn't deserve.

Hemos adquirido una colección de sellos. We've bought a stamp collection.

Con el tiempo **adquirió** cierta madurez. Over the years he gained a certain maturity.

Remember that subject pronouns are not used very often in Spanish.

adquirir

	FUTURE	CONDITIONAL
(yo)	adquiriré	adquiriría
(tú)	adquirirás	adquirirías
(él/ella/usted)	adquirirá	adquiriría
(nosotros/as)	adquiriremos	adquiriríamos
(vosotros/as)	adquiriréis	adquiriríais
(ellos/ellas/ ustedes)	adquirirán	adquirirían

	PRESENT SUBJUNCTIVE	IMPERFECT SUBJUNCTIVE
(yo)	adquiera	adquiriera or adquiriese
(tú)	adquieras	adquirieras or adquirieses
(él/ella/usted)	adquiera	adquiriera or adquiriese
(nosotros/as)	adquiramos	adquiriéramos or adquiriésemos
(vosotros/as)	adquiráis	adquirierais or adquirieseis
(ellos/ellas/ ustedes)	adquieran	adquirieran or adquiriesen

IMPERATIVE
adquiere / adquirid

Use the present subjunctive in all cases other than these **tú** and **vosotros** affirmative forms.

EXAMPLE PHRASES
Al final **adquirirán** los derechos de publicación. They will get the publishing rights in the end.

¿Lo **adquirirías** por ese precio? Would you buy it for that price?

Adquiera o no la nacionalidad, podrá permanecer en el país. She'll be able to stay in the country whether she becomes naturalized or not.

Tenía gran interés en que **adquiriera** el cuadro. He was very keen that she should buy the picture.

Remember that subject pronouns are not used very often in Spanish.

advertir (to warn; to notice)

	PRESENT	PRESENT PERFECT
(yo)	advierto	he advertido
(tú)	adviertes	has advertido
(él/ella/usted)	advierte	ha advertido
(nosotros/as)	advertimos	hemos advertido
(vosotros/as)	advertís	habéis advertido
(ellos/ellas/ ustedes)	advierten	han advertido

	PRETERITE	IMPERFECT
(yo)	advertí	advertía
(tú)	advertiste	advertías
(él/ella/usted)	advirtió	advertía
(nosotros/as)	advertimos	advertíamos
(vosotros/as)	advertisteis	advertíais
(ellos/ellas/ ustedes)	advirtieron	advertían

GERUND	PAST PARTICIPLE
advirtiendo	advertido

EXAMPLE PHRASES

Te **advierto** que no va a ser nada fácil. I must warn you that it won't be at all easy.

No **he advertido** nada extraño en su comportamiento. I haven't noticed anything strange about his behaviour.

Ya te **advertí** que no intervinieras. I warned you not to get involved.

Las señales **advertían** del peligro. The signs warned of danger.

Remember that subject pronouns are not used very often in Spanish.

advertir

	FUTURE	CONDITIONAL
(yo)	advertiré	advertiría
(tú)	advertirás	advertirías
(él/ella/usted)	advertirá	advertiría
(nosotros/as)	advertiremos	advertiríamos
(vosotros/as)	advertiréis	advertiríais
(ellos/ellas/ ustedes)	advertirán	advertirían

	PRESENT SUBJUNCTIVE	IMPERFECT SUBJUNCTIVE
(yo)	advierta	advirtiera or advirtiese
(tú)	adviertas	advirtieras or advirtieses
(él/ella/usted)	advierta	advirtiera or advirtiese
(nosotros/as)	advirtamos	advirtiéramos or advirtiésemos
(vosotros/as)	advirtáis	advirtierais or advirtieseis
(ellos/ellas/ ustedes)	adviertan	advirtieran or advirtiesen

IMPERATIVE
advierte / advertid

Use the present subjunctive in all cases other than these **tú** and **vosotros** affirmative forms.

EXAMPLE PHRASES

Si **advirtiera** algún cambio, llámenos. If you should notice any change, give us a call.

Adviértele del riesgo que entraña. Warn him about the risk involved.

almorzar (to have lunch)

	PRESENT		PRESENT PERFECT
(yo)	almuerzo		he almorzado
(tú)	almuerzas		has almorzado
(él/ella/usted)	almuerza		ha almorzado
(nosotros/as)	almorzamos		hemos almorzado
(vosotros/as)	almorzáis		habéis almorzado
(ellos/ellas/ ustedes)	almuerzan		han almorzado

	PRETERITE		IMPERFECT
(yo)	almorcé		almorzaba
(tú)	almorzaste		almorzabas
(él/ella/usted)	almorzó		almorzaba
(nosotros/as)	almorzamos		almorzábamos
(vosotros/as)	almorzasteis		almorzabais
(ellos/ellas/ ustedes)	almorzaron		almorzaban

GERUND	PAST PARTICIPLE
almorzando	almorzado

EXAMPLE PHRASES

¿Dónde vais a **almorzar**? Where are you going to have lunch?

¿A qué hora **almuerzas**? What time do you have lunch?

Ya **hemos almorzado**. We've already had lunch.

Almorcé en un bar. I had lunch in a bar.

Siempre **almorzaba** un bocadillo. He always had a sandwich for lunch.

Remember that subject pronouns are not used very often in Spanish.

almorzar

	FUTURE	CONDITIONAL
(yo)	almorzaré	almorzaría
(tú)	almorzarás	almorzarías
(él/ella/usted)	almorzará	almorzaría
(nosotros/as)	almorzaremos	almorzaríamos
(vosotros/as)	almorzaréis	almorzaríais
(ellos/ellas/ ustedes)	almorzarán	almorzarían

	PRESENT SUBJUNCTIVE	IMPERFECT SUBJUNCTIVE
(yo)	almuerce	almorzara or almorzase
(tú)	almuerces	almorzaras or almorzases
(él/ella/usted)	almuerce	almorzara or almorzase
(nosotros/as)	almorcemos	almorzáramos or almorzásemos
(vosotros/as)	almorcéis	almorzarais or almorzaseis
(ellos/ellas/ ustedes)	almuercen	almorzaran or almorzasen

IMPERATIVE
almuerza / almorzad

Use the present subjunctive in all cases other than these tú and vosotros affirmative forms.

EXAMPLE PHRASES

Mañana **almorzaremos** todos juntos. We'll all have lunch together tomorrow.

Almuerce o no siempre me entra sueño a esta hora. I always feel sleepy at this time of the day, regardless of whether I've had lunch or not.

Si **almorzara** así todos los días, estaría mucho más gordo. I'd be much fatter if I had this sort of lunch every day.

Remember that subject pronouns are not used very often in Spanish.

amanecer (to get light; to wake up)

	PRESENT		PRESENT PERFECT
(yo)	amanezco		he amanecido
(tú)	amaneces		has amanecido
(él/ella/usted)	amanece		ha amanecido
(nosotros/as)	amanecemos		hemos amanecido
(vosotros/as)	amanecéis		habéis amanecido
(ellos/ellas/ ustedes)	amanecen		han amanecido

	PRETERITE		IMPERFECT
(yo)	amanecí		amanecía
(tú)	amaneciste		amanecías
(él/ella/usted)	amaneció		amanecía
(nosotros/as)	amanecimos		amanecíamos
(vosotros/as)	amanecisteis		amanecíais
(ellos/ellas/ ustedes)	amanecieron		amanecían

GERUND	PAST PARTICIPLE
amaneciendo	amanecido

EXAMPLE PHRASES

Siempre **amanece** nublado. The day always starts off cloudy.

Justo en ese momento **estaba amaneciendo**. Just then, dawn was breaking.

Hoy **ha amanecido** a las ocho. Today it got light at eight o'clock.

La ciudad **amaneció** desierta. In the morning, the town was deserted.

Amanecía de un humor de perros. She would wake up in a really bad mood.

Remember that subject pronouns are not used very often in Spanish.

amanecer

	FUTURE	CONDITIONAL
(yo)	amaneceré	amanecería
(tú)	amanecerás	amanecerías
(él/ella/usted)	amanecerá	amanecería
(nosotros/as)	amaneceremos	amaneceríamos
(vosotros/as)	amaneceréis	amaneceríais
(ellos/ellas/ ustedes)	amanecerán	amanecerían

	PRESENT SUBJUNCTIVE	IMPERFECT SUBJUNCTIVE
(yo)	amanezca	amaneciera or amaneciese
(tú)	amanezcas	amanecieras or amanecieses
(él/ella/usted)	amanezca	amaneciera or amaneclese
(nosotros/as)	amanezcamos	amaneciéramos or amaneciésemos
(vosotros/as)	amanezcáis	amanecierals or amanecieseis
(ellos/ellas/ ustedes)	amanezcan	amanecieran or amaneciesen

IMPERATIVE
amanece / amaneced
Use the present subjunctive in all cases other than these **tú** and **vosotros** affirmative forms.

EXAMPLE PHRASES
Pronto **amanecerá**. It will soon be daylight.
Saldremos en cuanto **amanezca**. We'll set off as soon as it gets light.
Si **amanecieras** con fiebre, toma una de estas pastillas. If you should wake up with a temperature, take one of these pills.

Remember that subject pronouns are not used very often in Spanish.

andar (to walk)

	PRESENT		PRESENT PERFECT
(yo)	ando		he andado
(tú)	andas		has andado
(él/ella/usted)	anda		ha andado
(nosotros/as)	andamos		hemos andado
(vosotros/as)	andáis		habéis andado
(ellos/ellas/ ustedes)	andan		han andado

	PRETERITE	IMPERFECT
(yo)	anduve	andaba
(tú)	anduviste	andabas
(él/ella/usted)	anduvo	andaba
(nosotros/as)	anduvimos	andábamos
(vosotros/as)	anduvisteis	andabais
(ellos/ellas/ ustedes)	anduvieron	andaban

GERUND	PAST PARTICIPLE
andando	andado

EXAMPLE PHRASES

Andar es un ejercicio muy sano. Walking is very good exercise.

Hemos andado todo el camino hasta aquí. We walked all the way here.

Anduvimos al menos 10 km. We walked at least 10 km.

Por aquel entonces **andaban** mal de dinero. Back then they were short of money.

Voy **andando** al trabajo todos los días. I walk to work every day.

Remember that subject pronouns are not used very often in Spanish.

andar

	FUTURE	CONDITIONAL
(yo)	andaré	andaría
(tú)	andarás	andarías
(él/ella/usted)	andará	andaría
(nosotros/as)	andaremos	andaríamos
(vosotros/as)	andaréis	andaríais
(ellos/ellas/ ustedes)	andarán	andarían

	PRESENT SUBJUNCTIVE	IMPERFECT SUBJUNCTIVE
(yo)	ande	anduviera or anduviese
(tú)	andes	anduvieras or anduvieses
(él/ella/usted)	ande	anduviera or anduviese
(nosotros/as)	andemos	anduviéramos or anduviésemos
(vosotros/as)	andéis	anduvierais or anduvieseis
(ellos/ellas/ ustedes)	anden	anduvieran or anduviesen

IMPERATIVE
anda / andad

Use the present subjunctive in all cases other than these **tú** and **vosotros** affirmative forms.

EXAMPLE PHRASES

Andará por los cuarenta. He must be about forty.

Yo **me andaría** con pies de plomo. I'd tread very carefully.

El médico le ha aconsejado que **ande** varios kilómetros al día. The doctor has advised him to walk several kilometres a day.

Si **anduvieras** con más cuidado, no te pasarían esas cosas. If you were more careful, this sort of thing wouldn't happen to you.

Remember that subject pronouns are not used very often in Spanish.

apoderarse (to take possession)

	PRESENT	PRESENT PERFECT
(yo)	me apodero	me he apoderado
(tú)	te apoderas	te has apoderado
(él/ella/usted)	se apodera	se ha apoderado
(nosotros/as)	nos apoderamos	nos hemos apoderado
(vosotros/as)	os apoderáis	os habéis apoderado
(ellos/ellas/ ustedes)	se apoderan	se han apoderado

	PRETERITE	IMPERFECT
(yo)	me apoderé	me apoderaba
(tú)	te apoderaste	te apoderabas
(él/ella/usted)	se apoderó	se apoderaba
(nosotros/as)	nos apoderamos	nos apoderábamos
(vosotros/as)	os apoderasteis	os apoderabais
(ellos/ellas/ ustedes)	se apoderaron	se apoderaban

GERUND	PAST PARTICIPLE
apoderando	apoderado

EXAMPLE PHRASES

En esas situaciones, el miedo **se apodera** de mí. In situations like that,
   I find myself gripped by fear.

Poco a poco **se han ido apoderando** de las riquezas del país. Little by little,
   they've seized the country's riches.

Se apoderaron de las joyas y huyeron. They ran off with the jewels.

El desánimo **se apoderaba** de nosotros por momentos. We were feeling more
   and more discouraged by the minute.

Remember that subject pronouns are not used very often in Spanish.

apoderarse

	FUTURE	CONDITIONAL
(yo)	me apoderaré	me apoderaría
(tú)	te apoderarás	te apoderarías
(él/ella/usted)	se apoderará	se apoderaría
(nosotros/as)	nos apoderaremos	nos apoderaríamos
(vosotros/as)	os apoderaréis	os apoderaríais
(ellos/ellas/ ustedes)	se apoderarán	se apoderarían

	PRESENT SUBJUNCTIVE	IMPERFECT SUBJUNCTIVE
(yo)	me apodere	me apoderara or apoderase
(tú)	te apoderes	te apoderaras or apoderases
(él/ella/usted)	se apodere	se apoderara or apoderase
(nosotros/as)	nos apoderemos	nos apoderáramos or apoderásemos
(vosotros/as)	os apoderéis	os apoderarais or apoderaseis
(ellos/ellas/ ustedes)	se apoderen	se apoderaran or apoderasen

IMPERATIVE
apodérate / apoderaos

Use the present subjunctive in all cases other than these **tú** and **vosotros** affirmative forms.

EXAMPLE PHRASES
No dejes que la curiosidad **se apodere** de ti. Don't let curiosity get the better of you.

aprobar (to pass; to approve of)

	PRESENT	PRESENT PERFECT
(yo)	apruebo	he aprobado
(tú)	apruebas	has aprobado
(él/ella/usted)	aprueba	ha aprobado
(nosotros/as)	aprobamos	hemos aprobado
(vosotros/as)	aprobáis	habéis aprobado
(ellos/ellas/ ustedes)	aprueban	han aprobado

	PRETERITE	IMPERFECT
(yo)	aprobé	aprobaba
(tú)	aprobaste	aprobabas
(él/ella/usted)	aprobó	aprobaba
(nosotros/as)	aprobamos	aprobábamos
(vosotros/as)	aprobasteis	aprobabais
(ellos/ellas/ ustedes)	aprobaron	aprobaban

GERUND	PAST PARTICIPLE
aprobando	aprobado

EXAMPLE PHRASES

No **apruebo** esa conducta. I don't approve of that sort of behaviour.

Este año lo **estoy aprobando** todo. So far this year I've passed everything.

Han aprobado una ley antitabaco. They've passed an anti-smoking law.

¿**Aprobaste** el examen? Did you pass the exam?

La decisión **fue aprobada** por mayoría. The decision was approved by a majority.

Remember that subject pronouns are not used very often in Spanish.

aprobar

	FUTURE	CONDITIONAL
(yo)	aprobaré	aprobaría
(tú)	aprobarás	aprobarías
(él/ella/usted)	aprobará	aprobaría
(nosotros/as)	aprobaremos	aprobaríamos
(vosotros/as)	aprobaréis	aprobaríais
(ellos/ellas/ ustedes)	aprobarán	aprobarían

	PRESENT SUBJUNCTIVE	IMPERFECT SUBJUNCTIVE
(yo)	apruebe	aprobara or aprobase
(tú)	apruebes	aprobaras or aprobases
(él/ella/usted)	apruebe	aprobara or aprobase
(nosotros/as)	aprobemos	aprobáramos or aprobásemos
(vosotros/as)	aprobéis	aprobarais or aprobaseis
(ellos/ellas/ ustedes)	aprueben	aprobaran or aprobasen

IMPERATIVE
aprueba / aprobad

Use the present subjunctive in all cases other than these **tú** and **vosotros** affirmative forms.

Remember that subject pronouns are not used very often in Spanish.

arrancar (to pull up)

	PRESENT		PRESENT PERFECT
(yo)	arranco		he arrancado
(tú)	arrancas		has arrancado
(él/ella/usted)	arranca		ha arrancado
(nosotros/as)	arrancamos		hemos arrancado
(vosotros/as)	arrancáis		habéis arrancado
(ellos/ellas/ ustedes)	arrancan		han arrancado

	PRETERITE		IMPERFECT
(yo)	arranqué		arrancaba
(tú)	arrancaste		arrancabas
(él/ella/usted)	arrancó		arrancaba
(nosotros/as)	arrancamos		arrancábamos
(vosotros/as)	arrancasteis		arrancabais
(ellos/ellas/ ustedes)	arrancaron		arrancaban

GERUND	PAST PARTICIPLE
arrancando	arrancado

EXAMPLE PHRASES

Lo tienes que **arrancar** de raíz. You must pull it up by its roots.

Estaba arrancando malas hierbas. I was pulling up weeds.

Me **has arrancado** un botón. You've pulled off one of my buttons.

El viento **arrancó** varios árboles. Several trees were uprooted in the wind.

Remember that subject pronouns are not used very often in Spanish.

arrancar

	FUTURE	CONDITIONAL
(yo)	arrancaré	arrancaría
(tú)	arrancarás	arrancarías
(él/ella/usted)	arrancará	arrancaría
(nosotros/as)	arrancaremos	arrancaríamos
(vosotros/as)	arrancaréis	arrancaríais
(ellos/ellas/ ustedes)	arrancarán	arrancarían

	PRESENT SUBJUNCTIVE	IMPERFECT SUBJUNCTIVE
(yo)	arranque	arrancara or arrancase
(tú)	arranques	arrancaras or arrancases
(él/ella/usted)	arranque	arrancara or arrancase
(nosotros/as)	arranquemos	arrancáramos or arrancásemos
(vosotros/as)	arranquéis	arrancarais or arrancaseis
(ellos/ellas/ ustedes)	arranquen	arrancaran or arrancasen

IMPERATIVE
arranca / arrancad

Use the present subjunctive in all cases other than these **tú** and **vosotros** affirmative forms.

EXAMPLE PHRASES
No **arranques** hojas del cuaderno. Don't go tearing pages out of the exercise book.

Arranca y vámonos. Start the engine and let's get going.

Remember that subject pronouns are not used very often in Spanish.

arrepentirse (to be sorry)

	PRESENT	PRESENT PERFECT
(yo)	me arrepiento	me he arrepentido
(tú)	te arrepientes	te has arrepentido
(él/ella/usted)	se arrepiente	se ha arrepentido
(nosotros/as)	nos arrepentimos	nos hemos arrepentido
(vosotros/as)	os arrepentís	os habéis arrepentido
(ellos/ellas/ ustedes)	se arrepienten	se han arrepentido

	PRETERITE	IMPERFECT
(yo)	me arrepentí	me arrepentía
(tú)	te arrepentiste	te arrepentías
(él/ella/usted)	se arrepintió	se arrepentía
(nosotros/as)	nos arrepentimos	nos arrepentíamos
(vosotros/as)	os arrepentisteis	os arrepentíais
(ellos/ellas/ ustedes)	se arrepintieron	se arrepentían

GERUND
arrepintiéndose, etc

PAST PARTICIPLE
arrepentido

EXAMPLE PHRASES

¡**Te** vas a **arrepentir** de esto! You'll be sorry you did that!

No **me arrepiento** de nada. I don't regret anything.

Arrepintiéndote en serio, seguro que te perdonarán. If you're truly sorry, I'm sure they'll forgive you.

Se arrepintieron y decidieron no vender la casa. They changed their minds and decided not to sell the house.

Remember that subject pronouns are not used very often in Spanish.

arrepentirse

	FUTURE	CONDITIONAL
(yo)	me arrepentiré	me arrepentiría
(tú)	te arrepentirás	te arrepentirías
(él/ella/usted)	se arrepentirá	se arrepentiría
(nosotros/as)	nos arrepentiremos	nos arrepentiríamos
(vosotros/as)	os arrepentiréis	os arrepentiríais
(ellos/ellas/ ustedes)	se arrepentirán	se arrepentirían

	PRESENT SUBJUNCTIVE	IMPERFECT SUBJUNCTIVE
(yo)	me arrepienta	me arrepintiera or arrepintiese
(tú)	te arrepientas	te arrepintieras or arrepintieses
(él/ella/usted)	se arrepienta	se arrepintiera or arrepintiese
(nosotros/as)	nos arrepintamos	nos arrepintiéramos or arrepintiésemos
(vosotros/as)	os arrepintáis	os arrepintierais or arrepintieseis
(ellos/ellas/ ustedes)	se arrepientan	se arrepintieran or arrepintiesen

IMPERATIVE
arrepiéntete / arrepentíos

Use the present subjunctive in all cases other than these **tú** and **vosotros** affirmative forms.

EXAMPLE PHRASES
Algún día **se arrepentirá** de no haber estudiado una carrera. One day he'll be sorry he didn't go to university.

No **te arrepientas** nunca de haber dicho la verdad. Don't ever regret having told the truth.

Remember that subject pronouns are not used very often in Spanish.

atravesar (to cross; to go through)

	PRESENT	PRESENT PERFECT
(yo)	atravieso	he atravesado
(tú)	atraviesas	has atravesado
(él/ella/usted)	atraviesa	ha atravesado
(nosotros/as)	atravesamos	hemos atravesado
(vosotros/as)	atravesáis	habéis atravesado
(ellos/ellas/ ustedes)	atraviesan	han atravesado

	PRETERITE	IMPERFECT
(yo)	atravesé	atravesaba
(tú)	atravesaste	atravesabas
(él/ella/usted)	atravesó	atravesaba
(nosotros/as)	atravesamos	atravesábamos
(vosotros/as)	atravesasteis	atravesabais
(ellos/ellas/ ustedes)	atravesaron	atravesaban

GERUND	PAST PARTICIPLE
atravesando	atravesado

EXAMPLE PHRASES

Atravesamos un mal momento. We're going through a bad patch.

En este momento **está atravesando** la ciudad en un coche descubierto. Right now he's driving through the city in an open-topped vehicle.

Hemos atravesado el río a nado. We swam across the river.

La bala le **atravesó** el cráneo. The bullet went through his skull.

Un camión **se** nos **atravesó** en la carretera. A lorry pulled out in front of us on the road.

Remember that subject pronouns are not used very often in Spanish.

atravesar

	FUTURE	CONDITIONAL
(yo)	atravesaré	atravesaría
(tú)	atravesarás	atravesarías
(él/ella/usted)	atravesará	atravesaría
(nosotros/as)	atravesaremos	atravesaríamos
(vosotros/as)	atravesaréis	atravesaríais
(ellos/ellas/ ustedes)	atravesarán	atravesarían

	PRESENT SUBJUNCTIVE	IMPERFECT SUBJUNCTIVE
(yo)	atravlese	atravesara or atravesase
(tú)	atravieses	atravesaras or atravesases
(él/ella/usted)	atraviese	atravesara or atravesase
(nosotros/as)	atravesemos	atravesáramos or atravesásemos
(vosotros/as)	atraveséis	atravesarais or atravesaseis
(ellos/ellas/ ustedes)	atraviesen	atravesaran or atravesasen

IMPERATIVE
atraviesa / atravesad

Use the present subjunctive in all cases other than these **tú** and **vosotros** affirmative forms.

EXAMPLE PHRASES
El túnel **atravesará** la montaña. The tunnel will go through the mountain.

aunar (to join together)

	PRESENT		PRESENT PERFECT
(yo)	aúno		he aunado
(tú)	aúnas		has aunado
(él/ella/usted)	aúna		ha aunado
(nosotros/as)	aunamos		hemos aunado
(vosotros/as)	aunáis		habéis aunado
(ellos/ellas/ ustedes)	aúnan		han aunado

	PRETERITE		IMPERFECT
(yo)	auné		aunaba
(tú)	aunaste		aunabas
(él/ella/usted)	aunó		aunaba
(nosotros/as)	aunamos		aunábamos
(vosotros/as)	aunasteis		aunabais
(ellos/ellas/ ustedes)	aunaron		aunaban

GERUND	PAST PARTICIPLE
aunando	aunado

EXAMPLE PHRASES

En esta obra **se han aunado** imaginación y técnica. This play combines imagination and technique.

Aunaron esfuerzos. They joined forces.

La pintura barroca **aunaba** conocimientos de geometría y anatomía.
Baroque painting brought knowledge of geometry and anatomy together.

aunar

	FUTURE	CONDITIONAL
(yo)	aunaré	aunaría
(tú)	aunarás	aunarías
(él/ella/usted)	aunará	aunaría
(nosotros/as)	aunaremos	aunaríamos
(vosotros/as)	aunaréis	aunaríais
(ellos/ellas/ ustedes)	aunarán	aunarían

	PRESENT SUBJUNCTIVE	IMPERFECT SUBJUNCTIVE
(yo)	aúne	aunara or aunase
(tú)	aúnes	aunaras or aunases
(él/ella/usted)	aúne	aunara or aunase
(nosotros/as)	aunemos	aunáramos or aunásemos
(vosotros/as)	aunéis	aunarais or aunaseis
(ellos/ellas/ ustedes)	aúnen	aunaran or aunasen

IMPERATIVE
aúna / aunad

Use the present subjunctive in all cases other than these **tú** and **vosotros** affirmative forms.

Remember that subject pronouns are not used very often in Spanish.

avergonzar (to shame)

	PRESENT	PRESENT PERFECT
(yo)	avergüenzo	he avergonzado
(tú)	avergüenzas	has avergonzado
(él/ella/usted)	avergüenza	ha avergonzado
(nosotros/as)	avergonzamos	hemos avergonzado
(vosotros/as)	avergonzáis	habéis avergonzado
(ellos/ellas/ ustedes)	avergüenzan	han avergonzado

	PRETERITE	IMPERFECT
(yo)	avergoncé	avergonzaba
(tú)	avergonzaste	avergonzabas
(él/ella/usted)	avergonzó	avergonzaba
(nosotros/as)	avergonzamos	avergonzábamos
(vosotros/as)	avergonzasteis	avergonzabais
(ellos/ellas/ ustedes)	avergonzaron	avergonzaban

GERUND	PAST PARTICIPLE
avergonzando	avergonzado

EXAMPLE PHRASES

Tendrías que **avergonzarte**. You should be ashamed of yourself.

Le **avergüenza** no tener dinero. He's ashamed of having no money.

Cuando me lo dijo **me avergoncé**. I was embarrassed when he told me.

Se avergonzaba de su familia. He was ashamed of his family.

Avergonzándote no arreglas nada. Being ashamed doesn't solve anything.

Remember that subject pronouns are not used very often in Spanish.

avergonzar

	FUTURE	CONDITIONAL
(yo)	avergonzaré	avergonzaría
(tú)	avergonzarás	avergonzarías
(él/ella/usted)	avergonzará	avergonzaría
(nosotros/as)	avergonzaremos	avergonzaríamos
(vosotros/as)	avegonzaréis	avergonzaríais
(ellos/ellas/ ustedes)	avergonzarán	avergonzarían

	PRESENT SUBJUNCTIVE	IMPERFECT SUBJUNCTIVE
(yo)	avergüence	avergonzara or avergonzase
(tú)	avergüences	avergonzaras or avergonzases
(él/ella/usted)	avergüence	avergonzara or avergonzase
(nosotros/as)	avergoncemos	avergonzáramos or avergonzásemos
(vosotros/as)	avergoncéis	avergonzarais or avergonzaseis
(ellos/ellas/ ustedes)	avergüencen	avergonzaran or avergonzasen

IMPERATIVE
avergüenza / avergonzad

Use the present subjunctive in all cases other than these **tú** and **vosotros** affirmative forms.

EXAMPLE PHRASES

Si hubiera sabido que **te avergonzarías** tanto, no te lo habría dicho.
I wouldn't have told you if I'd known you'd be so embarrassed.
Si de verdad **se avergonzaran**, no se comportarían así. They wouldn't behave
like that if they were really ashamed.

Remember that subject pronouns are not used very often in Spanish.

averiguar (to find out)

	PRESENT		PRESENT PERFECT
(yo)	averiguo		he averiguado
(tú)	averiguas		has averiguado
(él/ella/usted)	averigua		ha averiguado
(nosotros/as)	averiguamos		hemos averiguado
(vosotros/as)	averiguáis		habéis averiguado
(ellos/ellas/ ustedes)	averiguan		han averiguado

	PRETERITE		IMPERFECT
(yo)	averigüé		averiguaba
(tú)	averiguaste		averiguabas
(él/ella/usted)	averiguó		averiguaba
(nosotros/as)	averiguamos		averiguábamos
(vosotros/as)	averiguasteis		averiguabais
(ellos/ellas/ ustedes)	averiguaron		averiguaban

GERUND	PAST PARTICIPLE
averiguando	averiguado

EXAMPLE PHRASES

Trataron de **averiguar** su paradero. They tried to find out his whereabouts.

Poco a poco van **averiguando** más cosas sobre su vida. They're gradually finding out more about his life.

¿Cómo **has averiguado** dónde vivo? How did you find out where I lived?

¿Cuándo lo **averiguaron**? When did they find out?

Remember that subject pronouns are not used very often in Spanish.

averiguar

	FUTURE	CONDITIONAL
(yo)	averiguaré	averiguaría
(tú)	averiguarás	averiguarías
(él/ella/usted)	averiguará	averiguaría
(nosotros/as)	averiguaremos	averiguaríamos
(vosotros/as)	averiguaréis	averiguaríais
(ellos/ellas/ ustedes)	averiguarán	averiguarían

	PRESENT SUBJUNCTIVE	IMPERFECT SUBJUNCTIVE
(yo)	averigüe	averiguara or averiguase
(tú)	averigües	averiguaras or averiguases
(él/ella/usted)	averigüe	averiguara or averiguase
(nosotros/as)	averigüemos	averiguáramos or averiguásemos
(vosotros/as)	averigüéis	averiguarais or averiguaseis
(ellos/ellas/ ustedes)	averigüen	averiguaran or averiguasen

IMPERATIVE
averigua / averiguad

Use the present subjunctive in all cases other than these **tú** and **vosotros** affirmative forms.

EXAMPLE PHRASES

Lo **averiguaré** pronto. I'll find out soon.

Dijo que si le dábamos tiempo lo **averiguaría**. She said that she'd find out if we gave her time.

En cuanto lo **averigüe** te lo digo. I'll tell you as soon as I find out.

¡**Averígualo** inmediatamente! Check it out immediately!

Remember that subject pronouns are not used very often in Spanish.

bendecir (to bless)

	PRESENT		PRESENT PERFECT
(yo)	bendigo		he bendecido
(tú)	bendices		has bendecido
(él/ella/usted)	bendice		ha bendecido
(nosotros/as)	bendecimos		hemos bendecido
(vosotros/as)	bendecís		habéis bendecido
(ellos/ellas/ ustedes)	bendicen		han bendecido

	PRETERITE		IMPERFECT
(yo)	bendije		bendecía
(tú)	bendijiste		bendecías
(él/ella/usted)	bendijo		bendecía
(nosotros/as)	bendijimos		bendecíamos
(vosotros/as)	bendijisteis		bendecíais
(ellos/ellas/ ustedes)	bendijeron		bendecían

GERUND

bendiciendo

PAST PARTICIPLE

bendecido

EXAMPLE PHRASES

Su padre **bendice** siempre la mesa. His father always says grace.

La vida me **ha bendecido** con unos hijos maravillosos. I've been blessed with
   wonderful children.

Jesús **bendijo** los panes y los peces. Jesus blessed the fish and the bread.

Bendecía el día en que lo conoció. She blessed the day she met him.

Remember that subject pronouns are not used very often in Spanish.

bendecir

	FUTURE	CONDITIONAL
(yo)	bendeciré	bendeciría
(tú)	bendecirás	bendecirías
(él/ella/usted)	bendecirá	bendeciría
(nosotros/as)	bendeciremos	bendeciríamos
(vosotros/as)	bendeciréis	bendeciríais
(ellos/ellas/ ustedes)	bendecirán	bendecirían

	PRESENT SUBJUNCTIVE	IMPERFECT SUBJUNCTIVE
(yo)	bendiga	bendijera or bendijese
(tú)	bendigas	bendijeras or bendijeses
(él/ella/usted)	bendiga	bendijera or bendijese
(nosotros/as)	bendigamos	bendijéramos or bendijésemos
(vosotros/as)	bendigáis	bendijerais or bendijeseis
(ellos/ellas/ ustedes)	bendigan	bendijeran or bendijesen

IMPERATIVE
bendice / bendecid

Use the present subjunctive in all cases other than these **tú** and **vosotros** affirmative forms.

EXAMPLE PHRASES
El Papa **bendecirá** a los fieles desde el balcón. The Pope will bless the faithful from the balcony.

Quieren que sea él quien **bendiga** su unión. They want him to marry them.

Pidieron a un sacerdote que **bendijera** su nueva casa. They asked a priest to bless their new house.

Remember that subject pronouns are not used very often in Spanish.

caber (to fit)

	PRESENT		PRESENT PERFECT
(yo)	quepo		he cabido
(tú)	cabes		has cabido
(él/ella/usted)	cabe		ha cabido
(nosotros/as)	cabemos		hemos cabido
(vosotros/as)	cabéis		habéis cabido
(ellos/ellas/ ustedes)	caben		han cabido

	PRETERITE		IMPERFECT
(yo)	cupe		cabía
(tú)	cupiste		cabías
(él/ella/usted)	cupo		cabía
(nosotros/as)	cupimos		cabíamos
(vosotros/as)	cupisteis		cabíais
(ellos/ellas/ ustedes)	cupieron		cabían

GERUND	PAST PARTICIPLE
cabiendo	cabido

EXAMPLE PHRASES

No te preocupes, que va a **caber**. Don't worry, it will fit.

Aquí no **cabe**. There isn't enough room for it here.

Al final **ha cabido** todo. In the end everything went in.

No le **cupo** la menor duda. She wasn't in any doubt.

No **cabía** en sí de gozo. She was beside herself with joy.

Remember that subject pronouns are not used very often in Spanish.

caber

	FUTURE		CONDITIONAL
(yo)	cabré		cabría
(tú)	cabrás		cabrías
(él/ella/usted)	cabrá		cabría
(nosotros/as)	cabremos		cabríamos
(vosotros/as)	cabréis		cabríais
(ellos/ellas/ ustedes)	cabrán		cabrían

	PRESENT SUBJUNCTIVE	IMPERFECT SUBJUNCTIVE
(yo)	quepa	cupiera or cupiese
(tú)	quepas	cupieras or cupieses
(él/ella/usted)	quepa	cupiera or cupiese
(nosotros/as)	quepamos	cupiéramos or cupiésemos
(vosotros/as)	quepáis	cupierais or cupleseis
(ellos/ellas/ ustedes)	quepan	cupieran or cupiesen

IMPERATIVE
cabe / cabed

Use the present subjunctive in all cases other than these **tú** and **vosotros** affirmative forms.

EXAMPLE PHRASES

¿Crees que **cabrá**? Do you think there will be enough room for it?

Cabría cuestionarse si es la mejor solución. We should ask ourselves whether it's the best solution.

Hizo lo imposible para que le **cupiera** la redacción en una página.
He did everything he could to fit the composition onto one page.

Remember that subject pronouns are not used very often in Spanish.

caer (to fall)

	PRESENT	PRESENT PERFECT
(yo)	caigo	he caído
(tú)	caes	has caído
(él/ella/usted)	cae	ha caído
(nosotros/as)	caemos	hemos caído
(vosotros/as)	caéis	habéis caído
(ellos/ellas/ ustedes)	caen	han caído

	PRETERITE	IMPERFECT
(yo)	caí	caía
(tú)	caíste	caías
(él/ella/usted)	cayó	caía
(nosotros/as)	caímos	caíamos
(vosotros/as)	caísteis	caíais
(ellos/ellas/ ustedes)	cayeron	caían

GERUND	PAST PARTICIPLE
cayendo	caído

EXAMPLE PHRASES

Su cumpleaños **cae** en viernes. Her birthday falls on a Friday.

Ese edificio se **está cayendo**. That building's falling down.

Se me **ha caído** un guante. I've dropped one of my gloves.

Me **caí** por las escaleras. I fell down the stairs.

Me **caía** muy bien. I really liked him.

Remember that subject pronouns are not used very often in Spanish.

caer

	FUTURE	CONDITIONAL
(yo)	caeré	caería
(tú)	caerás	caerías
(él/ella/usted)	caerá	caería
(nosotros/as)	caeremos	caeríamos
(vosotros/as)	caeréis	caeríais
(ellos/ellas/ ustedes)	caerán	caerían

	PRESENT SUBJUNCTIVE	IMPERFECT SUBJUNCTIVE
(yo)	caiga	cayera or cayese
(tú)	caigas	cayeras or cayeses
(él/ella/usted)	caiga	cayera or cayese
(nosotros/as)	caigamos	cayéramos or cayésemos
(vosotros/as)	caigáis	cayerais or cayesels
(ellos/ellas/ ustedes)	caigan	cayeran or cayesen

IMPERATIVE

cae / caed

*Use the present subjunctive in all cases other than these **tú** and **vosotros** affirmative forms.*

EXAMPLE PHRASES

Tarde o temprano, **caerá** en manos del enemigo. Sooner or later, it will fall into enemy hands.

Yo me **caería** con esos tacones. I'd fall over if I wore heels like those.

Seguirá adelante **caiga** quien **caiga**. She'll go ahead no matter how many heads have to roll.

No **caigas** tan bajo. Don't stoop so low.

Remember that subject pronouns are not used very often in Spanish.

cambiar (to change)

	PRESENT		PRESENT PERFECT
(yo)	cambio		he cambiado
(tú)	cambias		has cambiado
(él/ella/usted)	cambia		ha cambiado
(nosotros/as)	cambiamos		hemos cambiado
(vosotros/as)	cambiáis		habéis cambiado
(ellos/ellas/ ustedes)	cambian		han cambiado

	PRETERITE		IMPERFECT
(yo)	cambié		cambiaba
(tú)	cambiaste		cambiabas
(él/ella/usted)	cambió		cambiaba
(nosotros/as)	cambiamos		cambiábamos
(vosotros/as)	cambiasteis		cambiabais
(ellos/ellas/ ustedes)	cambiaron		cambiaban

GERUND	PAST PARTICIPLE
cambiando	cambiado

EXAMPLE PHRASES

Necesito **cambiar** de ambiente. I need a change of scene.

Te **cambio** mi bolígrafo por tu goma. I'll swap my pen for your rubber.

He cambiado de idea. I've changed my mind.

Cambié varias veces de trabajo. I changed jobs several times.

Cambiaban de coche cada año. They changed their car every year.

Remember that subject pronouns are not used very often in Spanish.

cambiar

	FUTURE	CONDITIONAL
(yo)	cambiaré	cambiaría
(tú)	cambiarás	cambiarías
(él/ella/usted)	cambiará	cambiaría
(nosotros/as)	cambiaremos	cambiaríamos
(vosotros/as)	cambiaréis	cambiaríais
(ellos/ellas/ ustedes)	cambiarán	cambiarían

	PRESENT SUBJUNCTIVE	IMPERFECT SUBJUNCTIVE
(yo)	cambie	cambiara or cambiase
(tú)	cambies	cambiaras or cambiases
(él/ella/usted)	cambie	cambiara or cambiase
(nosotros/as)	cambiemos	cambiáramos or cambiásemos
(vosotros/as)	cambiéis	cambiarais or cambiaseis
(ellos/ellas/ ustedes)	cambien	cambiaran or cambiasen

IMPERATIVE
cambia / cambiad

Use the present subjunctive in all cases other than these **tú** and **vosotros** affirmative forms.

EXAMPLE PHRASES

Cuando la conozcas, **cambiarás** de idea. You'll change your mind when you meet her.

Si pudiéramos, **nos cambiaríamos** de casa. If we could, we'd move house.

No quiero que **cambies**. I don't want you to change.

Cámbiate, que se nos hace tarde. Get changed, it's getting late.

Remember that subject pronouns are not used very often in Spanish.

cazar (to hunt; to shoot)

	PRESENT		PRESENT PERFECT
(yo)	cazo		he cazado
(tú)	cazas		has cazado
(él/ella/usted)	caza		ha cazado
(nosotros/as)	cazamos		hemos cazado
(vosotros/as)	cazáis		habéis cazado
(ellos/ellas/ ustedes)	cazan		han cazado

	PRETERITE		IMPERFECT
(yo)	cacé		cazaba
(tú)	cazaste		cazabas
(él/ella/usted)	cazó		cazaba
(nosotros/as)	cazamos		cazábamos
(vosotros/as)	cazasteis		cazabais
(ellos/ellas/ ustedes)	cazaron		cazaban

GERUND
cazando

PAST PARTICIPLE
cazado

EXAMPLE PHRASES

Salieron a **cazar** ciervos. They went deer-hunting.

Caza las cosas al vuelo. She's very quick on the uptake.

No **he cazado** nada de lo que ha dicho. I didn't understand a word he said.

Los **cacé** robando. I caught them stealing.

Cazaban con lanza. They hunted with spears.

Remember that subject pronouns are not used very often in Spanish.

cazar

	FUTURE	CONDITIONAL
(yo)	cazaré	cazaría
(tú)	cazarás	cazarías
(él/ella/usted)	cazará	cazaría
(nosotros/as)	cazaremos	cazaríamos
(vosotros/as)	cazaréis	cazaríais
(ellos/ellas/ustedes)	cazarán	cazarían

	PRESENT SUBJUNCTIVE	IMPERFECT SUBJUNCTIVE
(yo)	cace	cazara or cazase
(tú)	caces	cazaras or cazases
(él/ella/usted)	cace	cazara or cazase
(nosotros/as)	cacemos	cazáramos or cazásemos
(vosotros/as)	cacéis	cazarais or cazaseis
(ellos/ellas/ustedes)	cacen	cazaran or cazasen

IMPERATIVE

caza / cazad

Use the present subjunctive in all cases other than these tú and vosotros affirmative forms.

EXAMPLE PHRASES

¡Quién **cazara** a un millonario! I wish I could land myself a millionaire!

cerrar (to close)

	PRESENT	PRESENT PERFECT
(yo)	cierro	he cerrado
(tú)	cierras	has cerrado
(él/ella/usted)	cierra	ha cerrado
(nosotros/as)	cerramos	hemos cerrado
(vosotros/as)	cerráis	habéis cerrado
(ellos/ellas/ustedes)	cierran	han cerrado

	PRETERITE	IMPERFECT
(yo)	cerré	cerraba
(tú)	cerraste	cerrabas
(él/ella/usted)	cerró	cerraba
(nosotros/as)	cerramos	cerrábamos
(vosotros/as)	cerrasteis	cerrabais
(ellos/ellas/ustedes)	cerraron	cerraban

GERUND	PAST PARTICIPLE
cerrando	cerrado

EXAMPLE PHRASES

No puedo **cerrar** la maleta. I can't shut my suitcase.

No **cierran** al mediodía. They don't close at lunchtime.

Ha cerrado la puerta con llave. She's locked the door.

Cerró el libro. He closed the book.

Se le **cerraban** los ojos. She couldn't keep her eyes open.

Remember that subject pronouns are not used very often in Spanish.

cerrar

	FUTURE	CONDITIONAL
(yo)	cerraré	cerraría
(tú)	cerrarás	cerrarías
(él/ella/usted)	cerrará	cerraría
(nosotros/as)	cerraremos	cerraríamos
(vosotros/as)	cerraréis	cerraríais
(ellos/ellas/ ustedes)	cerrrarán	cerrarían

	PRESENT SUBJUNCTIVE	IMPERFECT SUBJUNCTIVE
(yo)	cierre	cerrara or cerrase
(tú)	cierres	cerraras or cerrases
(él/ella/usted)	cierre	cerrara or cerrase
(nosotros/as)	cerremos	cerráramos or cerrásemos
(vosotros/as)	cerréis	cerrarais or cerraseis
(ellos/ellas/ ustedes)	cierren	cerraran or cerrasen

IMPERATIVE
cierra / cerrad

Use the present subjunctive in all cases other than these **tú** and **vosotros** affirmative forms.

EXAMPLE PHRASES
No dejes que **se cierre** la puerta de golpe. Don't let the door slam shut.

No **cierres** la ventana. Don't close the window.

Cierra el grifo. Turn off the tap.

cocer (to boil; to cook)

	PRESENT		PRESENT PERFECT
(yo)	cuezo		he cocido
(tú)	cueces		has cocido
(él/ella/usted)	cuece		ha cocido
(nosotros/as)	cocemos		hemos cocido
(vosotros/as)	cocéis		habéis cocido
(ellos/ellas/ ustedes)	cuecen		han cocido

	PRETERITE		IMPERFECT
(yo)	cocí		cocía
(tú)	cociste		cocías
(él/ella/usted)	coció		cocía
(nosotros/as)	cocimos		cocíamos
(vosotros/as)	cocisteis		cocíais
(ellos/ellas/ ustedes)	cocieron		cocían

GERUND

cociendo

PAST PARTICIPLE

cocido

EXAMPLE PHRASES

Las gambas **se cuecen** en un momento. Prawns take no time to cook.

Aquí nos **estamos cociendo**. It's boiling in here.

He cocido todo junto. I've cooked everything together.

Coció el pan en el horno. He baked the bread in the oven.

Remember that subject pronouns are not used very often in Spanish.

cocer

	FUTURE	CONDITIONAL
(yo)	coceré	cocería
(tú)	cocerás	cocerías
(él/ella/usted)	cocerá	cocería
(nosotros/as)	coceremos	coceríamos
(vosotros/as)	coceréis	coceríais
(ellos/ellas/ustedes)	cocerán	cocerían

	PRESENT SUBJUNCTIVE	IMPERFECT SUBJUNCTIVE
(yo)	cueza	cociera or cociese
(tú)	cuezas	cocieras or cocieses
(él/ella/usted)	cueza	cociera or cociese
(nosotros/as)	cozamos	cociéramos or cociésemos
(vosotros/as)	cozáis	cocierais or cocieseis
(ellos/ellas/ustedes)	cuezan	cocieran or cociesen

IMPERATIVE

cuece / coced

Use the present subjunctive in all cases other than these **tú** and **vosotros** affirmative forms.

EXAMPLE PHRASES

Así se **cocerá** antes. This way it will be ready sooner.

Te dije que lo **cocieras** tapado. I told you to cook it with the lid on.

No lo **cuezas** demasiado. Don't overcook it.

Cuécelo a fuego lento. Cook it over a gentle heat.

Remember that subject pronouns are not used very often in Spanish.

coger (to catch; to take)

	PRESENT	PRESENT PERFECT
(yo)	cojo	he cogido
(tú)	coges	has cogido
(él/ella/usted)	coge	ha cogido
(nosotros/as)	cogemos	hemos cogido
(vosotros/as)	cogéis	habéis cogido
(ellos/ellas/ ustedes)	cogen	han cogido

	PRETERITE	IMPERFECT
(yo)	cogí	cogía
(tú)	cogiste	cogías
(él/ella/usted)	cogió	cogía
(nosotros/as)	cogimos	cogíamos
(vosotros/as)	cogisteis	cogíais
(ellos/ellas/ ustedes)	cogieron	cogían

GERUND	PAST PARTICIPLE
cogiendo	cogido

EXAMPLE PHRASES

¿Por qué no **coges** el tren de las seis? Why don't you get the six o'clock train?

Estuvimos cogiendo setas. We were picking mushrooms.

Le **he cogido** cariño al gato. I've grown fond of the cat.

La **cogí** entre mis brazos. I took her in my arms.

Cogía el metro todos los días. I used to take the tube every day.

Remember that subject pronouns are not used very often in Spanish.

coger

	FUTURE		CONDITIONAL
(yo)	cogeré		cogería
(tú)	cogerás		cogerías
(él/ella/usted)	cogerá		cogería
(nosotros/as)	cogeremos		cogeríamos
(vosotros/as)	cogeréis		cogeríais
(ellos/ellas/ ustedes)	cogerán		cogerían

	PRESENT SUBJUNCTIVE		IMPERFECT SUBJUNCTIVE
(yo)	coja		cogiera or cogiese
(tú)	cojas		cogieras or cogieses
(él/ella/usted)	coja		cogiera or cogiese
(nosotros/as)	cojamos		cogiéramos or cogiésemos
(vosotros/as)	cojáis		cogierais or cogieseis
(ellos/ellas/ ustedes)	cojan		cogieran or cogiesen

IMPERATIVE

coge / coged

*Use the present subjunctive in all cases other than these **tú** and **vosotros** affirmative forms.*

EXAMPLE PHRASES

Se **cogerá** un resfriado. He'll catch a cold.

Yo **cogería** el azul. I'd take the blue one.

No le **cojas** los juguetes a tu hermana. Don't take your sister's toys.

Coja la primera calle a la derecha. Take the first street on the right.

Remember that subject pronouns are not used very often in Spanish.

colgar (to hang)

	PRESENT		PRESENT PERFECT
(yo)	cuelgo		he colgado
(tú)	cuelgas		has colgado
(él/ella/usted)	cuelga		ha colgado
(nosotros/as)	colgamos		hemos colgado
(vosotros/as)	colgáis		habéis colgado
(ellos/ellas/ ustedes)	cuelgan		han colgado

	PRETERITE		IMPERFECT
(yo)	colgué		colgaba
(tú)	colgaste		colgabas
(él/ella/usted)	colgó		colgaba
(nosotros/as)	colgamos		colgábamos
(vosotros/as)	colgasteis		colgabais
(ellos/ellas/ ustedes)	colgaron		colgaban

GERUND	PAST PARTICIPLE
colgando	colgado

EXAMPLE PHRASES

Cada día **cuelgan** el cartel de "no hay billetes". Every day the "sold out" sign goes up.

Hay telarañas **colgando** del techo. There are cobwebs hanging from the ceiling.

Te **he colgado** la chaqueta en la percha. I've hung your jacket on the hanger.

Me **colgó** el teléfono. He hung up on me.

De la pared **colgaba** un espejo. There was a mirror hanging on the wall.

Remember that subject pronouns are not used very often in Spanish.

colgar

	FUTURE	CONDITIONAL
(yo)	colgaré	colgaría
(tú)	colgarás	colgarías
(él/ella/usted)	colgará	colgaría
(nosotros/as)	colgaremos	colgaríamos
(vosotros/as)	colgaréis	colgaríais
(ellos/ellas/ ustedes)	colgarán	colgarían

	PRESENT SUBJUNCTIVE	IMPERFECT SUBJUNCTIVE
(yo)	cuelgue	colgara or colgase
(tú)	cuelgues	colgaras or colgases
(él/ella/usted)	cuelgue	colgara or colgase
(nosotros/as)	colguemos	colgáramos or colgásemos
(vosotros/as)	colguéis	colgarais or colgaseis
(ellos/ellas/ ustedes)	cuelguen	colgaran or colgasen

IMPERATIVE
cuelga / colgad

Use the present subjunctive in all cases other than these tú and vosotros affirmative forms.

EXAMPLE PHRASES
Colgaremos el cuadro en esa pared. We'll hang the picture on that wall.

¡Que lo **cuelguen**! Hang him!

No **cuelgue**, por favor. Please don't hang up.

¡**Cuelga**, por favor, que quiero hacer una llamada! Please hang up. I want to use the phone!

Remember that subject pronouns are not used very often in Spanish.

comer (to eat)

	PRESENT		PRESENT PERFECT
(yo)	como		he comido
(tú)	comes		has comido
(él/ella/usted)	come		ha comido
(nosotros/as)	comemos		hemos comido
(vosotros/as)	coméis		habéis comido
(ellos/ellas/ ustedes)	comen		han comido

	PRETERITE		IMPERFECT
(yo)	comí		comía
(tú)	comiste		comías
(él/ella/usted)	comió		comía
(nosotros/as)	comimos		comíamos
(vosotros/as)	comisteis		comíais
(ellos/ellas/ ustedes)	comieron		comían

GERUND

comiendo

PAST PARTICIPLE

comido

EXAMPLE PHRASES

No **come** carne. He doesn't eat meat.

Se lo **ha comido** todo. He's eaten it all.

Comimos en un restaurante. We had lunch in a restaurant.

Siempre **comían** demasiado. They always ate too much.

Remember that subject pronouns are not used very often in Spanish.

comer

	FUTURE	CONDITIONAL
(yo)	comeré	comería
(tú)	comerás	comerías
(él/ella/usted)	comerá	comería
(nosotros/as)	comeremos	comeríamos
(vosotros/as)	comeréis	comeríais
(ellos/ellas/ ustedes)	comerán	comerían

	PRESENT SUBJUNCTIVE	IMPERFECT SUBJUNCTIVE
(yo)	coma	comiera or comiese
(tú)	comas	comieras or comieses
(él/ella/usted)	coma	comiera or comiese
(nosotros/as)	comamos	comiéramos or comiésemos
(vosotros/as)	comáis	comierais or comieseis
(ellos/ellas/ ustedes)	coman	comieran or comiesen

IMPERATIVE
come / comed

Use the present subjunctive in all cases other than these **tú** and **vosotros** affirmative forms.

EXAMPLE PHRASES

Me lo **comeré** yo. I'll eat it.

Si no fuera por mí, no **comeríamos**. We wouldn't eat if it weren't for me.

Si **comieras** más, no estarías tan delgado. You wouldn't be so thin if you ate more.

No **comas** tan deprisa. Don't eat so fast.

Remember that subject pronouns are not used very often in Spanish.

conducir (to drive; to lead)

	PRESENT		PRESENT PERFECT
(yo)	conduzco		he conducido
(tú)	conduces		has conducido
(él/ella/usted)	conduce		ha conducido
(nosotros/as)	conducimos		hemos conducido
(vosotros/as)	conducís		habéis conducido
(ellos/ellas/ ustedes)	conducen		han conducido

	PRETERITE		IMPERFECT
(yo)	conduje		conducía
(tú)	condujiste		conducías
(él/ella/usted)	condujo		conducía
(nosotros/as)	condujimos		conducíamos
(vosotros/as)	condujisteis		conducíais
(ellos/ellas/ ustedes)	condujeron		conducían

GERUND	PAST PARTICIPLE
conduciendo	conducido

EXAMPLE PHRASES

No sé **conducir**. I can't drive.

Conduces muy bien. You're a very good driver.

Enfadarte no te **ha conducido** a nada. Getting angry hasn't got you anywhere.

La pista nos **condujo** hasta él. The clue led us to him.

¿**Conducías** tú? Was it you driving?

Remember that subject pronouns are not used very often in Spanish.

conducir

	FUTURE	CONDITIONAL
(yo)	conduciré	conduciría
(tú)	conducirás	conducirías
(él/ella/usted)	conducirá	conduciría
(nosotros/as)	conduciremos	conduciríamos
(vosotros/as)	conduciréis	conduciríais
(ellos/ellas/ ustedes)	conducirán	conducirían

	PRESENT SUBJUNCTIVE	IMPERFECT SUBJUNCTIVE
(yo)	conduzca	condujera or condujese
(tú)	conduzcas	condujeras or condujeses
(él/ella/usted)	conduzca	condujera or condujese
(nosotros/as)	conduzcamos	condujéramos or condujésemos
(vosotros/as)	conduzcáis	condujerais or condujeseis
(ellos/ellas/ ustedes)	conduzcan	condujeran or condujesen

IMPERATIVE
conduce / conducid
Use the present subjunctive in all cases other than these tú and vosotros affirmative forms.

EXAMPLE PHRASES
El camarero les **conducirá** a su mesa. The waiter will show you to your table.
Si bebes, no **conduzcas**. Don't drink and drive.
Le pedí que **condujera** más despacio. I asked him to drive more slowly.
Conduzca con cuidado. Drive carefully.

Remember that subject pronouns are not used very often in Spanish.

conocer (to know)

	PRESENT		PRESENT PERFECT
(yo)	conozco		he conocido
(tú)	conoces		has conocido
(él/ella/usted)	conoce		ha conocido
(nosotros/as)	conocemos		hemos conocido
(vosotros/as)	conocéis		habéis conocido
(ellos/ellas/ ustedes)	conocen		han conocido

	PRETERITE		IMPERFECT
(yo)	conocí		conocía
(tú)	conociste		conocías
(él/ella/usted)	conoció		conocía
(nosotros/as)	conocimos		conocíamos
(vosotros/as)	conocisteis		conocíais
(ellos/ellas/ ustedes)	conocieron		conocían

GERUND
conociendo

PAST PARTICIPLE
conocido

EXAMPLE PHRASES

Conozco un restaurante donde se come bien. I know a restaurant where the food is very good.

Nunca **he conocido** a nadie así. I've never met anybody like that.

La **conocí** en una fiesta. I met her at a party.

Nos conocíamos desde hacía años. We'd known each other for years.

Remember that subject pronouns are not used very often in Spanish.

conocer

	FUTURE	CONDITIONAL
(yo)	conoceré	conocería
(tú)	conocerás	conocerías
(él/ella/usted)	conocerá	conocería
(nosotros/as)	conoceremos	conoceríamos
(vosotros/as)	conoceréis	conoceríais
(ellos/ellas/ ustedes)	conocerán	conocerían

	PRESENT SUBJUNCTIVE	IMPERFECT SUBJUNCTIVE
(yo)	conozca	conociera or conociese
(tú)	conozcas	conocieras or conocieses
(él/ella/usted)	conozca	conociera or conociese
(nosotros/as)	conozcamos	conociéramos or conociésemos
(vosotros/as)	conozcáis	conocierais or conocieseis
(ellos/ellas/ ustedes)	conozcan	conocieran or conociesen

IMPERATIVE
conoce / conoced

Use the present subjunctive in all cases other than these **tú** and **vosotros** affirmative forms.

EXAMPLE PHRASES
No sé si la **conocerás** cuando la veas. I don't know if you'll recognize her when you see her.

No quiero que mis padres le **conozcan**. I don't want my parents to meet him.

Si no la **conociera**, pensaría que lo hizo queriendo. If I didn't know her better, I'd think she had done it on purpose.

Remember that subject pronouns are not used very often in Spanish.

construir (to build)

	PRESENT		PRESENT PERFECT
(yo)	construyo		he construido
(tú)	construyes		has construido
(él/ella/usted)	construye		ha construido
(nosotros/as)	construimos		hemos construido
(vosotros/as)	construís		habéis construido
(ellos/ellas/ ustedes)	construyen		han construido

	PRETERITE		IMPERFECT
(yo)	construí		construía
(tú)	construiste		construías
(él/ella/usted)	construyó		construía
(nosotros/as)	construimos		construíamos
(vosotros/as)	construisteis		construíais
(ellos/ellas/ ustedes)	construyeron		construían

GERUND

construyendo

PAST PARTICIPLE

construido

EXAMPLE PHRASES

Construyen casas de madera. They build wooden houses.

Están construyendo una escuela. They're building a new school.

Ha construido la casa él solo. He built the house on his own.

Lo **construyó** sin planos. He built it without any plans.

Su empresa **construía** puentes. His company built bridges.

Remember that subject pronouns are not used very often in Spanish.

construir

	FUTURE	CONDITIONAL
(yo)	construiré	construiría
(tú)	construirás	construirías
(él/ella/usted)	construirá	construiría
(nosotros/as)	construiremos	construiríamos
(vosotros/as)	construiréis	construiríais
(ellos/ellas/ ustedes)	construirán	construirían

	PRESENT SUBJUNCTIVE	IMPERFECT SUBJUNCTIVE
(yo)	construya	construyera or construyese
(tú)	construyas	construyeras or construyeses
(él/ella/usted)	construya	construyera or construyese
(nosotros/as)	construyamos	construyéramos or construyésemos
(vosotros/as)	construyáis	construyerais or construyeseis
(ellos/ellas/ ustedes)	construyan	construyeran or construyesen

IMPERATIVE
construye / construid

Use the present subjunctive in all cases other than these tú and vosotros affirmative forms.

EXAMPLE PHRASES
Aquí **construirán** una autopista. They're going to build a new motorway here.
Yo **construiría** la oración de otra forma. I'd construct the sentence differently.
Le pedí que lo **construyera** así. I asked him to build it like this.

contar (to tell; to count)

	PRESENT		PRESENT PERFECT
(yo)	cuento		he contado
(tú)	cuentas		has contado
(él/ella/usted)	cuenta		ha contado
(nosotros/as)	contamos		hemos contado
(vosotros/as)	contáis		habéis contado
(ellos/ellas/ ustedes)	cuentan		han contado

	PRETERITE		IMPERFECT
(yo)	conté		contaba
(tú)	contaste		contabas
(él/ella/usted)	contó		contaba
(nosotros/as)	contamos		contábamos
(vosotros/as)	contasteis		contabais
(ellos/ellas/ ustedes)	contaron		contaban

GERUND

contando

PAST PARTICIPLE

contado

EXAMPLE PHRASES

Sabe **contar** hasta diez. She can count up to ten.

Estoy contando los días. I'm counting the days.

¿**Has contado** el dinero? Have you counted the money?

Nos **contó** un secreto. He told us a secret.

Para él sólo **contaba** su carrera. The only thing that mattered to him was his career.

Remember that subject pronouns are not used very often in Spanish.

contar

	FUTURE	CONDITIONAL
(yo)	contaré	contaría
(tú)	contarás	contarías
(él/ella/usted)	contará	contaría
(nosotros/as)	contaremos	contaríamos
(vosotros/as)	contaréis	contaríais
(ellos/ellas/ ustedes)	contarán	contarían

	PRESENT SUBJUNCTIVE	IMPERFECT SUBJUNCTIVE
(yo)	cuente	contara or contase
(tú)	cuentes	contaras or contases
(él/ella/usted)	cuente	contara or contase
(nosotros/as)	contemos	contáramos or contásemos
(vosotros/as)	contéis	contarais or contaseis
(ellos/ellas/ ustedes)	cuenten	contaran or contasen

IMPERATIVE
cuenta / contad

Use the present subjunctive in all cases other than these **tú** and **vosotros** affirmative forms.

EXAMPLE PHRASES

Prométeme que no se lo **contarás** a nadie. Promise you won't tell anyone.

Quiero que me **cuente** exactamente qué pasó. I want you to tell me exactly what happened.

Quería que le **contara** un cuento. She wanted me to tell her a story.

No **cuentes** conmigo. Don't count on me.

Venga, **cuéntamelo**. Come on, tell me.

Remember that subject pronouns are not used very often in Spanish.

crecer (to grow)

	PRESENT		PRESENT PERFECT
(yo)	crezco		he crecido
(tú)	creces		has crecido
(él/ella/usted)	crece		ha crecido
(nosotros/as)	crecemos		hemos crecido
(vosotros/as)	crecéis		habéis crecido
(ellos/ellas/ ustedes)	crecen		han crecido

	PRETERITE		IMPERFECT
(yo)	crecí		crecía
(tú)	creciste		crecías
(él/ella/usted)	creció		crecía
(nosotros/as)	crecimos		crecíamos
(vosotros/as)	crecisteis		crecíais
(ellos/ellas/ ustedes)	crecieron		crecían

GERUND

creciendo

PAST PARTICIPLE

crecido

EXAMPLE PHRASES

Esas plantas **crecen** en Chile. Those plants grow in Chile.

¡Cómo **has crecido**! Haven't you grown!

Crecimos juntos. We grew up together.

La ciudad **crecía** a pasos agigantados. The city was growing by leaps and bounds.

Sigue **creciendo** la inflación. Inflation is still going up.

Remember that subject pronouns are not used very often in Spanish.

crecer

	FUTURE	CONDITIONAL
(yo)	creceré	crecería
(tú)	crecerás	crecerías
(él/ella/usted)	crecerá	crecería
(nosotros/as)	creceremos	creceríamos
(vosotros/as)	creceréis	creceríais
(ellos/ellas/ ustedes)	crecerán	crecerían

	PRESENT SUBJUNCTIVE	IMPERFECT SUBJUNCTIVE
(yo)	crezca	creciera or creciese
(tú)	crezcas	crecieras or crecieses
(él/ella/usted)	crezca	creciera or creciese
(nosotros/as)	crezcamos	creciéramos or creciésemos
(vosotros/as)	crezcáis	crecierais or crecieseis
(ellos/ellas/ ustedes)	crezcan	crecieran or creciesen

IMPERATIVE
crece / creced

Use the present subjunctive in all cases other than these tú and vosotros affirmative forms.

EXAMPLE PHRASES
Este año la economía **crecerá** un 2%. The economy will grow by 2% this year.

Crecería mejor en un ambiente húmedo. It would grow better in a humid environment.

Cuando **crezca**, ya verás. When he grows up, you'll see.

Quería que sus hijos **crecieran** en otro ambiente. She wanted her children to grow up in a different environment.

Remember that subject pronouns are not used very often in Spanish.

cruzar (to cross)

	PRESENT	PRESENT PERFECT
(yo)	cruzo	he cruzado
(tú)	cruzas	has cruzado
(él/ella/usted)	cruza	ha cruzado
(nosotros/as)	cruzamos	hemos cruzado
(vosotros/as)	cruzáis	habéis cruzado
(ellos/ellas/ ustedes)	cruzan	han cruzado

	PRETERITE	IMPERFECT
(yo)	crucé	cruzaba
(tú)	cruzaste	cruzabas
(él/ella/usted)	cruzó	cruzaba
(nosotros/as)	cruzamos	cruzábamos
(vosotros/as)	cruzasteis	cruzabais
(ellos/ellas/ ustedes)	cruzaron	cruzaban

GERUND	PAST PARTICIPLE
cruzando	cruzado

EXAMPLE PHRASES

Hace tiempo que no **me cruzo** con él. I haven't seen him for a long time.

La caravana **está cruzando** el desierto. The caravan is crossing the dessert.

Se me **han cruzado** los cables. I got mixed up.

Cruzaron el puente. They crossed the bridge.

La carretera **cruzaba** la urbanización. The road went through the housing estate.

Remember that subject pronouns are not used very often in Spanish.

cruzar

	FUTURE	CONDITIONAL
(yo)	cruzaré	cruzaría
(tú)	cruzarás	cruzarías
(él/ella/usted)	cruzará	cruzaría
(nosotros/as)	cruzaremos	cruzaríamos
(vosotros/as)	cruzaréis	cruzaríais
(ellos/ellas/ ustedes)	cruzarán	cruzarían

	PRESENT SUBJUNCTIVE	IMPERFECT SUBJUNCTIVE
(yo)	cruce	cruzara or cruzase
(tú)	cruces	cruzaras or cruzases
(él/ella/usted)	cruce	cruzara or cruzase
(nosotros/as)	crucemos	cruzáramos or cruzásemos
(vosotros/as)	crucéis	cruzarais or cruzaseis
(ellos/ellas/ ustedes)	crucen	cruzaran or cruzasen

IMPERATIVE
cruza / cruzad

Use the present subjunctive in all cases other than these **tú** and **vosotros** affirmative forms.

EXAMPLE PHRASES
Cruzarán varias especies distintas. They'll cross several different species.

Crucemos los dedos. Let's keep our fingers crossed.

Le dije que **cruzara** por el paso de cebra. I told her to cross at the pedestrian crossing.

No **cruces** la calle con el semáforo en rojo. Don't cross the road when the lights are red.

Remember that subject pronouns are not used very often in Spanish.

cubrir (to cover)

	PRESENT		PRESENT PERFECT
(yo)	cubro		he cubierto
(tú)	cubres		has cubierto
(él/ella/usted)	cubre		ha cubierto
(nosotros/as)	cubrimos		hemos cubierto
(vosotros/as)	cubrís		habéis cubierto
(ellos/ellas/ ustedes)	cubren		han cubierto

	PRETERITE		IMPERFECT
(yo)	cubrí		cubría
(tú)	cubriste		cubrías
(él/ella/usted)	cubrió		cubría
(nosotros/as)	cubrimos		cubríamos
(vosotros/as)	cubristeis		cubríais
(ellos/ellas/ ustedes)	cubrieron		cubrían

GERUND	PAST PARTICIPLE
cubriendo	cubierto

EXAMPLE PHRASES

Esto no **cubre** los gastos. This isn't enough to cover expenses.

Le **han cubierto** con una manta. They've covered him with a blanket.

Se cubrió la cara con las manos. She covered her face with her hands.

La nieve **cubría** la montaña. The mountain was covered in snow.

Remember that subject pronouns are not used very often in Spanish.

cubrir

	FUTURE	CONDITIONAL
(yo)	cubriré	cubriría
(tú)	cubrirás	cubrirías
(él/ella/usted)	cubrirá	cubriría
(nosotros/as)	cubriremos	cubriríamos
(vosotros/as)	cubriréis	cubriríais
(ellos/ellas/ustedes)	cubrirán	cubrirían

	PRESENT SUBJUNCTIVE	IMPERFECT SUBJUNCTIVE
(yo)	cubra	cubriera or cubriese
(tú)	cubras	cubrieras or cubrieses
(él/ella/usted)	cubra	cubriera or cubriese
(nosotros/as)	cubramos	cubriéramos or cubriésemos
(vosotros/as)	cubráis	cubrierais or cubrieseis
(ellos/ellas/ustedes)	cubran	cubrieran or cubriesen

IMPERATIVE
cubre / cubrid

Use the present subjunctive in all cases other than these tú and vosotros affirmative forms.

EXAMPLE PHRASES

Los corredores **cubrirán** una distancia de 2 km. The runners will cover a distance of 2 km.

¿Quién **cubriría** la vacante? Who'd fill the vacancy?

Quiero que **cubras** la noticia. I want you to cover the story.

Remember that subject pronouns are not used very often in Spanish.

dar (to give)

	PRESENT		PRESENT PERFECT
(yo)	doy		he dado
(tú)	das		has dado
(él/ella/usted)	da		ha dado
(nosotros/as)	damos		hemos dado
(vosotros/as)	dais		habéis dado
(ellos/ellas/ ustedes)	dan		han dado

	PRETERITE		IMPERFECT
(yo)	di		daba
(tú)	diste		dabas
(él/ella/usted)	dio		daba
(nosotros/as)	dimos		dábamos
(vosotros/as)	disteis		dabais
(ellos/ellas/ ustedes)	dieron		daban

GERUND	PAST PARTICIPLE
dando	dado

EXAMPLE PHRASES

Me **da** miedo la oscuridad. I'm afraid of the dark.

Le **han dado** varios premios a su película. His film has been awarded several prizes.

Nos **dieron** un par de entradas gratis. They gave us a couple of free tickets.

Mi ventana **daba** al jardín. My window looked out on the garden.

Remember that subject pronouns are not used very often in Spanish.

dar

	FUTURE	CONDITIONAL
(yo)	daré	daría
(tú)	darás	darías
(él/ella/usted)	dará	daría
(nosotros/as)	daremos	daríamos
(vosotros/as)	daréis	daríais
(ellos/ellas/ ustedes)	darán	darían

	PRESENT SUBJUNCTIVE	IMPERFECT SUBJUNCTIVE
(yo)	dé	diera or diese
(tú)	des	dieras or dieses
(él/ella/usted)	dé	diera or diese
(nosotros/as)	demos	diéramos or diésemos
(vosotros/as)	deis	dierais or dieseis
(ellos/ellas/ ustedes)	den	dieran or diesen

IMPERATIVE
da / dad

Use the present subjunctive in all cases other than these tú *and* vosotros *affirmative forms.*

EXAMPLE PHRASES
Te **daré** el número de mi móvil. I'll give you my mobile phone number.

Me **daría** mucha alegría volver a verla. It would be really good to see her again.

Quiero que me lo **des** ahora mismo. I want you to give it to me right now.

Déme 2 kilos. 2 kilos please.

Remember that subject pronouns are not used very often in Spanish.

decir (to say; to tell)

	PRESENT		PRESENT PERFECT
(yo)	digo		he dicho
(tú)	dices		has dicho
(él/ella/usted)	dice		ha dicho
(nosotros/as)	decimos		hemos dicho
(vosotros/as)	decís		habéis dicho
(ellos/ellas/ ustedes)	dicen		han dicho

	PRETERITE		IMPERFECT
(yo)	dije		decía
(tú)	dijiste		decías
(él/ella/usted)	dijo		decía
(nosotros/as)	dijimos		decíamos
(vosotros/as)	dijisteis		decíais
(ellos/ellas/ ustedes)	dijeron		decían

GERUND

diciendo

PAST PARTICIPLE

dicho

EXAMPLE PHRASES

Pero ¿qué **dices**? What are you saying?

¿Te **ha dicho** lo de la boda? Has he told you about the wedding?

Me lo **dijo** ayer. He told me yesterday.

Siempre nos **decía** que tuviéramos cuidado. She always used to tell us to be careful.

Remember that subject pronouns are not used very often in Spanish.

decir

	FUTURE	CONDITIONAL
(yo)	diré	diría
(tú)	dirás	dirías
(él/ella/usted)	dirá	diría
(nosotros/as)	diremos	diríamos
(vosotros/as)	diréis	diríais
(ellos/ellas/ ustedes)	dirán	dirían

	PRESENT SUBJUNCTIVE	IMPERFECT SUBJUNCTIVE
(yo)	diga	dijera *or* dijese
(tú)	digas	dijeras *or* dijeses
(él/ella/usted)	diga	dijera *or* dijese
(nosotros/as)	digamos	dijéramos *or* dijésemos
(vosotros/as)	digáis	dijerais *or* dijeseis
(ellos/ellas/ ustedes)	digan	dijeran *or* dijesen

IMPERATIVE
di / decid

Use the present subjunctive in all cases other than these tú *and* **vosotros** *affirmative forms.*

EXAMPLE PHRASES

Yo **diría** que miente. I'd say he's lying.

Diga lo que **diga**, no le voy a creer. Whatever he says, I won't believe him.

Si me **dijeras** lo que pasa, a lo mejor podría ayudar. If you told me what was going on, I could maybe help.

No le **digas** que me has visto. Don't tell him you've seen me.

Remember that subject pronouns are not used very often in Spanish.

desapreocuparse (to stop worrying)

	PRESENT		PRESENT PERFECT
(yo)	me despreocupo		me he despreocupado
(tú)	te despreocupas		te has despreocupado
(él/ella/usted)	se despreocupa		se ha despreocupado
(nosotros/as)	nos despreocupamos		nos hemos despreocupado
(vosotros/as)	os despreocupáis		os habéis despreocupado
(ellos/ellas/ ustedes)	se despreocupan		se han despreocupado

	PRETERITE		IMPERFECT
(yo)	me despreocupé		me despreocupaba
(tú)	te despreocupaste		te despreocupabas
(él/ella/usted)	se despreocupó		se despreocupaba
(nosotros/as)	nos despreocupamos		nos despreocupábamos
(vosotros/as)	os despreocupasteis		os despreocupabais
(ellos/ellas/ ustedes)	se despreocuparon		se despreocupaban

GERUND
despreocupándose, etc

PAST PARTICIPLE
despreocupado

EXAMPLE PHRASES

Deberías **despreocuparte** un poco más de las cosas. You shouldn't worry so much about things.

Se despreocupa de todo. He shows no concern for anything.

Se despreocupó del asunto. He forgot about the matter.

Remember that subject pronouns are not used very often in Spanish.

despreocuparse

	FUTURE	CONDITIONAL
(yo)	me despreocuparé	me despreocuparía
(tú)	te despreocuparás	te despreocuparías
(él/ella/usted)	se despreocupará	se despreocuparía
(nosotros/as)	nos despreocuparemos	nos despreocuparíamos
(vosotros/as)	os despreocuparéis	os despreocuparíais
(ellos/ellas/ ustedes)	se despreocuparán	se despreocuparían

	PRESENT SUBJUNCTIVE	IMPERFECT SUBJUNCTIVE
(yo)	me despreocupe	me despreocupara or despreocupase
(tú)	te despreocupes	te despreocuparas or despreocupases
(él/ella/usted)	se despreocupe	se despreocupara or despreocupase
(nosotros/as)	nos despreocupemos	nos despreocupáramos or despreocupásemos
(vosotros/as)	os despreocupéis	os despreocuparais or despreocupaseis
(ellos/ellas/ ustedes)	se despreocupen	se despreocuparan or despreocupasen

IMPERATIVE
despreocúpate / despreocupaos

Use the present subjunctive in all cases other than these **tú** and **vosotros** affirmative forms.

EXAMPLE PHRASES
Yo **me despreocuparía** de él. I wouldn't worry about him.

Despreocúpate porque ya no tiene remedio. Stop worrying because there's nothing we can do about it now.

Remember that subject pronouns are not used very often in Spanish.

detener (to stop; to arrest)

	PRESENT	PRESENT PERFECT
(yo)	detengo	he detenido
(tú)	detienes	has detenido
(él/ella/usted)	detiene	ha detenido
(nosotros/as)	detenemos	hemos detenido
(vosotros/as)	detenéis	habéis detenido
(ellos/ellas/ ustedes)	detienen	han detenido

	PRETERITE	IMPERFECT
(yo)	detuve	detenía
(tú)	detuviste	detenías
(él/ella/usted)	detuvo	detenía
(nosotros/as)	detuvimos	deteníamos
(vosotros/as)	detuvisteis	deteníais
(ellos/ellas/ ustedes)	detuvieron	detenían

GERUND	PAST PARTICIPLE
deteniendo	detenido

EXAMPLE PHRASES

Han detenido a los ladrones. They've arrested the thieves.

Nos detuvimos en el semáforo. We stopped at the lights.

¡Queda **detenido**! You are under arrest!

Remember that subject pronouns are not used very often in Spanish.

detener

	FUTURE	CONDITIONAL
(yo)	detendré	detendría
(tú)	detendrás	detendrías
(él/ella/usted)	detendrá	detendría
(nosotros/as)	detendremos	detendríamos
(vosotros/as)	detendréis	detendríais
(ellos/ellas/ ustedes)	detendrán	detendrían

	PRESENT SUBJUNCTIVE	IMPERFECT SUBJUNCTIVE
(yo)	detenga	detuviera *or* detuviese
(tú)	detengas	detuvieras *or* detuvieses
(él/ella/usted)	detenga	detuviera *or* detuviese
(nosotros/as)	detengamos	detuviéramos *or* detuviésemos
(vosotros/as)	detengáis	detuvierais *or* detuvieseis
(ellos/ellas/ ustedes)	detengan	detuvieran *or* detuviesen

IMPERATIVE
detén / detened

Use the present subjunctive in all cases other than these **tú** *and* **vosotros** *affirmative forms.*

EXAMPLE PHRASES
Nada la **detendrá**. Nothing will stop her.

Si **te detuvieras** a pensar, nunca harías nada. If you stopped to think, you'd never do anything.

¡**Deténgase**! Stop!

¡No **te detengas**! Don't stop!

Remember that subject pronouns are not used very often in Spanish.

dirigir (to direct; to run)

	PRESENT		PRESENT PERFECT
(yo)	dirijo		he dirigido
(tú)	diriges		has dirigido
(él/ella/usted)	dirige		ha dirigido
(nosotros/as)	dirigimos		hemos dirigido
(vosotros/as)	dirigís		habéis dirigido
(ellos/ellas/ ustedes)	dirigen		han dirigido

	PRETERITE		IMPERFECT
(yo)	dirigí		dirigía
(tú)	dirigiste		dirigías
(él/ella/usted)	dirigió		dirigía
(nosotros/as)	dirigimos		dirigíamos
(vosotros/as)	dirigisteis		dirigíais
(ellos/ellas/ ustedes)	dirigieron		dirigían

GERUND	PAST PARTICIPLE
dirigiendo	dirigido

EXAMPLE PHRASES

Dirijo esta empresa desde hace dos años. I've been running this company for two years.

Ha dirigido varias películas. She has directed several films.

No le **dirigió** la palabra. She didn't say a word to him.

Se dirigía a la parada de autobús. He was making his way to the bus stop.

Remember that subject pronouns are not used very often in Spanish.

dirigir

	FUTURE	CONDITIONAL
(yo)	dirigiré	dirigiría
(tú)	dirigirás	dirigirías
(él/ella/usted)	dirigirá	dirigiría
(nosotros/as)	dirigiremos	dirigiríamos
(vosotros/as)	dirigiréis	dirigiríais
(ellos/ellas/ ustedes)	dirigirán	dirigirían

	PRESENT SUBJUNCTIVE	IMPERFECT SUBJUNCTIVE
(yo)	dirija	dirigiera or dirigiese
(tú)	dirijas	dirigieras or dirigieses
(él/ella/usted)	dirija	dirigiera or dirigiese
(nosotros/as)	dirijamos	dirigiéramos or dirigiésemos
(vosotros/as)	dirijáis	dirigierais or dirigieseis
(ellos/ellas/ ustedes)	dirijan	dirigieran or dirigiesen

IMPERATIVE
dirige / dirigid

Use the present subjunctive in all cases other than these tú and vosotros affirmative forms.

EXAMPLE PHRASES
Dirigirá la expedición. He'll be leading the expedition.

Para más información **diríjase** al apartado de correos número 1002.
   For further information write to PO Box 1002.

distinguir (to distinguish)

	PRESENT		PRESENT PERFECT
(yo)	distingo		he distinguido
(tú)	distingues		has distinguido
(él/ella/usted)	distingue		ha distinguido
(nosotros/as)	distinguimos		hemos distinguido
(vosotros/as)	distinguís		habéis distinguido
(ellos/ellas/ ustedes)	distinguen		han distinguido

	PRETERITE		IMPERFECT
(yo)	distinguí		distinguía
(tú)	distinguiste		distinguías
(él/ella/usted)	distinguió		distinguía
(nosotros/as)	distinguimos		distinguíamos
(vosotros/as)	distinguisteis		distinguíais
(ellos/ellas/ ustedes)	distinguieron		distinguían

GERUND

distinguiendo

PAST PARTICIPLE

distinguido

EXAMPLE PHRASES

No lo **distingo** del azul. I can't tell the difference between it and the blue one.

Nos **ha distinguido** con su presencia. He has honoured us with his presence.

Se **distinguió** por su gran valentía. He distinguished himself by his bravery.

Se **distinguía** desde lejos. You could see it from the distance.

Remember that subject pronouns are not used very often in Spanish.

distinguir

	FUTURE	CONDITIONAL
(yo)	distinguiré	distinguiría
(tú)	distinguirás	distinguirías
(él/ella/usted)	distinguirá	distinguiría
(nosotros/as)	distinguiremos	distinguiríamos
(vosotros/as)	distinguiréis	distinguiríais
(ellos/ellas/ ustedes)	distinguirán	distinguirían

	PRESENT SUBJUNCTIVE	IMPERFECT SUBJUNCTIVE
(yo)	distinga	distinguiera or distinguiese
(tú)	distingas	distinguleras or distinguieses
(él/ella/usted)	distinga	distinguiera or distinguiese
(nosotros/as)	distingamos	distinguiéramos or distinguiésemos
(vosotros/as)	distingáis	distinguierais or distinguieseis
(ellos/ellas/ ustedes)	distingan	distinguieran or distinguiesen

IMPERATIVE
distingue / distinguid

*Use the present subjunctive in all cases other than these **tú** and **vosotros** affirmative forms.*

EXAMPLE PHRASES
Al final **distinguirás** unas notas de otras. Eventually you'll be able to tell one
note from another.
No los **distinguiría**. I wouldn't be able to tell them apart.

Remember that subject pronouns are not used very often in Spanish.

divertir (to entertain)

	PRESENT	PRESENT PERFECT
(yo)	divierto	he divertido
(tú)	diviertes	has divertido
(él/ella/usted)	divierte	ha divertido
(nosotros/as)	divertimos	hemos divertido
(vosotros/as)	divertís	habéis divertido
(ellos/ellas/ ustedes)	divierten	han divertido

	PRETERITE	IMPERFECT
(yo)	divertí	divertía
(tú)	divertiste	divertías
(él/ella/usted)	divirtió	divertía
(nosotros/as)	divertimos	divertíamos
(vosotros/as)	divertisteis	divertíais
(ellos/ellas/ ustedes)	divirtieron	divertían

GERUND	PAST PARTICIPLE
divirtiendo	divertido

EXAMPLE PHRASES

Cantamos sólo para **divertirnos**. We sing just for fun.

Me **divierte** verlos tan serios. It's amusing to see them looking so serious.

¿**Os habéis divertido** en la fiesta? Did you enjoy the party?

Nos **divirtió** con sus anécdotas. He entertained us with his stories.

Nos divertíamos mucho jugando en la playa. We were having a great time playing on the beach.

Remember that subject pronouns are not used very often in Spanish.

divertir

	FUTURE	CONDITIONAL
(yo)	divertiré	divertiría
(tú)	divertirás	divertirías
(él/ella/usted)	divertirá	divertiría
(nosotros/as)	divertiremos	divertiríamos
(vosotros/as)	divertiréis	divertiríais
(ellos/ellas/ ustedes)	divertirán	divertirían

	PRESENT SUBJUNCTIVE	IMPERFECT SUBJUNCTIVE
(yo)	divierta	divirtiera or divirtiese
(tú)	diviertas	divirtieras or divirtieses
(él/ella/usted)	divierta	divirtiera or divirtiese
(nosotros/as)	divirtamos	divirtiéramos or divirtiésemos
(vosotros/as)	divirtáis	divirtierais or divirtieseis
(ellos/ellas/ ustedes)	diviertan	divirtieran or divirtiesen

IMPERATIVE
divierte / divertid

Use the present subjunctive in all cases other than these **tú** and **vosotros** affirmative forms.

EXAMPLE PHRASES

Si fueras, **te divertirías** mucho. If you went you'd have a great time.

Hizo lo posible por que **se divirtieran**. He did everything he could to make it fun for them.

¡Que **te diviertas**! Have a good time!

Remember that subject pronouns are not used very often in Spanish.

dormir (to sleep)

	PRESENT		PRESENT PERFECT
(yo)	duermo		he dormido
(tú)	duermes		has dormido
(él/ella/usted)	duerme		ha dormido
(nosotros/as)	dormimos		hemos dormido
(vosotros/as)	dormís		habéis dormido
(ellos/ellas/ ustedes)	duermen		han dormido

	PRETERITE		IMPERFECT
(yo)	dormí		dormía
(tú)	dormiste		dormías
(él/ella/usted)	durmió		dormía
(nosotros/as)	dormimos		dormíamos
(vosotros/as)	dormisteis		dormíais
(ellos/ellas/ ustedes)	durmieron		dormían

GERUND	PAST PARTICIPLE
durmiendo	dormido

EXAMPLE PHRASES

No **duermo** muy bien. I don't sleep very well.

Está durmiendo. She's asleep.

He dormido de un tirón. I slept like a log.

Se me **durmió** la pierna. My leg went to sleep.

Se dormía en clase. She would fall asleep in class.

Remember that subject pronouns are not used very often in Spanish.

dormir

	FUTURE	CONDITIONAL
(yo)	dormiré	dormiría
(tú)	dormirás	dormirías
(él/ella/usted)	dormirá	dormiría
(nosotros/as)	dormiremos	dormiríamos
(vosotros/as)	dormiréis	dormiríais
(ellos/ellas/ ustedes)	dormirán	dormirían

	PRESENT SUBJUNCTIVE	IMPERFECT SUBJUNCTIVE
(yo)	duerma	durmiera or durmiese
(tú)	duermas	durmieras or durmieses
(él/ella/usted)	duerma	durmiera or durmiese
(nosotros/as)	durmamos	durmiéramos or durmiésemos
(vosotros/as)	durmáis	durmierais or durmieseis
(ellos/ellas/ ustedes)	duerman	durmieran or durmiesen

IMPERATIVE
duerme / dormid
Use the present subjunctive in all cases other than these **tú** *and* **vosotros** *affirmative forms.*

EXAMPLE PHRASES
Si no tomo café, **me dormiré**. I'll fall asleep if I don't have some coffee.

Yo no **dormiría** en esa casa. I wouldn't sleep in that house.

Quiero que **duermas** la siesta. I want you to have a nap.

Si **durmieras** más horas, no estarías tan cansada. You wouldn't be so tired if you slept for longer.

Remember that subject pronouns are not used very often in Spanish.

elegir (to choose)

	PRESENT	PRESENT PERFECT
(yo)	elijo	he elegido
(tú)	eliges	has elegido
(él/ella/usted)	elige	ha elegido
(nosotros/as)	elegimos	hemos elegido
(vosotros/as)	elegís	habéis elegido
(ellos/ellas/ ustedes)	eligen	han elegido

	PRETERITE	IMPERFECT
(yo)	elegí	elegía
(tú)	elegiste	elegías
(él/ella/usted)	eligió	elegía
(nosotros/as)	elegimos	elegíamos
(vosotros/as)	elegisteis	elegíais
(ellos/ellas/ ustedes)	eligieron	elegían

GERUND	PAST PARTICIPLE
eligiendo	elegido

EXAMPLE PHRASES

Te dan a **elegir** entre dos modelos. You get a choice of two models.

Nosotros no **elegimos** a nuestros padres, ni ellos nos **eligen** a nosotros.

  We don't choose our parents and they don't choose us either.

Creo que **ha elegido** bien. I think he's made a good choice.

No lo **eligieron** ellos. It wasn't them who chose it.

Remember that subject pronouns are not used very often in Spanish.

elegir

	FUTURE	CONDITIONAL
(yo)	elegiré	elegiría
(tú)	elegirás	elegirías
(él/ella/usted)	elegirá	elegiría
(nosotros/as)	elegiremos	elegiríamos
(vosotros/as)	elegiréis	elegiríais
(ellos/ellas/ ustedes)	elegirán	elegirían

	PRESENT SUBJUNCTIVE	IMPERFECT SUBJUNCTIVE
(yo)	elija	eligiera or eligiese
(tú)	elijas	eligieras or ellgieses
(él/ella/usted)	elija	eligiera or eligiese
(nosotros/as)	elijamos	eligiéramos or eligiésemos
(vosotros/as)	elijáis	eligierais or eligieseis
(ellos/ellas/ ustedes)	elijan	eligieran or eligiesen

IMPERATIVE
elige / elegid

Use the present subjunctive in all cases other than these **tú** and **vosotros** affirmative forms.

EXAMPLE PHRASES
Yo **elegiría** el más caro. I'd choose the most expensive one.
Elija una carta. Choose a card.

Remember that subject pronouns are not used very often in Spanish.

empezar (to begin)

	PRESENT		PRESENT PERFECT
(yo)	empiezo		he empezado
(tú)	empiezas		has empezado
(él/ella/usted)	empieza		ha empezado
(nosotros/as)	empezamos		hemos empezado
(vosotros/as)	empezáis		habéis empezado
(ellos/ellas/ ustedes)	empiezan		han empezado

	PRETERITE		IMPERFECT
(yo)	empecé		empezaba
(tú)	empezaste		empezabas
(él/ella/usted)	empezó		empezaba
(nosotros/as)	empezamos		empezábamos
(vosotros/as)	empezasteis		empezabais
(ellos/ellas/ ustedes)	empezaron		empezaban

GERUND	PAST PARTICIPLE
empezando	empezado

EXAMPLE PHRASES

Está a punto de **empezar**. It's about to start.

¿Cuándo **empiezas** a trabajar en el sitio nuevo? When do you start work at the new place?

Ha empezado a nevar. It's started snowing.

Las vacaciones **empezaron** el quince. The holidays started on the fifteenth.

Empezaba por *p*. It began with *p*.

Remember that subject pronouns are not used very often in Spanish.

empezar

	FUTURE	CONDITIONAL
(yo)	empezaré	empezaría
(tú)	empezarás	empezarías
(él/ella/usted)	empezará	empezaría
(nosotros/as)	empezaremos	empezaríamos
(vosotros/as)	empezaréis	empezaríais
(ellos/ellas/ustedes)	empezarán	empezarían

	PRESENT SUBJUNCTIVE	IMPERFECT SUBJUNCTIVE
(yo)	empiece	empezara or empezase
(tú)	empieces	empezaras or empezases
(él/ella/usted)	empiece	empezara or empezase
(nosotros/as)	empecemos	empezáramos or empezásemos
(vosotros/as)	empecéis	empezarais or empezaseis
(ellos/ellas/ustedes)	empiecen	empezaran or empezasen

IMPERATIVE
empieza / empezad

Use the present subjunctive in all cases other than these **tú** and **vosotros** affirmative forms.

EXAMPLE PHRASES

La semana que viene **empezaremos** un curso nuevo. We'll start a new course next week.

Yo **empezaría** desde cero. I'd start from scratch.

Quiero que **empieces** ya. I want you to start now.

Si **empezáramos** ahora, acabaríamos a las diez. If we started now, we'd be finished by ten.

Empieza por aquí. Start here.

Remember that subject pronouns are not used very often in Spanish.

enfrentarse (a) (to face)

	PRESENT		PRESENT PERFECT
(yo)	me enfrento		me he enfrentado
(tú)	te enfrentas		te has enfrentado
(él/ella/usted)	se enfrenta		se ha enfrentado
(nosotros/as)	nos enfrentamos		nos hemos enfrentado
(vosotros/as)	os enfrentáis		os habéis enfrentado
(ellos/ellas/ ustedes)	se enfrentan		se han enfrentado

	PRETERITE		IMPERFECT
(yo)	me enfrenté		me enfrentaba
(tú)	te enfrentaste		te enfrentabas
(él/ella/usted)	se enfrentó		se enfrentaba
(nosotros/as)	nos enfrentamos		nos enfrentábamos
(vosotros/as)	os enfrentasteis		os enfrentabais
(ellos/ellas/ ustedes)	se enfrentaron		se enfrentaban

GERUND

enfrentándose, etc

PAST PARTICIPLE

enfrentado

EXAMPLE PHRASES

Tienes que **enfrentarte al** problema. You have to face up to the problem.

Hoy **se enfrentan** los dos semifinalistas. The two semifinalists meet today.

Padre e hijo **se han enfrentado** varias veces. Father and son have had several confrontations.

Se enfrentaban a un futuro incierto. They faced an uncertain future.

Remember that subject pronouns are not used very often in Spanish.

enfrentarse

	FUTURE	CONDITIONAL
(yo)	me enfrentaré	me enfrentaría
(tú)	te enfrentarás	te enfrentarías
(él/ella/usted)	se enfrentará	se enfrentaría
(nosotros/as)	nos enfrentaremos	nos enfrentaríamos
(vosotros/as)	os enfrentaréis	os enfrentaríais
(ellos/ellas/ ustedes)	se enfrentarán	se enfrentarían

	PRESENT SUBJUNCTIVE	IMPERFECT SUBJUNCTIVE
(yo)	me enfrente	me enfrentara or enfrentase
(tú)	te enfrentes	te enfrentaras or enfrentases
(él/ella/usted)	se enfrente	se enfrentara or enfrentase
(nosotros/as)	nos enfrentemos	nos enfrentáramos or enfrentásemos
(vosotros/as)	os enfrentéis	os enfrentarais or enfrentaseis
(ellos/ellas/ ustedes)	se enfrenten	se enfrentaran or enfrentasen

IMPERATIVE
enfréntate / enfrentaos

Use the present subjunctive in all cases other than these tú and vosotros affirmative forms.

EXAMPLE PHRASES

El héroe **se enfrentará** a todo tipo de peligros. The hero will have to face all kinds of dangers.

No **te enfrentes** con él. Don't confront him.

Remember that subject pronouns are not used very often in Spanish.

entender (to understand)

	PRESENT	PRESENT PERFECT
(yo)	entiendo	he entendido
(tú)	entiendes	has entendido
(él/ella/usted)	entiende	ha entendido
(nosotros/as)	entendemos	hemos entendido
(vosotros/as)	entendéis	habéis entendido
(ellos/ellas/ ustedes)	entienden	han entendido

	PRETERITE	IMPERFECT
(yo)	entendí	entendía
(tú)	entendiste	entendías
(él/ella/usted)	entendió	entendía
(nosotros/as)	entendimos	entendíamos
(vosotros/as)	entendisteis	entendíais
(ellos/ellas/ ustedes)	entendieron	entendían

GERUND	PAST PARTICIPLE
entendiendo	entendido

EXAMPLE PHRASES

No lo vas a **entender**. You won't understand.

No lo **entiendo**. I don't understand.

Estás entendiéndolo todo al revés. You're getting the wrong end of the stick.

Creo que lo **he entendido** mal. I think I've misunderstood.

¿**Entendiste** lo que dijo? Did you understand what she said?

Mi padre **entendía** mucho de caballos. My father knew a lot about horses.

Remember that subject pronouns are not used very often in Spanish.

entender

	FUTURE	CONDITIONAL
(yo)	entenderé	entendería
(tú)	entenderás	entenderías
(él/ella/usted)	entenderá	entendería
(nosotros/as)	entenderemos	entenderíamos
(vosotros/as)	entenderéis	entenderíais
(ellos/ellas/ ustedes)	entenderán	entenderían

	PRESENT SUBJUNCTIVE	IMPERFECT SUBJUNCTIVE
(yo)	entienda	entendiera or entendiese
(tú)	entiendas	entendieras or entendieses
(él/ella/usted)	entienda	entendiera or entendiese
(nosotros/as)	entendamos	entendiéramos or entendiésemos
(vosotros/as)	entendáis	entendierais or entendieseis
(ellos/ellas/ ustedes)	entiendan	entendieran or entendiesen

IMPERATIVE
entiende / entended

Use the present subjunctive in all cases other than these **tú** and **vosotros** affirmative forms.

EXAMPLE PHRASES
Con el tiempo lo **entenderás**. You'll understand one day.

Yo no lo **entendería** así. I wouldn't interpret it like that.

Si de verdad me **entendieras**, no habrías dicho eso. If you really understood me, you would never have said that.

No me **entiendas** mal. Don't misunderstand me.

Remember that subject pronouns are not used very often in Spanish.

enviar (to send)

	PRESENT		PRESENT PERFECT
(yo)	envío		he enviado
(tú)	envías		has enviado
(él/ella/usted)	envía		ha enviado
(nosotros/as)	enviamos		hemos enviado
(vosotros/as)	enviáis		habéis enviado
(ellos/ellas/ ustedes)	envían		han enviado

	PRETERITE		IMPERFECT
(yo)	envié		enviaba
(tú)	enviaste		enviabas
(él/ella/usted)	envió		enviaba
(nosotros/as)	enviamos		enviábamos
(vosotros/as)	enviasteis		enviabais
(ellos/ellas/ ustedes)	enviaron		enviaban

GERUND	PAST PARTICIPLE
enviando	enviado

EXAMPLE PHRASES

¿Cómo lo vas a **enviar**? How are you going to send it?

Les **envío** el trabajo por correo electrónico. I send them my work by email.

Ya **está enviando** las invitaciones. She has already started sending out the invitations.

La **han enviado** a Guatemala. They've sent her to Guatemala.

Le **envió** el regalo por correo. He posted her the present.

Me **enviaba** siempre a mí a hacer los recados. She always sent me to do the errands.

Remember that subject pronouns are not used very often in Spanish.

enviar

	FUTURE		CONDITIONAL
(yo)	enviaré		enviaría
(tú)	enviarás		enviarías
(él/ella/usted)	enviará		enviaría
(nosotros/as)	enviaremos		enviaríamos
(vosotros/as)	enviaréis		enviaríais
(ellos/ellas/ ustedes)	enviarán		enviarían

	PRESENT SUBJUNCTIVE	IMPERFECT SUBJUNCTIVE
(yo)	envíe	enviara or enviase
(tú)	envíes	enviaras or enviases
(él/ella/usted)	envíe	enviara or enviase
(nosotros/as)	enviemos	enviáramos or enviásemos
(vosotros/as)	enviéis	enviarais or enviaseis
(ellos/ellas/ ustedes)	envíen	enviaran or enviasen

IMPERATIVE

envía / enviad

Use the present subjunctive in all cases other than these tú and vosotros affirmative forms.

EXAMPLE PHRASES

Nos **enviarán** más información. They'll send us further information.

Yo lo **enviaría** por mensajero. I'd send it by courier.

Necesitamos que lo **envíes** inmediatamente. We need you to send it immediately.

Si lo **enviaras** ahora, llegaría el lunes. If you sent it now it would get there on Monday.

No lo **envíes** sin repasarlo antes. Don't send it in without checking it first.

Envíe sus datos personales. Send in your details.

Remember that subject pronouns are not used very often in Spanish.

equivocarse (to make a mistake; to be wrong)

	PRESENT		PRESENT PERFECT
(yo)	me equivoco		me he equivocado
(tú)	te equivocas		te has equivocado
(él/ella/usted)	se equivoca		se ha equivocado
(nosotros/as)	nos equivocamos		nos hemos equivocado
(vosotros/as)	os equivocáis		os habéis equivocado
(ellos/ellas/ ustedes)	se equivocan		se han equivocado

	PRETERITE		IMPERFECT
(yo)	me equivoqué		me equivocaba
(tú)	te equivocaste		te equivocabas
(él/ella/usted)	se equivocó		se equivocaba
(nosotros/as)	nos equivocamos		nos equivocábamos
(vosotros/as)	os equivocasteis		os equivocabais
(ellos/ellas/ ustedes)	se equivocaron		se equivocaban

GERUND

equivocándose, etc

PAST PARTICIPLE

equivocado

EXAMPLE PHRASES

Si crees que voy a dejarte ir, **te equivocas**. If you think I'm going to let you go, you're mistaken.

Perdone, **me he equivocado** de número. Sorry, I've got the wrong number.

Se equivocaron de tren. They got the wrong train.

Siempre **se equivocaba** de calle. He always went down the wrong street.

Remember that subject pronouns are not used very often in Spanish.

equivocarse

	FUTURE	CONDITIONAL
(yo)	me equivocaré	me equivocaría
(tú)	te equivocarás	te equivocarías
(él/ella/usted)	se equivocará	se equivocaría
(nosotros/as)	nos equivocaremos	nos equivocaríamos
(vosotros/as)	os equivocaréis	os equivocaríais
(ellos/ellas/ ustedes)	se equivocarán	se equivocarían

	PRESENT SUBJUNCTIVE	IMPERFECT SUBJUNCTIVE
(yo)	me equivoque	me equivocara or equivocase
(tú)	te equivoques	te equivocaras or equivocases
(él/ella/usted)	se equivoque	se equivocara or equivocase
(nosotros/as)	nos equivoquemos	nos equivocáramos or equivocásemos
(vosotros/as)	os equivoquéis	os equivocarais or equivocaseis
(ellos/ellas/ ustedes)	se equivoquen	se equivocaran or equivocasen

IMPERATIVE
equivócate / equivocaos

Use the present subjunctive in all cases other than these **tú** and **vosotros** affirmative forms.

EXAMPLE PHRASES
Sobre todo, no **te equivoques** de hora. Above all, don't get the time wrong.

Si **te equivocaras**, quedarías eliminado del juego. If you made a mistake, you'd be out of the game.

erguir (to erect)

	PRESENT	PRESENT PERFECT
(yo)	yergo	he erguido
(tú)	yergues	has erguido
(él/ella/usted)	yergue	ha erguido
(nosotros/as)	erguimos	hemos erguido
(vosotros/as)	erguís	habéis erguido
(ellos/ellas/ ustedes)	yerguen	han erguido

	PRETERITE	IMPERFECT
(yo)	erguí	erguía
(tú)	erguiste	erguías
(él/ella/usted)	irguió	erguía
(nosotros/as)	erguimos	erguíamos
(vosotros/as)	erguisteis	erguías
(ellos/ellas/ ustedes)	irguieron	erguían

GERUND	PAST PARTICIPLE
irguiendo	erguido

EXAMPLE PHRASES

El perro **irguió** las orejas. The dog pricked up its ears.

La montaña **se erguía** majestuosa sobre el valle. The mountain rose majestically above the valley.

Tú mantén siempre la cabeza bien **erguida**. You must always hold your head high.

erguir

	FUTURE	CONDITIONAL
(yo)	erguiré	erguiría
(tú)	erguirás	erguirías
(él/ella/usted)	erguirá	erguiría
(nosotros/as)	erguiremos	erguiríamos
(vosotros/as)	erguiréis	erguiríais
(ellos/ellas/ ustedes)	erguirán	erguirían

	PRESENT SUBJUNCTIVE	IMPERFECT SUBJUNCTIVE
(yo)	yerga	irguiera or irguiese
(tú)	yergas	irguieras or irguieses
(él/ella/usted)	yerga	irguiera or irgulese
(nosotros/as)	irgamos	irguiéramos or irguiésemos
(vosotros/as)	irgáis	irguierais or irguieseis
(ellos/ellas/ ustedes)	yergan	irguieran or irguiesen

IMPERATIVE

yergue / erguid

Use the present subjunctive in all cases other than these tú and vosotros affirmative forms.

errar (to err)

	PRESENT		PRESENT PERFECT
(yo)	yerro		he errado
(tú)	yerras		has errado
(él/ella/usted)	yerra		ha errado
(nosotros/as)	erramos		hemos errado
(vosotros/as)	erráis		habéis errado
(ellos/ellas/ ustedes)	yerran		han errado

	PRETERITE		IMPERFECT
(yo)	erré		erraba
(tú)	erraste		errabas
(él/ella/usted)	erró		erraba
(nosotros/as)	erramos		errábamos
(vosotros/as)	errasteis		errabais
(ellos/ellas/ ustedes)	erraron		erraban

GERUND	PAST PARTICIPLE
errando	errado

EXAMPLE PHRASES

Errar es humano. To err is human.

Ha errado en su decisión. She has made the wrong decision.

Erró el tiro. He missed.

errar

	FUTURE	CONDITIONAL
(yo)	erraré	erraría
(tú)	errarás	errarías
(él/ella/usted)	errará	erraría
(nosotros/as)	erraremos	erraríamos
(vosotros/as)	erraréis	erraríais
(ellos/ellas/ ustedes)	errarán	errarían

	PRESENT SUBJUNCTIVE	IMPERFECT SUBJUNCTIVE
(yo)	yerre	errara *or* errase
(tú)	yerres	erraras *or* errases
(él/ella/usted)	yerre	errara *or* errase
(nosotros/as)	erremos	erráramos *or* errásemos
(vosotros/as)	erréis	errarais *or* erraseis
(ellos/ellas/ ustedes)	yerren	erraran *or* errasen

IMPERATIVE

yerra / errad

Use the present subjunctive in all cases other than these **tú** *and* **vosotros** *affirmative forms.*

Remember that subject pronouns are not used very often in Spanish.

escribir (to write)

	PRESENT	PRESENT PERFECT
(yo)	escribo	he escrito
(tú)	escribes	has escrito
(él/ella/usted)	escribe	ha escrito
(nosotros/as)	escribimos	hemos escrito
(vosotros/as)	escribís	habéis escrito
(ellos/ellas/ustedes)	escriben	han escrito

	PRETERITE	IMPERFECT
(yo)	escribí	escribía
(tú)	escribiste	escribías
(él/ella/usted)	escribió	escribía
(nosotros/as)	escribimos	escribíamos
(vosotros/as)	escribisteis	escribíais
(ellos/ellas/ustedes)	escribieron	escribían

GERUND	PAST PARTICIPLE
escribiendo	escrito

EXAMPLE PHRASES

¿Cómo **se escribe** su nombre? How do you spell your name?

¿**Estás escribiendo** la carta? Are you writing the letter?

Eso lo **he escrito** yo. I wrote that.

Nos escribimos durante un tiempo. We wrote to each other for a while.

Escribía canciones. She wrote songs.

Remember that subject pronouns are not used very often in Spanish.

escribir

	FUTURE	CONDITIONAL
(yo)	escribiré	escribiría
(tú)	escribirás	escribirías
(él/ella/usted)	escribirá	escribiría
(nosotros/as)	escribiremos	escribiríamos
(vosotros/as)	escribiréis	escribiríais
(ellos/ellas/ ustedes)	escribirán	escribirían

	PRESENT SUBJUNCTIVE	IMPERFECT SUBJUNCTIVE
(yo)	escriba	escribiera or escribiese
(tú)	escribas	escribieras or escribieses
(él/ella/usted)	escriba	escribiera or escribiese
(nosotros/as)	escribamos	escribiéramos or escribiésemos
(vosotros/as)	escribáis	escribierais or escribieseis
(ellos/ellas/ ustedes)	escriban	escribieran or escribiesen

IMPERATIVE

escribe / escribid

Use the present subjunctive in all cases other than these **tú** and **vosotros** affirmative forms.

EXAMPLE PHRASES

¿Me **escribirás**? Will you write to me?

Yo lo **escribiría** con mayúscula. I'd write it with a capital letter.

Te he dicho que no **escribas** en la mesa. I've told you not to write on the table.

Si de verdad **escribiera** bien, ya le habrían publicado algún libro. If he really was a good writer, he'd have had a book published by now.

Escríbelo en la pizarra. Write it on the blackboard.

Remember that subject pronouns are not used very often in Spanish.

esforzarse (to make an effort)

	PRESENT		PRESENT PERFECT
(yo)	me esfuerzo		me he esforzado
(tú)	te esfuerzas		te has esforzado
(él/ella/usted)	se esfuerza		se ha esforzado
(nosotros/as)	nos esforzamos		nos hemos esforzado
(vosotros/as)	os esforzáis		os habéis esforzado
(ellos/ellas/ ustedes)	se esfuerzan		se han esforzado

	PRETERITE		IMPERFECT
(yo)	me esforcé		me esforzaba
(tú)	te esforzaste		te esforzabas
(él/ella/usted)	se esforzó		se esforzaba
(nosotros/as)	nos esforzamos		nos esforzábamos
(vosotros/as)	os esforzasteis		os esforzabais
(ellos/ellas/ ustedes)	se esforzaron		se esforzaban

GERUND
esforzándose, etc

PAST PARTICIPLE
esforzado

EXAMPLE PHRASES

Tienes que **esforzarte** si quieres ganar. You have to make an effort if you want to win.

No **te esfuerzas** lo suficiente. You don't make enough effort.

Me he esforzado, pero nada. I've tried my best but haven't got anywhere.

Se esforzó todo lo que pudo por aprobar el examen. He did his best to pass the exam.

Me esforzaba por entenderla. I tried hard to understand her.

Remember that subject pronouns are not used very often in Spanish.

esforzarse

	FUTURE	CONDITIONAL
(yo)	me esforzaré	me esforzaría
(tú)	te esforzarás	te esforzarías
(él/ella/usted)	se esforzará	se esforzaría
(nosotros/as)	nos esforzaremos	nos esforzaríamos
(vosotros/as)	os esforzaréis	os esforzaríais
(ellos/ellas/ ustedes)	se esforzarán	se esforzarían

	PRESENT SUBJUNCTIVE	IMPERFECT SUBJUNCTIVE
(yo)	me esfuerce	me esforzara or esforzase
(tú)	te esfuerces	te esforzaras or esforzases
(él/ella/usted)	se esfuerce	se esforzara or esforzase
(nosotros/as)	nos esforcemos	nos esforzáramos or esforzásemos
(vosotros/as)	os esforcéis	os esforzarais or esforzaseis
(ellos/ellas/ ustedes)	se esfuercen	se esforzaran or esforzasen

IMPERATIVE
esfuérzate / esforzaos

Use the present subjunctive in all cases other than these **tú** and **vosotros** affirmative forms.

EXAMPLE PHRASES

No **te esfuerces**, no me vas a convencer. Stop struggling, you're not going to convince me.

Si **te esforzaras** un poco más, lo conseguirías. You'd manage it if you made a bit more of an effort.

Remember that subject pronouns are not used very often in Spanish.

establecer (to establish)

	PRESENT	PRESENT PERFECT
(yo)	establezco	he establecido
(tú)	estableces	has establecido
(él/ella/usted)	establece	ha establecido
(nosotros/as)	establecemos	hemos establecido
(vosotros/as)	establecéis	habéis establecido
(ellos/ellas/ ustedes)	establecen	han establecido

	PRETERITE	IMPERFECT
(yo)	establecí	establecía
(tú)	estableciste	establecías
(él/ella/usted)	estableció	establecía
(nosotros/as)	establecimos	establecíamos
(vosotros/as)	establecisteis	establecíais
(ellos/ellas/ ustedes)	establecieron	establecían

GERUND	PAST PARTICIPLE
estableciendo	establecido

EXAMPLE PHRASES

Han logrado **establecer** contacto con el barco. They've managed to make contact with the boat.

La ley **establece** que... The law states that...

Se ha establecido una buena relación entre los dos países. A good relationship has been established between the two countries.

En 1945, la familia **se estableció** en Madrid. In 1945, the family settled in Madrid.

Remember that subject pronouns are not used very often in Spanish.

establecer

	FUTURE	CONDITIONAL
(yo)	estableceré	establecería
(tú)	establecerás	establecerías
(él/ella/usted)	establecerá	establecería
(nosotros/as)	estableceremos	estableceríamos
(vosotros/as)	estableceréis	estableceríais
(ellos/ellas/ ustedes)	establecerán	establecerían

	PRESENT SUBJUNCTIVE	IMPERFECT SUBJUNCTIVE
(yo)	establezca	estableciera or estableciese
(tú)	establezcas	establecieras or establecieses
(él/ella/usted)	establezca	estableciera or estableciese
(nosotros/as)	establezcamos	estableciéramos or estableciésemos
(vosotros/as)	establezcáis	establecierais or establecieseis
(ellos/ellas/ ustedes)	establezcan	establecieran or estableciesen

IMPERATIVE

establece / estableced

Use the present subjunctive in all cases other than these tú and vosotros affirmative forms.

EXAMPLE PHRASES

El año que viene **se establecerá** por su cuenta. Next year she'll set up on her own.

estar (to be)

	PRESENT		PRESENT PERFECT
(yo)	estoy		he estado
(tú)	estás		has estado
(él/ella/usted)	está		ha estado
(nosotros/as)	estamos		hemos estado
(vosotros/as)	estáis		habéis estado
(ellos/ellas/ ustedes)	están		han estado

	PRETERITE		IMPERFECT
(yo)	estuve		estaba
(tú)	estuviste		estabas
(él/ella/usted)	estuvo		estaba
(nosotros/as)	estuvimos		estábamos
(vosotros/as)	estuvisteis		estabais
(ellos/ellas/ ustedes)	estuvieron		estaban

GERUND	PAST PARTICIPLE
estando	estado

EXAMPLE PHRASES

Estoy cansado. I'm tired.

¿Cómo **estás**? How are you?

¿**Has estado** alguna vez en París? Have you ever been to Paris?

Estuvimos en casa de mis padres. We were at my parents'.

¿Dónde **estabas**? Where were you?

Remember that subject pronouns are not used very often in Spanish.

estar

	FUTURE	CONDITIONAL
(yo)	estaré	estaría
(tú)	estarás	estarías
(él/ella/usted)	estará	estaría
(nosotros/as)	estaremos	estaríamos
(vosotros/as)	estaréis	estaríais
(ellos/ellas/ ustedes)	estarán	estarían

	PRESENT SUBJUNCTIVE	IMPERFECT SUBJUNCTIVE
(yo)	esté	estuviera or estuviese
(tú)	estés	estuvieras or estuvieses
(él/ella/usted)	esté	estuviera or estuviese
(nosotros/as)	estemos	estuviéramos or estuviésemos
(vosotros/as)	estéis	estuvierais or estuvieseis
(ellos/ellas/ ustedes)	estén	estuvieran or estuviesen

IMPERATIVE
está / estad

Use the present subjunctive in all cases other than these **tú** and **vosotros** affirmative forms.

EXAMPLE PHRASES
¿A qué hora **estarás** en casa? What time will you be home?
Dijo que **estaría** aquí a las ocho. She said she'd be here at eight o'clock.
Avísame cuando **estés** lista. Let me know when you're ready.
No sabía que **estuviera** tan lejos. I didn't know it was so far.
¡**Estáte** quieto! Stay still!

Remember that subject pronouns are not used very often in Spanish.

evacuar (to evacuate)

	PRESENT		PRESENT PERFECT
(yo)	evacuo		he evacuado
(tú)	evacuas		has evacuado
(él/ella/usted)	evacua		ha evacuado
(nosotros/as)	evacuamos		hemos evacuado
(vosotros/as)	evacuáis		habéis evacuado
(ellos/ellas/ ustedes)	evacuan		han evacuado

	PRETERITE		IMPERFECT
(yo)	evacué		evacuaba
(tú)	evacuaste		evacuabas
(él/ella/usted)	evacuó		evacuaba
(nosotros/as)	evacuamos		evacuábamos
(vosotros/as)	evacuasteis		evacuabais
(ellos/ellas/ ustedes)	evacuaron		evacuaban

GERUND

evacuando

PAST PARTICIPLE

evacuado

EXAMPLE PHRASES

Van a **evacuar** a los heridos. They're going to evacuate the injured.

Han evacuado la zona. The area has been evacuated.

evacuar

	FUTURE	CONDITIONAL
(yo)	evacuaré	evacuaría
(tú)	evacuarás	evacuarías
(él/ella/usted)	evacuará	evacuaría
(nosotros/as)	evacuaremos	evacuaríamos
(vosotros/as)	evacuaréis	evacuaríais
(ellos/ellas/ ustedes)	evacuarán	evacuarían

	PRESENT SUBJUNCTIVE	IMPERFECT SUBJUNCTIVE
(yo)	evacue	evacuara or evacuase
(tú)	evacues	evacuaras or evacuases
(él/ella/usted)	evacue	evacuara or evacuase
(nosotros/as)	evacuemos	evacuáramos or evacuásemos
(vosotros/as)	evacuéis	evacuarais or evacuaseis
(ellos/ellas/ ustedes)	evacuen	evacuaran or evacuasen

IMPERATIVE
evacua / evacuad

Use the present subjunctive in all cases other than these **tú** and **vosotros** affirmative forms.

EXAMPLE PHRASES

Seguirá existiendo peligro mientras no **evacuen** el edificio. The danger won't be over until the building has been evacuated.

freír (to fry)

	PRESENT		PRESENT PERFECT
(yo)	frío		he frito
(tú)	fríes		has frito
(él/ella/usted)	fríe		ha frito
(nosotros/as)	freímos		hemos frito
(vosotros/as)	freís		habéis frito
(ellos/ellas/ustedes)	fríen		han frito

	PRETERITE		IMPERFECT
(yo)	freí		freía
(tú)	freíste		freías
(él/ella/usted)	frio		freía
(nosotros/as)	freímos		freíamos
(vosotros/as)	freísteis		freíais
(ellos/ellas/ustedes)	frieron		freían

GERUND
friendo

PAST PARTICIPLE
frito

EXAMPLE PHRASES

No sabe ni **freír** un huevo. He can't even fry an egg.

He frito el pescado. I've fried the fish.

Se está friendo demasiado por ese lado. It's getting overdone on that side.

Lo **frio** en manteca. She fried it in lard.

Nos **freíamos** de calor. We were roasting in the heat.

Remember that subject pronouns are not used very often in Spanish.

freír

	FUTURE	CONDITIONAL
(yo)	freiré	freiría
(tú)	freirás	freirías
(él/ella/usted)	freirá	freiría
(nosotros/as)	freiremos	freiríamos
(vosotros/as)	freiréis	freiríais
(ellos/ellas/ ustedes)	freirán	freirían

	PRESENT SUBJUNCTIVE	IMPERFECT SUBJUNCTIVE
(yo)	fría	friera or friese
(tú)	frías	frieras or frieses
(él/ella/usted)	fría	friera or friese
(nosotros/as)	friamos	friéramos or friésemos
(vosotros/as)	friais	frierais or frieseis
(ellos/ellas/ ustedes)	frían	frieran or friesen

IMPERATIVE
fríe / freíd

Use the present subjunctive in all cases other than these *tú* and *vosotros* affirmative forms.

EXAMPLE PHRASES

Yo lo **freiría** con menos aceite. I'd fry it using less oil.

Fríelo en esa sartén. Fry it in that pan.

Remember that subject pronouns are not used very often in Spanish.

gruñir (to grumble; to growl)

	PRESENT		PRESENT PERFECT
(yo)	gruño		he gruñido
(tú)	gruñes		has gruñido
(él/ella/usted)	gruñe		ha gruñido
(nosotros/as)	gruñimos		hemos gruñido
(vosotros/as)	gruñís		habéis gruñido
(ellos/ellas/ ustedes)	gruñen		han gruñido

	PRETERITE		IMPERFECT
(yo)	gruñí		gruñía
(tú)	gruñiste		gruñías
(él/ella/usted)	gruñó		gruñía
(nosotros/as)	gruñimos		gruñíamos
(vosotros/as)	gruñisteis		gruñíais
(ellos/ellas/ ustedes)	gruñeron		gruñían

GERUND	PAST PARTICIPLE
gruñendo	gruñido

EXAMPLE PHRASES

¿A quién **gruñe** el perro? Who's the dog growling at?

Siempre **está gruñendo**. He's always grumbling.

El oso nos **gruñía** sin parar. The bear kept growling at us.

Remember that subject pronouns are not used very often in Spanish.

gruñir

	FUTURE	CONDITIONAL
(yo)	gruñiré	gruñiría
(tú)	gruñirás	gruñirías
(él/ella/usted)	gruñirá	gruñiría
(nosotros/as)	gruñiremos	gruñiríamos
(vosotros/as)	gruñiréis	gruñiríais
(ellos/ellas/ ustedes)	gruñirán	gruñirían

	PRESENT SUBJUNCTIVE	IMPERFECT SUBJUNCTIVE
(yo)	gruña	gruñera or gruñese
(tú)	gruñas	gruñeras or gruñeses
(él/ella/usted)	gruña	gruñera or gruñese
(nosotros/as)	gruñamos	gruñéramos or gruñésemos
(vosotros/as)	gruñáis	gruñerais or gruñeseis
(ellos/ellas/ ustedes)	gruñan	gruñeran or gruñesen

IMPERATIVE
gruñe / gruñid

Use the present subjunctive in all cases other than these **tú** and **vosotros** affirmative forms.

EXAMPLE PHRASES
¡No **gruñas** tanto! Don't grumble so much.

Remember that subject pronouns are not used very often in Spanish.

guiar (to guide)

	PRESENT		PRESENT PERFECT
(yo)	guío		he guiado
(tú)	guías		has guiado
(él/ella/usted)	guía		ha guiado
(nosotros/as)	guiamos		hemos guiado
(vosotros/as)	guiais		habéis guiado
(ellos/ellas/ ustedes)	guían		han guiado

	PRETERITE		IMPERFECT
(yo)	guie		guiaba
(tú)	guiaste		guiabas
(él/ella/usted)	guio		guiaba
(nosotros/as)	guiamos		guiábamos
(vosotros/as)	guiasteis		guiabais
(ellos/ellas/ ustedes)	guiaron		guiaban

GERUND	PAST PARTICIPLE
guiando	guiado

EXAMPLE PHRASES

Los perros **se guían** por su olfato. Dogs follow their sense of smell.

Me he guiado por el instinto. I followed my instinct.

Nos guiamos por un mapa que teníamos. We found our way using a map we had.

Siempre me protegía y me **guiaba**. He always protected me and guided me.

Remember that subject pronouns are not used very often in Spanish.

guiar

	FUTURE	CONDITIONAL
(yo)	guiaré	guiaría
(tú)	guiarás	guiarías
(él/ella/usted)	guiará	guiaría
(nosotros/as)	guiaremos	guiaríamos
(vosotros/as)	guiaréis	guiaríais
(ellos/ellas/ ustedes)	guiarán	guiarían

	PRESENT SUBJUNCTIVE	IMPERFECT SUBJUNCTIVE
(yo)	guíe	guiara or guiase
(tú)	guíes	guiaras or guiases
(él/ella/usted)	guíe	guiara or guiase
(nosotros/as)	guiemos	guiáramos or guiásemos
(vosotros/as)	guieis	guiarais or guiaseis
(ellos/ellas/ ustedes)	guíen	guiaran or guiasen

IMPERATIVE
guía / guiad

Use the present subjunctive in all cases other than these **tú** *and* **vosotros** *affirmative forms.*

EXAMPLE PHRASES
Les **guiaré** hasta allí. I'll take you there.
Guíate por la razón. Use reason as your guide.

haber (to have – *auxiliary*)

	PRESENT		PRESENT PERFECT
(yo)	he		*not used except impersonally*
(tú)	has		*See* **hay**
(él/ella/usted)	ha		
(nosotros/as)	hemos		
(vosotros/as)	habéis		
(ellos/ellas/ ustedes)	han		

	PRETERITE	IMPERFECT
(yo)	hube	había
(tú)	hubiste	habías
(él/ella/usted)	hubo	había
(nosotros/as)	hubimos	habíamos
(vosotros/as)	hubisteis	habíais
(ellos/ellas/ ustedes)	hubieron	habían

GERUND	PAST PARTICIPLE
habiendo	habido

EXAMPLE PHRASES

De **haberlo** sabido, **habría** ido. If I'd known, I would have gone.

¿**Has** visto eso? Did you see that?

Eso nunca **había** pasado antes. That had never happened before.

Remember that subject pronouns are not used very often in Spanish.

haber

	FUTURE	CONDITIONAL
(yo)	habré	habría
(tú)	habrás	habrías
(él/ella/usted)	habrá	habría
(nosotros/as)	habremos	habríamos
(vosotros/as)	habréis	habríais
(ellos/ellas/ ustedes)	habrán	habrían

	PRESENT SUBJUNCTIVE	IMPERFECT SUBJUNCTIVE
(yo)	haya	hubiera or hubiese
(tú)	hayas	hubieras or hubieses
(él/ella/usted)	haya	hubiera or hubiese
(nosotros/as)	hayamos	hubiéramos or hubiésemos
(vosotros/as)	hayáis	hubierais or hubleseis
(ellos/ellas/ ustedes)	hayan	hubieran or hubiesen

IMPERATIVE

not used

EXAMPLE PHRASES

Habrá que repasarlo. We'll have to check it.

Habría que limpiarlo. We should clean it.

Como se **hayan** olvidado los mato. I'll kill them if they've forgotten.

Si me lo **hubieras** dicho, te lo **habría** traído. I'd have brought it, if you'd said.

Remember that subject pronouns are not used very often in Spanish.

hablar (to speak; to talk)

	PRESENT		PRESENT PERFECT
(yo)	hablo		he hablado
(tú)	hablas		has hablado
(él/ella/usted)	habla		ha hablado
(nosotros/as)	hablamos		hemos hablado
(vosotros/as)	habláis		habéis hablado
(ellos/ellas/ ustedes)	hablan		han hablado

	PRETERITE		IMPERFECT
(yo)	hablé		hablaba
(tú)	hablaste		hablabas
(él/ella/usted)	habló		hablaba
(nosotros/as)	hablamos		hablábamos
(vosotros/as)	hablasteis		hablabais
(ellos/ellas/ ustedes)	hablaron		hablaban

GERUND
hablando

PAST PARTICIPLE
hablado

EXAMPLE PHRASES

María no **habla** inglés. María doesn't speak English.

No **nos hablamos** desde hace tiempo. We haven't spoken to each other for a long time.

Está hablando por teléfono. He's on the phone.

Hoy **he hablado** con mi hermana. I've spoken to my sister today.

¿**Has hablado** ya con el profesor? Have you spoken to the teacher yet?

Remember that subject pronouns are not used very often in Spanish.

hablar

	FUTURE	CONDITIONAL
(yo)	hablaré	hablaría
(tú)	hablarás	hablarías
(él/ella/usted)	hablará	hablaría
(nosotros/as)	hablaremos	hablaríamos
(vosotros/as)	hablaréis	hablaríais
(ellos/ellas/ustedes)	hablarán	hablarían

	PRESENT SUBJUNCTIVE	IMPERFECT SUBJUNCTIVE
(yo)	hable	hablara or hablase
(tú)	hables	hablaras or hablases
(él/ella/usted)	hable	hablara or hablase
(nosotros/as)	hablemos	habláramos or hablásemos
(vosotros/as)	habléis	hablarais or hablaseis
(ellos/ellas/ustedes)	hablen	hablaran or hablasen

IMPERATIVE
habla / hablad

Use the present subjunctive in all cases other than these **tú** and **vosotros** affirmative forms.

EXAMPLE PHRASES
Luego **hablaremos** de ese tema. We'll talk about that later.

Recuérdame que **hable** con Daniel. Remind me to speak to Daniel.

¿Quieres que **hablemos**? Shall we talk?

Hay que darles una oportunidad para que **hablen**. We need to give them an opportunity to speak.

Remember that subject pronouns are not used very often in Spanish.

hacer (to do; to make)

	PRESENT		PRESENT PERFECT
(yo)	hago		he hecho
(tú)	haces		has hecho
(él/ella/usted)	hace		ha hecho
(nosotros/as)	hacemos		hemos hecho
(vosotros/as)	hacéis		habéis hecho
(ellos/ellas/ ustedes)	hacen		han hecho

	PRETERITE		IMPERFECT
(yo)	hice		hacía
(tú)	hiciste		hacías
(él/ella/usted)	hizo		hacía
(nosotros/as)	hicimos		hacíamos
(vosotros/as)	hicisteis		hacíais
(ellos/ellas/ ustedes)	hicieron		hacían

GERUND

haciendo

PAST PARTICIPLE

hecho

EXAMPLE PHRASES

¿Qué **hace** tu padre? What does your father do?

Están haciendo mucho ruido. They're making a lot of noise.

¿Quién **hizo** eso? Who did that?

Hicieron pintar la fachada del colegio. They had the front of the school painted.

Lo **hacía** para fastidiarme. He did it to annoy me.

Remember that subject pronouns are not used very often in Spanish.

hacer

	FUTURE	CONDITIONAL
(yo)	haré	haría
(tú)	harás	harías
(él/ella/usted)	hará	haría
(nosotros/as)	haremos	haríamos
(vosotros/as)	haréis	haríais
(ellos/ellas/ ustedes)	harán	harían

	PRESENT SUBJUNCTIVE	IMPERFECT SUBJUNCTIVE
(yo)	haga	hiciera *or* hiciese
(tú)	hagas	hicieras *or* hicieses
(él/ella/usted)	haga	hiciera *or* hiciese
(nosotros/as)	hagamos	hiciéramos *or* hiciésemos
(vosotros/as)	hagáis	hicierais *or* hicieseis
(ellos/ellas/ ustedes)	hagan	hicieran *or* hiciesen

IMPERATIVE

haz / haced

*Use the present subjunctive in all cases other than these **tú** and **vosotros** affirmative forms.*

EXAMPLE PHRASES

Lo **haré** yo mismo. I'll do it myself.

Dijiste que lo **harías.** You said you'd do it.

¿Quieres que **haga** las camas? Do you want me to make the beds?

Preferiría que **hiciera** menos calor. I'd rather it weren't so hot.

Hazlo como te he dicho. Do it the way I told you.

Remember that subject pronouns are not used very often in Spanish.

hay (there is; there are)

PRESENT
hay

PRESENT PERFECT
ha habido

PRETERITE
hubo

IMPERFECT
había

GERUND
habiendo

PAST PARTICIPLE
habido

EXAMPLE PHRASES

Esta tarde va a **haber** una manifestación. There's going to be a demonstration this evening.

Hay una iglesia en la esquina. There's a church on the corner.

Ha habido una tormenta. There's been a storm.

Hubo una guerra. There was a war.

Había mucha gente. There were a lot of people.

Remember that subject pronouns are not used very often in Spanish.

hay

FUTURE
habrá

CONDITIONAL
habría

PRESENT SUBJUNCTIVE
haya

IMPERFECT SUBJUNCTIVE
hubiera *or* hubiese

IMPERATIVE
not used

EXAMPLE PHRASES

¿**Habrá** suficiente? Will there be enough?

De este modo **habría** menos accidentes. That way there would be fewer accidents.

No creo que **haya** mucha gente en el recital. I don't think there'll be many people at the concert.

Si **hubiera** más espacio, pondría un sofá. I'd have a sofa if there were more room.

Remember that subject pronouns are not used very often in Spanish.

herir (to injure)

	PRESENT		PRESENT PERFECT
(yo)	hiero		he herido
(tú)	hieres		has herido
(él/ella/usted)	hiere		ha herido
(nosotros/as)	herimos		hemos herido
(vosotros/as)	herís		habéis herido
(ellos/ellas/ ustedes)	hieren		han herido

	PRETERITE		IMPERFECT
(yo)	herí		hería
(tú)	heriste		herías
(él/ella/usted)	hirió		hería
(nosotros/as)	herimos		heríamos
(vosotros/as)	heristeis		heríais
(ellos/ellas/ ustedes)	hirieron		herían

GERUND	PAST PARTICIPLE
hiriendo	herido

EXAMPLE PHRASES

Vas a **herir** sus sentimientos. You're going to hurt her feelings.

Me **hiere** que me digas eso. I'm hurt that you should say such a thing.

La **han herido** en el brazo. Her arm's been injured.

Lo **hirieron** en el pecho. He was wounded in the chest.

La **hería** en lo más hondo. She was deeply hurt.

Remember that subject pronouns are not used very often in Spanish.

herir

	FUTURE	CONDITIONAL
(yo)	heriré	heriría
(tú)	herirás	herirías
(él/ella/usted)	herirá	heriría
(nosotros/as)	heriremos	heriríamos
(vosotros/as)	heriréis	heriríais
(ellos/ellas/ ustedes)	herirán	herirían

	PRESENT SUBJUNCTIVE	IMPERFECT SUBJUNCTIVE
(yo)	hiera	hiriera or hiriese
(tú)	hieras	hirieras or hirieses
(él/ella/usted)	hiera	hiriera or hiriese
(nosotros/as)	hiramos	hiriéramos or hiriésemos
(vosotros/as)	hiráis	hirierais or hirieseis
(ellos/ellas/ ustedes)	hieran	hirieran or hiriesen

IMPERATIVE
hiere / herid

Use the present subjunctive in all cases other than these **tú** and **vosotros** affirmative forms.

EXAMPLE PHRASES
Mi madre siempre tenía miedo que nos **hiriéramos**. My mum was always scared we'd hurt ourselves.

Remember that subject pronouns are not used very often in Spanish.

huir (to escape)

	PRESENT		PRESENT PERFECT
(yo)	huyo		he huido
(tú)	huyes		has huido
(él/ella/usted)	huye		ha huido
(nosotros/as)	huimos		hemos huido
(vosotros/as)	huis		habéis huido
(ellos/ellas/ ustedes)	huyen		han huido

	PRETERITE		IMPERFECT
(yo)	hui		huía
(tú)	huiste		huías
(él/ella/usted)	huyó		huía
(nosotros/as)	huimos		huíamos
(vosotros/as)	huisteis		huíais
(ellos/ellas/ ustedes)	huyeron		huían

GERUND	PAST PARTICIPLE
huyendo	huido

EXAMPLE PHRASES

No sé por qué me **huye**. I don't know why he's avoiding me.

Salió **huyendo**. He ran away.

Ha huido de la cárcel. He has escaped from prison.

Huyeron del país. They fled the country.

Remember that subject pronouns are not used very often in Spanish.

huir

	FUTURE	CONDITIONAL
(yo)	huiré	huiría
(tú)	huirás	huirías
(él/ella/usted)	huirá	huiría
(nosotros/as)	huiremos	huiríamos
(vosotros/as)	huiréis	huiríais
(ellos/ellas/ ustedes)	huirán	huirían

	PRESENT SUBJUNCTIVE	IMPERFECT SUBJUNCTIVE
(yo)	huya	huyera or huyese
(tú)	huyas	huyeras or huyeses
(él/ella/usted)	huya	huyera or huyese
(nosotros/as)	huyamos	huyéramos or huyésemos
(vosotros/as)	huyáis	huyerais or huyeseis
(ellos/ellas/ ustedes)	huyan	huyeran or huyesen

IMPERATIVE
huye / huid

Use the present subjunctive in all cases other than these **tú** *and* **vosotros** *affirmative forms.*

EXAMPLE PHRASES

No quiero que **huyas** como un cobarde. I dont want you to run away like a coward.

¡**Huye**! Si te atrapan, te matarán. Run! If they catch you, they'll kill you.

Remember that subject pronouns are not used very often in Spanish.

imponer (to impose)

	PRESENT		PRESENT PERFECT
(yo)	impongo		he impuesto
(tú)	impones		has impuesto
(él/ella/usted)	impone		ha impuesto
(nosotros/as)	imponemos		hemos impuesto
(vosotros/as)	imponéis		habéis impuesto
(ellos/ellas/ ustedes)	imponen		han impuesto

	PRETERITE		IMPERFECT
(yo)	impuse		imponía
(tú)	impusiste		imponías
(él/ella/usted)	impuso		imponía
(nosotros/as)	impusimos		imponíamos
(vosotros/as)	impusisteis		imponíais
(ellos/ellas/ ustedes)	impusieron		imponían

GERUND

imponiendo

PAST PARTICIPLE

impuesto

EXAMPLE PHRASES

La vista desde el acantilado **impone** un poco. The view from the cliff top is quite impressive.

La minifalda **se está imponiendo** de nuevo. The miniskirt is back in fashion.

Han impuesto la enseñanza religiosa. They have made religious education compulsory.

El corredor nigeriano **se impuso** en la segunda carrera. The Nigerian runner triumphed in the second race.

Mi abuelo **imponía** mucho respeto. My grandfather commanded a lot of respect.

Remember that subject pronouns are not used very often in Spanish.

imponer

	FUTURE	CONDITIONAL
(yo)	impondré	impondría
(tú)	impondrás	impondrías
(él/ella/usted)	impondrá	impondría
(nosotros/as)	impondremos	impondríamos
(vosotros/as)	impondréis	impondríais
(ellos/ellas/ ustedes)	impondrán	impondrían

	PRESENT SUBJUNCTIVE	IMPERFECT SUBJUNCTIVE
(yo)	imponga	impusiera or impusiese
(tú)	impongas	impusieras or impusieses
(él/ella/usted)	imponga	impusiera or impuslese
(nosotros/as)	impongamos	impusiéramos or impusiésemos
(vosotros/as)	impongáis	impusierais or impusieseis
(ellos/ellas/ ustedes)	impongan	impusieran or impusiesen

IMPERATIVE
impón / imponed

Use the present subjunctive in all cases other than these **tú** and **vosotros** affirmative forms.

EXAMPLE PHRASES
Impondrán multas de hasta 50 euros. They'll impose fines of up to 50 euros.

imprimir (to print)

	PRESENT		PRESENT PERFECT
(yo)	imprimo		he imprimido
(tú)	imprimes		has imprimido
(él/ella/usted)	imprime		ha imprimido
(nosotros/as)	imprimimos		hemos imprimido
(vosotros/as)	imprimís		habéis imprimido
(ellos/ellas/ ustedes)	imprimen		han imprimido

	PRETERITE		IMPERFECT
(yo)	imprimí		imprimía
(tú)	imprimiste		imprimías
(él/ella/usted)	imprimió		imprimía
(nosotros/as)	imprimimos		imprimíamos
(vosotros/as)	imprimisteis		imprimíais
(ellos/ellas/ ustedes)	imprimieron		imprimían

GERUND	PAST PARTICIPLE
imprimiendo	imprimido, impreso

EXAMPLE PHRASES

Una experiencia así **imprime** carácter. An experience like that is character-building.

¿**Has imprimido** el documento? Have you printed out the file?

Se imprimieron sólo doce copias del libro. Only twelve copies of the book were printed.

El sillón **imprimía** un cierto aire de distinción al salón. The chair gave the living room a certain air of distinction.

Remember that subject pronouns are not used very often in Spanish.

imprimir

	FUTURE	CONDITIONAL
(yo)	imprimiré	imprimiría
(tú)	imprimirás	imprimirías
(él/ella/usted)	imprimirá	imprimiría
(nosotros/as)	imprimiremos	imprimiríamos
(vosotros/as)	imprimiréis	imprimiríais
(ellos/ellas/ ustedes)	imprimirán	imprimirían

	PRESENT SUBJUNCTIVE	IMPERFECT SUBJUNCTIVE
(yo)	imprima	imprimiera or imprimiese
(tú)	imprimas	imprimieras or imprimieses
(él/ella/usted)	imprima	imprimiera or imprimlese
(nosotros/as)	imprimamos	imprimiéramos or imprimiésemos
(vosotros/as)	imprimáis	imprimierais or imprimieseis
(ellos/ellas/ ustedes)	impriman	imprimieran or imprimiesen

IMPERATIVE
imprime / imprimid

Use the present subjunctive in all cases other than these **tú** and **vosotros** affirmative forms.

Remember that subject pronouns are not used very often in Spanish.

ir (to go)

	PRESENT		PRESENT PERFECT
(yo)	voy		he ido
(tú)	vas		has ido
(él/ella/usted)	va		ha ido
(nosotros/as)	vamos		hemos ido
(vosotros/as)	vais		habéis ido
(ellos/ellas/ ustedes)	van		han ido

	PRETERITE		IMPERFECT
(yo)	fui		iba
(tú)	fuiste		ibas
(él/ella/usted)	fue		iba
(nosotros/as)	fuimos		íbamos
(vosotros/as)	fuisteis		ibais
(ellos/ellas/ ustedes)	fueron		iban

GERUND	PAST PARTICIPLE
yendo	ido

EXAMPLE PHRASES

¿Puedo **ir** contigo? Can I come with you?

¿**Vamos** a comer al campo? Shall we have a picnic in the country?

Estoy yendo a clases de natación. I'm taking swimming lessons.

Ha ido a comprar el pan. She's gone to buy some bread.

Anoche **fuimos** al cine. We went to the cinema last night.

Remember that subject pronouns are not used very often in Spanish.

ir

	FUTURE	CONDITIONAL
(yo)	iré	iría
(tú)	irás	irías
(él/ella/usted)	irá	iría
(nosotros/as)	iremos	iríamos
(vosotros/as)	iréis	iríais
(ellos/ellas/ ustedes)	irán	irían

	PRESENT SUBJUNCTIVE	IMPERFECT SUBJUNCTIVE
(yo)	vaya	fuera or fuese
(tú)	vayas	fueras or fueses
(él/ella/usted)	vaya	fuera or fuese
(nosotros/as)	vayamos	fuéramos or fuésemos
(vosotros/as)	vayáis	fuerais or fueseis
(ellos/ellas/ ustedes)	vayan	fueran or fuesen

IMPERATIVE

ve / id

Use the present subjunctive in most cases other than these **tú** and **vosotros** affirmative forms.
However, in the 'let's' affirmative form, **vamos** is more common than **vayamos**.

EXAMPLE PHRASES

El domingo **iré** a Edimburgo. I'll go to Edinburgh on Sunday.

Dijeron que **irían** andando. They said they'd walk.

¡Que te **vaya** bien! Take care of yourself!

Quería pedirte que **fueras** en mi lugar. I wanted to ask you if you'd go
   instead of me.

No **te vayas** sin despedirte. Don't go without saying goodbye.

Vete a hacer los deberes. Go and do your homework.

Remember that subject pronouns are not used very often in Spanish.

jugar (to play)

	PRESENT		PRESENT PERFECT
(yo)	juego		he jugado
(tú)	juegas		has jugado
(él/ella/usted)	juega		ha jugado
(nosotros/as)	jugamos		hemos jugado
(vosotros/as)	jugáis		habéis jugado
(ellos/ellas/ ustedes)	juegan		han jugado

	PRETERITE		IMPERFECT
(yo)	jugué		jugaba
(tú)	jugaste		jugabas
(él/ella/usted)	jugó		jugaba
(nosotros/as)	jugamos		jugábamos
(vosotros/as)	jugasteis		jugabais
(ellos/ellas/ ustedes)	jugaron		jugaban

GERUND	PAST PARTICIPLE
jugando	jugado

EXAMPLE PHRASES

Juego al fútbol todos los domingos. I play football every Sunday.

Están jugando en el jardín. They're playing in the garden.

Le **han jugado** una mala pasada. They played a dirty trick on him.

Después de cenar **jugamos** a las cartas. After dinner we played cards.

Se jugaba la vida continuamente. She was constantly risking her life.

Remember that subject pronouns are not used very often in Spanish.

jugar

	FUTURE	CONDITIONAL
(yo)	jugaré	jugaría
(tú)	jugarás	jugarías
(él/ella/usted)	jugará	jugaría
(nosotros/as)	jugaremos	jugaríamos
(vosotros/as)	jugaréis	jugaríais
(ellos/ellas/ ustedes)	jugarán	jugarían

	PRESENT SUBJUNCTIVE	IMPERFECT SUBJUNCTIVE
(yo)	juegue	jugara or jugase
(tú)	juegues	jugaras or jugases
(él/ella/usted)	juegue	jugara or jugase
(nosotros/as)	juguemos	jugáramos or jugásemos
(vosotros/as)	juguéis	jugarais or jugaseis
(ellos/ellas/ ustedes)	jueguen	jugaran or jugasen

IMPERATIVE

juega / jugad

Use the present subjunctive in all cases other than these tú and vosotros affirmative forms.

EXAMPLE PHRASES

Jugarán contra el Real Madrid. They'll play Real Madrid.

Jugarías mejor si estuvieras más relajado. You'd play better if you were more relaxed.

No **juegues** con tu salud. Don't take risks with your health.

El médico le aconsejó que **jugara** más y leyera menos. The doctor advised him to play more and read less.

Remember that subject pronouns are not used very often in Spanish.

leer (to read)

	PRESENT		PRESENT PERFECT
(yo)	leo		he leído
(tú)	lees		has leído
(él/ella/usted)	lee		ha leído
(nosotros/as)	leemos		hemos leído
(vosotros/as)	leéis		habéis leído
(ellos/ellas/ ustedes)	leen		han leído

	PRETERITE		IMPERFECT
(yo)	leí		leía
(tú)	leíste		leías
(él/ella/usted)	leyó		leía
(nosotros/as)	leímos		leíamos
(vosotros/as)	leísteis		leíais
(ellos/ellas/ ustedes)	leyeron		leían

GERUND	PAST PARTICIPLE
leyendo	leído

EXAMPLE PHRASES

Hace mucho tiempo que no **leo** nada. I haven't read anything for ages.

Estoy leyendo un libro muy interesante. I'm reading a very interesting book.

¿**Has leído** esta novela? Have you read this novel?

Lo **leí** hace tiempo. I read it a while ago.

Antes **leía** mucho más. I used to read a lot more before.

Remember that subject pronouns are not used very often in Spanish.

leer

	FUTURE	CONDITIONAL
(yo)	leeré	leería
(tú)	leerás	leerías
(él/ella/usted)	leerá	leería
(nosotros/as)	leeremos	leeríamos
(vosotros/as)	leeréis	leeríais
(ellos/ellas/ustedes)	leerán	leerían

	PRESENT SUBJUNCTIVE	IMPERFECT SUBJUNCTIVE
(yo)	lea	leyera or leyese
(tú)	leas	leyeras or leyeses
(él/ella/usted)	lea	leyera or leyese
(nosotros/as)	leamos	leyéramos or leyésemos
(vosotros/as)	leáis	leyerais or leyeseis
(ellos/ellas/ustedes)	lean	leyeran or leyesen

IMPERATIVE

lee / leed

Use the present subjunctive in all cases other than these tú and vosotros affirmative forms.

EXAMPLE PHRASES

Si os portáis bien, os **leeré** un cuento. If you behave yourselves, I'll read you a story.

Yo **leería** también la letra pequeña. I'd read the small print as well.

Quiero que lo **leas** y me digas qué piensas. I want you to read it and tell me what you think.

No **leas** tan deprisa. Don't read so fast.

Remember that subject pronouns are not used very often in Spanish.

levantar (to lift)

	PRESENT		PRESENT PERFECT
(yo)	levanto		he levantado
(tú)	levantas		has levantado
(él/ella/usted)	levanta		ha levantado
(nosotros/as)	levantamos		hemos levantado
(vosotros/as)	levantáis		habéis levantado
(ellos/ellas/ ustedes)	levantan		han levantado

	PRETERITE		IMPERFECT
(yo)	levanté		levantaba
(tú)	levantaste		levantabas
(él/ella/usted)	levantó		levantaba
(nosotros/as)	levantamos		levantábamos
(vosotros/as)	levantasteis		levantabais
(ellos/ellas/ ustedes)	levantaron		levantaban

GERUND	PAST PARTICIPLE
levantando	levantado

EXAMPLE PHRASES

No me importa **levantarme** temprano. I don't mind getting up early.

Siempre **se levanta** de mal humor. He's always in a bad mood when he gets up.

Hoy **me he levantado** temprano. I got up early this morning.

Levantó la maleta como si no pesara nada. He lifted up the suitcase as if it weighed nothing.

Me levanté y seguí caminando. I got up and carried on walking.

Remember that subject pronouns are not used very often in Spanish.

levantar

	FUTURE	CONDITIONAL
(yo)	levantaré	levantaría
(tú)	levantarás	levantarías
(él/ella/usted)	levantará	levantaría
(nosotros/as)	levantaremos	levantaríamos
(vosotros/as)	levantaréis	levantaríais
(ellos/ellas/ ustedes)	levantarán	levantarían

	PRESENT SUBJUNCTIVE	IMPERFECT SUBJUNCTIVE
(yo)	levante	levantara or levantase
(tú)	levantes	levantaras or levantases
(él/ella/usted)	levante	levantara or levantase
(nosotros/as)	levantemos	levantáramos or levantásemos
(vosotros/as)	levantéis	levantarais or levantaseis
(ellos/ellas/ ustedes)	levanten	levantaran or levantasen

IMPERATIVE

levanta / levantad

Use the present subjunctive in all cases other than these **tú** and **vosotros** affirmative forms.

EXAMPLE PHRASES

La noticia le **levantará** el ánimo. This news will raise her spirits

Si pudiera **me levantaría** siempre tarde. I'd sleep in every day, if I could.

No me **levantes** la voz. Don't raise your voice to me.

Levanta la tapa. Lift the lid.

Levantad la mano si tenéis alguna duda. Put up your hands if you are unclear about anything.

Remember that subject pronouns are not used very often in Spanish.

llover (to rain)

PRESENT
llueve

PRESENT PERFECT
ha llovido

PRETERITE
llovió

IMPERFECT
llovía

GERUND
lloviendo

PAST PARTICIPLE
llovido

EXAMPLE PHRASES

Hace semanas que no **llueve**. It hasn't rained for weeks.

Está lloviendo. It's raining.

Le **han llovido** las ofertas. He's received lots of offers.

Llovió sin parar. It rained non-stop.

Llovía a cántaros. It was pouring down.

Remember that subject pronouns are not used very often in Spanish.

llover

FUTURE
lloverá

CONDITIONAL
llovería

PRESENT SUBJUNCTIVE
llueva

IMPERFECT SUBJUNCTIVE
lloviera *or* lloviese

IMPERATIVE
not used

EXAMPLE PHRASES

Sabía que le **lloverían** las críticas. She knew she would be much criticized.

Espero que no **llueva** este fin de semana. I hope it won't rain this weekend.

Si no **lloviera** podríamos salir a dar una vuelta. We could go for a walk if it wasn't raining.

Remember that subject pronouns are not used very often in Spanish.

lucir (to shine)

	PRESENT		PRESENT PERFECT
(yo)	luzco		he lucido
(tú)	luces		has lucido
(él/ella/usted)	luce		ha lucido
(nosotros/as)	lucimos		hemos lucido
(vosotros/as)	lucís		habéis lucido
(ellos/ellas/ustedes)	lucen		han lucido

	PRETERITE		IMPERFECT
(yo)	lucí		lucía
(tú)	luciste		lucías
(él/ella/usted)	lució		lucía
(nosotros/as)	lucimos		lucíamos
(vosotros/as)	lucisteis		lucíais
(ellos/ellas/ustedes)	lucieron		lucían

GERUND	PAST PARTICIPLE
luciendo	lucido

EXAMPLE PHRASES

Ahí no **luce** nada. It doesn't look very good there.

¡Anda, que **te has lucido**! Well, you've excelled yourself!

Lucían las estrellas. The stars were shining.

lucir

	FUTURE	CONDITIONAL
(yo)	luciré	luciría
(tú)	lucirás	lucirías
(él/ella/usted)	lucirá	luciría
(nosotros/as)	luciremos	luciríamos
(vosotros/as)	luciréis	luciríais
(ellos/ellas/ ustedes)	lucirán	lucirían

	PRESENT SUBJUNCTIVE	IMPERFECT SUBJUNCTIVE
(yo)	luzca	luciera or luciese
(tú)	luzcas	lucieras or lucieses
(él/ella/usted)	luzca	luciera or luciese
(nosotros/as)	luzcamos	luciéramos or luciésemos
(vosotros/as)	luzcáis	lucierais or lucieseis
(ellos/ellas/ ustedes)	luzcan	lucieran or luciesen

IMPERATIVE
luce / lucid

Use the present subjunctive in all cases other than these tú and vosotros affirmative forms.

EXAMPLE PHRASES

Lucirá un traje muy elegante. She will be wearing a very smart outfit.

Luciría más con otros zapatos. It would look much better with a different pair of shoes.

Quiero que esta noche **luzcas** tú el collar. I want you to wear the necklace tonight.

Remember that subject pronouns are not used very often in Spanish.

morir (to die)

	PRESENT		PRESENT PERFECT
(yo)	muero		he muerto
(tú)	mueres		has muerto
(él/ella/usted)	muere		ha muerto
(nosotros/as)	morimos		hemos muerto
(vosotros/as)	morís		habéis muerto
(ellos/ellas/ ustedes)	mueren		han muerto

	PRETERITE		IMPERFECT
(yo)	morí		moría
(tú)	moriste		morías
(él/ella/usted)	murió		moría
(nosotros/as)	morimos		moríamos
(vosotros/as)	moristeis		moríais
(ellos/ellas/ ustedes)	murieron		morían

GERUND	PAST PARTICIPLE
muriendo	muerto

EXAMPLE PHRASES

¡**Me muero** de hambre! I'm starving!

Se está muriendo. She's dying.

Se le **ha muerto** el gato. His cat has died.

Se murió el mes pasado. He died last month.

Me moría de ganas de contárselo. I was dying to tell her.

Remember that subject pronouns are not used very often in Spanish.

morir

	FUTURE	CONDITIONAL
(yo)	moriré	moriría
(tú)	morirás	morirías
(él/ella/usted)	morirá	moriría
(nosotros/as)	moriremos	moriríamos
(vosotros/as)	moriréis	moriríais
(ellos/ellas/ ustedes)	morirán	morirían

	PRESENT SUBJUNCTIVE	IMPERFECT SUBJUNCTIVE
(yo)	muera	muriera or muriese
(tú)	mueras	murieras or murieses
(él/ella/usted)	muera	muriera or muriese
(nosotros/as)	muramos	muriéramos or muriésemos
(vosotros/as)	muráis	murierais or murieseis
(ellos/ellas/ ustedes)	mueran	murieran or muriesen

IMPERATIVE

muere / morid

Use the present subjunctive in all cases other than these **tú** and **vosotros** affirmative forms.

EXAMPLE PHRASES

Cuando te lo cuente **te morirás** de risa. You'll kill yourself laughing when I tell you.

Yo **me moriría** de vergüenza. I'd die of shame.

Cuando **me muera**... When I die...

¡Por favor, no **te mueras**! Please don't die!

Estoy muerto de miedo. I'm scared stiff.

Remember that subject pronouns are not used very often in Spanish.

mover (to move)

	PRESENT	PRESENT PERFECT
(yo)	muevo	he movido
(tú)	mueves	has movido
(él/ella/usted)	mueve	ha movido
(nosotros/as)	movemos	hemos movido
(vosotros/as)	movéis	habéis movido
(ellos/ellas/ ustedes)	mueven	han movido

	PRETERITE	IMPERFECT
(yo)	moví	movía
(tú)	moviste	movías
(él/ella/usted)	movió	movía
(nosotros/as)	movimos	movíamos
(vosotros/as)	movisteis	movíais
(ellos/ellas/ ustedes)	movieron	movían

GERUND	PAST PARTICIPLE
moviendo	movido

EXAMPLE PHRASES

El perro no dejaba de **mover** la cola. The dog kept wagging its tail.

Se está moviendo. It's moving.

¿**Has movido** ese mueble de sitio? Have you moved that piece of furniture?

No **se movieron** de casa. They didn't leave the house.

Antes **se movía** en esos ambientes. He used to move in those circles.

Remember that subject pronouns are not used very often in Spanish.

mover

	FUTURE	CONDITIONAL
(yo)	moveré	movería
(tú)	moverás	moverías
(él/ella/usted)	moverá	movería
(nosotros/as)	moveremos	moveríamos
(vosotros/as)	moveréis	moveríais
(ellos/ellas/ ustedes)	moverán	moverían

	PRESENT SUBJUNCTIVE	IMPERFECT SUBJUNCTIVE
(yo)	mueva	moviera or moviese
(tú)	muevas	movieras or movieses
(él/ella/usted)	mueva	moviera or moviese
(nosotros/as)	movamos	moviéramos or moviésemos
(vosotros/as)	mováis	movierais or movieseis
(ellos/ellas/ ustedes)	muevan	movieran or moviesen

IMPERATIVE
mueve / moved

Use the present subjunctive in all cases other than these tú and vosotros affirmative forms.

EXAMPLE PHRASES
Prométeme que no **te moverás** de aquí. Promise me you won't move from here.

No **te muevas**. Don't move.

Mueve un poco las cajas para que podamos pasar. Move the boxes a bit so that we can get past.

Remember that subject pronouns are not used very often in Spanish.

nacer (to be born)

	PRESENT		PRESENT PERFECT
(yo)	nazco		he nacido
(tú)	naces		has nacido
(él/ella/usted)	nace		ha nacido
(nosotros/as)	nacemos		hemos nacido
(vosotros/as)	nacéis		habéis nacido
(ellos/ellas/ ustedes)	nacen		han nacido

	PRETERITE		IMPERFECT
(yo)	nací		nacía
(tú)	naciste		nacías
(él/ella/usted)	nació		nacía
(nosotros/as)	nacimos		nacíamos
(vosotros/as)	nacisteis		nacíais
(ellos/ellas/ ustedes)	nacieron		nacían

GERUND	PAST PARTICIPLE
naciendo	nacido

EXAMPLE PHRASES

Nacen cuatro niños por minuto. Four children are born every minute.

Ha nacido antes de tiempo. It was premature.

Nació en 1980. He was born in 1980.

¿Cuándo **naciste**? When were you born?

En aquella época había muchos más niños que **nacían** en casa. Many more babies were born at home in those days.

Remember that subject pronouns are not used very often in Spanish.

nacer

	FUTURE		CONDITIONAL
(yo)	naceré		nacería
(tú)	nacerás		nacerías
(él/ella/usted)	nacerá		nacería
(nosotros/as)	naceremos		naceríamos
(vosotros/as)	naceréis		naceríais
(ellos/ellas/ ustedes)	nacerán		nacerían

	PRESENT SUBJUNCTIVE	IMPERFECT SUBJUNCTIVE
(yo)	nazca	naciera or naciese
(tú)	nazcas	nacieras or nacieses
(él/ella/usted)	nazca	naciera or naciese
(nosotros/as)	nazcamos	naciéramos or naciésemos
(vosotros/as)	nazcáis	nacierais or nacieseis
(ellos/ellas/ ustedes)	nazcan	nacieran or naciesen

IMPERATIVE
nace / naced

Use the present subjunctive in all cases other than these **tú** and **vosotros** affirmative forms.

EXAMPLE PHRASES
Nacerá el año que viene. It will be born next year.

Queremos que **nazca** en España. We want it to be born in Spain.

Si **naciera** hoy, sería tauro. He'd be a Taurus if he were born today.

Remember that subject pronouns are not used very often in Spanish.

negar (to deny; to refuse)

	PRESENT		PRESENT PERFECT
(yo)	niego		he negado
(tú)	niegas		has negado
(él/ella/usted)	niega		ha negado
(nosotros/as)	negamos		hemos negado
(vosotros/as)	negáis		habéis negado
(ellos/ellas/ ustedes)	niegan		han negado

	PRETERITE		IMPERFECT
(yo)	negué		negaba
(tú)	negaste		negabas
(él/ella/usted)	negó		negaba
(nosotros/as)	negamos		negábamos
(vosotros/as)	negasteis		negabais
(ellos/ellas/ ustedes)	negaron		negaban

GERUND	PAST PARTICIPLE
negando	negado

EXAMPLE PHRASES

No lo puedes **negar**. You can't deny it.

Me niego a creerlo. I refuse to believe it.

Me **ha negado** el favor. He wouldn't do me this favour.

Se negó a venir con nosotros. She refused to come with us.

Decían que era el ladrón, pero él lo **negaba**. They said that he was the thief, but he denied it.

Remember that subject pronouns are not used very often in Spanish.

negar

	FUTURE	CONDITIONAL
(yo)	negaré	negaría
(tú)	negarás	negarías
(él/ella/usted)	negará	negaría
(nosotros/as)	negaremos	negaríamos
(vosotros/as)	negaréis	negaríais
(ellos/ellas/ ustedes)	negarán	negarían

	PRESENT SUBJUNCTIVE	IMPERFECT SUBJUNCTIVE
(yo)	niegue	negara or negase
(tú)	niegues	negaras or negases
(él/ella/usted)	niegue	negara or negase
(nosotros/as)	neguemos	negáramos or negásemos
(vosotros/as)	neguéis	negarais or negaseis
(ellos/ellas/ ustedes)	nieguen	negaran or negasen

IMPERATIVE
niega / negad

Use the present subjunctive in all cases other than these **tú** and **vosotros** affirmative forms.

EXAMPLE PHRASES
No me **negarás** que es barato. You can't say it's not cheap.
Si lo **negaras**, nadie te creería. If you denied it, nobody would believe you.
No lo **niegues**. Don't deny it.

Remember that subject pronouns are not used very often in Spanish.

oír (to hear)

	PRESENT		PRESENT PERFECT
(yo)	oigo		he oído
(tú)	oyes		has oído
(él/ella/usted)	oye		ha oído
(nosotros/as)	oímos		hemos oído
(vosotros/as)	oís		habéis oído
(ellos/ellas/ ustedes)	oyen		han oído

	PRETERITE		IMPERFECT
(yo)	oí		oía
(tú)	oíste		oías
(él/ella/usted)	oyó		oía
(nosotros/as)	oímos		oíamos
(vosotros/as)	oísteis		oíais
(ellos/ellas/ ustedes)	oyeron		oían

GERUND

oyendo

PAST PARTICIPLE

oído

EXAMPLE PHRASES

No **oigo** nada. I can't hear anything.

Hemos estado oyendo las noticias. We've been listening to the news.

¿**Has oído** eso? Did you hear that?

Lo **oí** por casualidad. I heard it by chance.

No **oía** muy bien. He couldn't hear very well.

Remember that subject pronouns are not used very often in Spanish.

oír

	FUTURE		CONDITIONAL
(yo)	oiré		oiría
(tú)	oirás		oirías
(él/ella/usted)	oirá		oiría
(nosotros/as)	oiremos		oiríamos
(vosotros/as)	oiréis		oiríais
(ellos/ellas/ ustedes)	oirán		oirían

	PRESENT SUBJUNCTIVE		IMPERFECT SUBJUNCTIVE
(yo)	oiga		oyera or oyese
(tú)	oigas		oyeras or oyeses
(él/ella/usted)	oiga		oyera or oyese
(nosotros/as)	oigamos		oyéramos or oyésemos
(vosotros/as)	oigáis		oyerais or oyeseis
(ellos/ellas/ ustedes)	oigan		oyeran or oyesen

IMPERATIVE
oye / oíd

Use the present subjunctive in all cases other than these **tú** *and* **vosotros** *affirmative forms.*

EXAMPLE PHRASES

Oirías mal. You must have misunderstood.

¡**Oiga**! ¡A ver si mira por dónde va! Excuse me! Why don't you look where you're going?

Óyeme bien, no vuelvas a hacer eso. Now listen carefully; don't do that again.

oler (to smell)

	PRESENT	PRESENT PERFECT
(yo)	huelo	he olido
(tú)	hueles	has olido
(él/ella/usted)	huele	ha olido
(nosotros/as)	olemos	hemos olido
(vosotros/as)	oléis	habéis olido
(ellos/ellas/ustedes)	huelen	han olido

	PRETERITE	IMPERFECT
(yo)	olí	olía
(tú)	oliste	olías
(él/ella/usted)	olió	olía
(nosotros/as)	olimos	olíamos
(vosotros/as)	olisteis	olíais
(ellos/ellas/ustedes)	olieron	olían

GERUND
oliendo

PAST PARTICIPLE
olido

EXAMPLE PHRASES

Huele a pescado. It smells of fish.

El perro **estaba oliendo** la basura. The dog was sniffing the rubbish.

Se ha olido algo. He's started to suspect.

A mí el asunto me **olió** mal. I thought there was something fishy about it.

Olía muy bien. It smelled really nice.

Remember that subject pronouns are not used very often in Spanish.

oler

	FUTURE	CONDITIONAL
(yo)	oleré	olería
(tú)	olerás	olerías
(él/ella/usted)	olerá	olería
(nosotros/as)	oleremos	oleríamos
(vosotros/as)	oleréis	oleríais
(ellos/ellas/ ustedes)	olerán	olerían

	PRESENT SUBJUNCTIVE	IMPERFECT SUBJUNCTIVE
(yo)	huela	oliera or oliese
(tú)	huelas	olieras or olieses
(él/ella/usted)	huela	oliera or oliese
(nosotros/as)	olamos	oliéramos or oliésemos
(vosotros/as)	oláis	olierais or olieseis
(ellos/ellas/ ustedes)	huelan	olieran or oliesen

IMPERATIVE
huele / oled

Use the present subjunctive in all cases other than these **tú** and **vosotros** affirmative forms.

EXAMPLE PHRASES
Con esto ya no **olerá**. This will take the smell away.
Si te **oliera** a quemado, apágalo. If you smell it burning, turn it off.

pagar (to pay; to pay for)

	PRESENT		PRESENT PERFECT
(yo)	pago		he pagado
(tú)	pagas		has pagado
(él/ella/usted)	paga		ha pagado
(nosotros/as)	pagamos		hemos pagado
(vosotros/as)	pagáis		habéis pagado
(ellos/ellas/ ustedes)	pagan		han pagado

	PRETERITE		IMPERFECT
(yo)	pagué		pagaba
(tú)	pagaste		pagabas
(él/ella/usted)	pagó		pagaba
(nosotros/as)	pagamos		pagábamos
(vosotros/as)	pagasteis		pagabais
(ellos/ellas/ ustedes)	pagaron		pagaban

GERUND	PAST PARTICIPLE
pagando	pagado

EXAMPLE PHRASES

Se puede **pagar** con tarjeta de crédito. You can pay by credit card.

¿Cuánto te **pagan** al mes? How much do they pay you a month?

No **han pagado** el alquiler. They haven't paid the rent.

Lo **pagué** en efectivo. I paid for it in cash.

Me **pagaban** muy poco. I got paid very little.

Remember that subject pronouns are not used very often in Spanish.

pagar

	FUTURE	CONDITIONAL
(yo)	pagaré	pagaría
(tú)	pagarás	pagarías
(él/ella/usted)	pagará	pagaría
(nosotros/as)	pagaremos	pagaríamos
(vosotros/as)	pagaréis	pagaríais
(ellos/ellas/ustedes)	pagarán	pagarían

	PRESENT SUBJUNCTIVE	IMPERFECT SUBJUNCTIVE
(yo)	pague	pagara or pagase
(tú)	pagues	pagaras or pagases
(él/ella/usted)	pague	pagara or pagase
(nosotros/as)	paguemos	pagáramos or pagásemos
(vosotros/as)	paguéis	pagarais or pagaseis
(ellos/ellas/ustedes)	paguen	pagaran or pagasen

IMPERATIVE

paga / pagad

Use the present subjunctive in all cases other than these tú and vosotros affirmative forms.

EXAMPLE PHRASES

Yo te **pagaré** la entrada. I'll pay for your ticket.

¡Quiero que **pague** por lo que me ha hecho! I want him to pay for what he's done to me!

Si **pagase** sus deudas, se quedaría sin nada. He'd be left with nothing if he paid his debts.

No les **pagues** hasta que lo hayan hecho. Don't pay them until they've done it.

Págame lo que me debes. Pay me what you owe me.

Remember that subject pronouns are not used very often in Spanish.

partir (to cut; to leave)

	PRESENT	PRESENT PERFECT
(yo)	parto	he partido
(tú)	partes	has partido
(él/ella/usted)	parte	ha partido
(nosotros/as)	partimos	hemos partido
(vosotros/as)	partís	habéis partido
(ellos/ellas/ ustedes)	parten	han partido

	PRETERITE	IMPERFECT
(yo)	partí	partía
(tú)	partiste	partías
(él/ella/usted)	partió	partía
(nosotros/as)	partimos	partíamos
(vosotros/as)	partisteis	partíais
(ellos/ellas/ ustedes)	partieron	partían

GERUND	PAST PARTICIPLE
partiendo	partido

EXAMPLE PHRASES

¿Te **parto** un trozo de queso? Shall I cut you a piece of cheese?

Partiendo de la base de que... Assuming that...

El remo **se partió** en dos. The oar broke in two.

Se partían de risa. They were splitting their sides laughing.

partir

	FUTURE	CONDITIONAL
(yo)	partiré	partiría
(tú)	partirás	partirías
(él/ella/usted)	partirá	partiría
(nosotros/as)	partiremos	partiríamos
(vosotros/as)	partiréis	partiríais
(ellos/ellas/ustedes)	partirán	partirían

	PRESENT SUBJUNCTIVE	IMPERFECT SUBJUNCTIVE
(yo)	parta	partiera or partiese
(tú)	partas	partieras or partieses
(él/ella/usted)	parta	partiera or partiese
(nosotros/as)	partamos	partiéramos or partiésemos
(vosotros/as)	partáis	partierais or partieseis
(ellos/ellas/ustedes)	partan	partieran or partiesen

IMPERATIVE

parte / partid

*Use the present subjunctive in all cases other than these **tú** and **vosotros** affirmative forms.*

EXAMPLE PHRASES

La expedición **partirá** mañana de París. The expedition will set off from Paris tomorrow.

Eso le **partiría** el corazón. That would break his heart.

No **partas** todavía el pan. Don't slice the bread yet.

Pártelo por la mitad. Cut it in half.

Remember that subject pronouns are not used very often in Spanish.

pedir (to ask for; to ask)

	PRESENT		PRESENT PERFECT
(yo)	pido		he pedido
(tú)	pides		has pedido
(él/ella/usted)	pide		ha pedido
(nosotros/as)	pedimos		hemos pedido
(vosotros/as)	pedís		habéis pedido
(ellos/ellas/ ustedes)	piden		han pedido

	PRETERITE		IMPERFECT
(yo)	pedí		pedía
(tú)	pediste		pedías
(él/ella/usted)	pidió		pedía
(nosotros/as)	pedimos		pedíamos
(vosotros/as)	pedisteis		pedíais
(ellos/ellas/ ustedes)	pidieron		pedían

GERUND	PAST PARTICIPLE
pidiendo	pedido

EXAMPLE PHRASES

¿Cuánto **pide** por el coche? How much is he asking for the car?

La casa **está pidiendo** a gritos una mano de pintura. The house is crying out to be painted.

Hemos pedido dos cervezas. We've ordered two beers.

No nos **pidieron** el pasaporte. They didn't ask us for our passports.

Pedían dos millones de rescate. They were demanding a two-million ransom.

Remember that subject pronouns are not used very often in Spanish.

pedir

	FUTURE	CONDITIONAL
(yo)	pediré	pediría
(tú)	pedirás	pedirías
(él/ella/usted)	pedirá	pediría
(nosotros/as)	pediremos	pediríamos
(vosotros/as)	pediréis	pediríais
(ellos/ellas/ustedes)	pedirán	pedirían

	PRESENT SUBJUNCTIVE	IMPERFECT SUBJUNCTIVE
(yo)	pida	pidiera or pidiese
(tú)	pidas	pidieras or pidieses
(él/ella/usted)	pida	pidiera or pidiese
(nosotros/as)	pidamos	pidiéramos or pidiésemos
(vosotros/as)	pidáis	pidierais or pidieseis
(ellos/ellas/ustedes)	pidan	pidieran or pidiesen

IMPERATIVE
pide / pedid
Use the present subjunctive in all cases other than these *tú* and *vosotros* affirmative forms.

EXAMPLE PHRASES

Si se entera, te **pedirá** explicaciones. If he finds out, he'll ask you for an explanation.

Nunca te **pediría** que hicieras una cosa así. I'd never ask you to do anything like that.

Y que sea lo último que me **pidas**. And don't ask me for anything else.

Pídele el teléfono. Ask her for her telephone number.

Remember that subject pronouns are not used very often in Spanish.

pensar (to think)

	PRESENT		PRESENT PERFECT
(yo)	pienso		he pensado
(tú)	piensas		has pensado
(él/ella/usted)	piensa		ha pensado
(nosotros/as)	pensamos		hemos pensado
(vosotros/as)	pensáis		habéis pensado
(ellos/ellas/ ustedes)	piensan		han pensado

	PRETERITE		IMPERFECT
(yo)	pensé		pensaba
(tú)	pensaste		pensabas
(él/ella/usted)	pensó		pensaba
(nosotros/as)	pensamos		pensábamos
(vosotros/as)	pensasteis		pensabais
(ellos/ellas/ ustedes)	pensaron		pensaban

GERUND	PAST PARTICIPLE
pensando	pensado

EXAMPLE PHRASES

¿**Piensas** que vale la pena? Do you think it's worth it?

¿Qué **piensas** del aborto? What do you think about abortion?

Está **pensando** en comprarse un piso. He's thinking about buying a flat.

¿Lo **has pensado** bien? Have you thought about it carefully?

Pensaba que vendrías. I thought you'd come.

Remember that subject pronouns are not used very often in Spanish.

pensar

	FUTURE	CONDITIONAL
(yo)	pensaré	pensaría
(tú)	pensarás	pensarías
(él/ella/usted)	pensará	pensaría
(nosotros/as)	pensaremos	pensaríamos
(vosotros/as)	pensaréis	pensaríais
(ellos/ellas/ ustedes)	pensarán	pensarían

	PRESENT SUBJUNCTIVE	IMPERFECT SUBJUNCTIVE
(yo)	piense	pensara or pensase
(tú)	pienses	pensaras or pensases
(él/ella/usted)	piense	pensara or pensase
(nosotros/as)	pensemos	pensáramos or pensásemos
(vosotros/as)	penséis	pensarais or pensaseis
(ellos/ellas/ ustedes)	piensen	pensaran or pensasen

IMPERATIVE

piensa / pensad

Use the present subjunctive in all cases other than these **tú** and **vosotros** affirmative forms.

EXAMPLE PHRASES

Yo no me lo **pensaría** dos veces. I wouldn't think about it twice.

Me da igual lo que **piensen**. I don't care what they think.

Si **pensara** eso, te lo diría. If I thought that, I'd tell you.

No **pienses** que no quiero ir. Don't think that I don't want to go.

No lo **pienses** más. Don't give it another thought.

Remember that subject pronouns are not used very often in Spanish.

perder (to lose)

	PRESENT		PRESENT PERFECT
(yo)	pierdo		he perdido
(tú)	pierdes		has perdido
(él/ella/usted)	pierde		ha perdido
(nosotros/as)	perdemos		hemos perdido
(vosotros/as)	perdéis		habéis perdido
(ellos/ellas/ ustedes)	pierden		han perdido

	PRETERITE		IMPERFECT
(yo)	perdí		perdía
(tú)	perdiste		perdías
(él/ella/usted)	perdió		perdía
(nosotros/as)	perdimos		perdíamos
(vosotros/as)	perdisteis		perdíais
(ellos/ellas/ ustedes)	perdieron		perdían

GERUND

perdiendo

PAST PARTICIPLE

perdido

EXAMPLE PHRASES

Siempre **pierde** las llaves. He's always losing his keys.

Ana es la que saldrá **perdiendo**. Ana is the one who will lose out.

He perdido dos kilos. I've lost two kilos.

Perdimos dos a cero. We lost two nil.

Perdían siempre. They always used to lose.

Remember that subject pronouns are not used very often in Spanish.

perder

	FUTURE	CONDITIONAL
(yo)	perderé	perdería
(tú)	perderás	perderías
(él/ella/usted)	perderá	perdería
(nosotros/as)	perderemos	perderíamos
(vosotros/as)	perderéis	perderíais
(ellos/ellas/ ustedes)	perderán	perderían

	PRESENT SUBJUNCTIVE	IMPERFECT SUBJUNCTIVE
(yo)	pierda	perdiera or perdiese
(tú)	pierdas	perdieras or perdieses
(él/ella/usted)	pierda	perdiera or perdiese
(nosotros/as)	perdamos	perdiéramos or perdiésemos
(vosotros/as)	perdáis	perdierais or perdieseis
(ellos/ellas/ ustedes)	pierdan	perdieran or perdiesen

IMPERATIVE
pierde / perded

Use the present subjunctive in all cases other than these **tú** and **vosotros** affirmative forms.

EXAMPLE PHRASES
Date prisa o **perderás** el tren. Hurry up or you'll miss the train.

¡No **te** lo **pierdas**! Don't miss it!

No **pierdas** esta oportunidad. Don't miss this opportunity.

Remember that subject pronouns are not used very often in Spanish.

poder (to be able to)

	PRESENT	PRESENT PERFECT
(yo)	puedo	he podido
(tú)	puedes	has podido
(él/ella/usted)	puede	ha podido
(nosotros/as)	podemos	hemos podido
(vosotros/as)	podéis	habéis podido
(ellos/ellas/ ustedes)	pueden	han podido

	PRETERITE	IMPERFECT
(yo)	pude	podía
(tú)	pudiste	podías
(él/ella/usted)	pudo	podía
(nosotros/as)	pudimos	podíamos
(vosotros/as)	pudisteis	podíais
(ellos/ellas/ ustedes)	pudieron	podían

GERUND	PAST PARTICIPLE
pudiendo	podido

EXAMPLE PHRASES

¿**Puedo** entrar? Can I come in?

Puede que llegue mañana. He may arrive tomorrow.

No **he podido** venir antes. I couldn't come before.

Pudiste haberte hecho daño. You could have hurt yourself.

¡Me lo **podías** haber dicho! You could have told me!

Remember that subject pronouns are not used very often in Spanish.

poder

	FUTURE		CONDITIONAL
(yo)	podré		podría
(tú)	podrás		podrías
(él/ella/usted)	podrá		podría
(nosotros/as)	podremos		podríamos
(vosotros/as)	podréis		podríais
(ellos/ellas/ ustedes)	podrán		podrían

	PRESENT SUBJUNCTIVE	IMPERFECT SUBJUNCTIVE
(yo)	pueda	pudiera or pudiese
(tú)	puedas	pudieras or pudieses
(él/ella/usted)	pueda	pudiera or pudiese
(nosotros/as)	podamos	pudiéramos or pudiésemos
(vosotros/as)	podáis	pudierais or pudieseis
(ellos/ellas/ ustedes)	puedan	pudieran or pudiesen

IMPERATIVE
puede / poded

Use the present subjunctive in all cases other than these **tú** and **vosotros** affirmative forms.

EXAMPLE PHRASES

Estoy segura de que **podrá** conseguirlo. I'm sure he'll succeed.

¿**Podrías** ayudarme? Could you help me?

Ven en cuanto **puedas**. Come as soon as you can.

Si no **pudiera** encontrar la casa, te llamaría al móvil. If I weren't able to find the house, I'd call you on your mobile.

Remember that subject pronouns are not used very often in Spanish.

poner (to put)

	PRESENT		PRESENT PERFECT
(yo)	pongo		he puesto
(tú)	pones		has puesto
(él/ella/usted)	pone		ha puesto
(nosotros/as)	ponemos		hemos puesto
(vosotros/as)	ponéis		habéis puesto
(ellos/ellas/ ustedes)	ponen		han puesto

	PRETERITE		IMPERFECT
(yo)	puse		ponía
(tú)	pusiste		ponías
(él/ella/usted)	puso		ponía
(nosotros/as)	pusimos		poníamos
(vosotros/as)	pusisteis		poníais
(ellos/ellas/ ustedes)	pusieron		ponían

GERUND	PAST PARTICIPLE
poniendo	puesto

EXAMPLE PHRASES

¿Dónde **pongo** mis cosas? Where shall I put my things?

¿Qué **pone** en la carta? What does the letter say?

¿Le **has puesto** azúcar a mi café? Have you put any sugar in my coffee?

Todos **nos pusimos** de acuerdo. We all agreed.

Remember that subject pronouns are not used very often in Spanish.

poner

	FUTURE	CONDITIONAL
(yo)	pondré	pondría
(tú)	pondrás	pondrías
(él/ella/usted)	pondrá	pondría
(nosotros/as)	pondremos	pondríamos
(vosotros/as)	pondréis	pondríais
(ellos/ellas/ ustedes)	pondrán	pondrían

	PRESENT SUBJUNCTIVE	IMPERFECT SUBJUNCTIVE
(yo)	ponga	pusiera or pusiese
(tú)	pongas	pusieras or pusieses
(él/ella/usted)	ponga	pusiera or pusiese
(nosotros/as)	pongamos	pusiéramos or pusiésemos
(vosotros/as)	pongáis	pusierais or pusieseis
(ellos/ellas/ ustedes)	pongan	pusieran or pusiesen

IMPERATIVE
pon / poned

Use the present subjunctive in all cases other than these **tú** and **vosotros** affirmative forms.

EXAMPLE PHRASES
Lo **pondré** aquí. I'll put it here.

¿Le **pondrías** más sal? Would you add more salt?

Ponlo ahí encima. Put it on there.

prohibir (to ban; to prohibit)

	PRESENT		PRESENT PERFECT
(yo)	prohíbo		he prohibido
(tú)	prohíbes		has prohibido
(él/ella/usted)	prohíbe		ha prohibido
(nosotros/as)	prohibimos		hemos prohibido
(vosotros/as)	prohibís		habéis prohibido
(ellos/ellas/ ustedes)	prohíben		han prohibido

	PRETERITE		IMPERFECT
(yo)	prohibí		prohibía
(tú)	prohibiste		prohibías
(él/ella/usted)	prohibió		prohibía
(nosotros/as)	prohibimos		prohibíamos
(vosotros/as)	prohibisteis		prohibíais
(ellos/ellas/ ustedes)	prohibieron		prohibían

GERUND	PAST PARTICIPLE
prohibiendo	prohibido

EXAMPLE PHRASES

Deberían **prohibirlo**. It should be banned.

Te **prohíbo** que me hables así. I won't have you talking to me like that!

Han prohibido el acceso a la prensa. The press have been banned.

Le **prohibieron** la entrada en el bingo. She was not allowed into the bingo hall.

El tratado **prohibía** el uso de armas químicas. The treaty prohibited the use of
   chemical weapons.

Remember that subject pronouns are not used very often in Spanish.

prohibir

	FUTURE	CONDITIONAL
(yo)	prohibiré	prohibiría
(tú)	prohibirás	prohibirías
(él/ella/usted)	prohibirá	prohibiría
(nosotros/as)	prohibiremos	prohibiríamos
(vosotros/as)	prohibiréis	prohibiríais
(ellos/ellas/ ustedes)	prohibirán	prohibirían

	PRESENT SUBJUNCTIVE	IMPERFECT SUBJUNCTIVE
(yo)	prohíba	prohibiera or prohibiese
(tú)	prohíbas	prohibieras or prohibieses
(él/ella/usted)	prohíba	prohibiera or prohibiese
(nosotros/as)	prohibamos	prohibiéramos or prohibiésemos
(vosotros/as)	prohibáis	prohibierais or prohibieseis
(ellos/ellas/ ustedes)	prohíban	prohibieran or prohibiesen

IMPERATIVE
prohíbe / prohibid

Use the present subjunctive in all cases other than these tú and vosotros affirmative forms.

EXAMPLE PHRASES
Lo **prohibirán** más tarde o más temprano. Sooner or later they'll ban it.

Yo esa música la **prohibiría**. If it were up to me, that music would be banned.

"**prohibido** fumar" "no smoking"

querer (to want; to love)

	PRESENT	PRESENT PERFECT
(yo)	quiero	he querido
(tú)	quieres	has querido
(él/ella/usted)	quiere	ha querido
(nosotros/as)	queremos	hemos querido
(vosotros/as)	queréis	habéis querido
(ellos/ellas/ ustedes)	quieren	han querido

	PRETERITE	IMPERFECT
(yo)	quise	quería
(tú)	quisiste	querías
(él/ella/usted)	quiso	quería
(nosotros/as)	quisimos	queríamos
(vosotros/as)	quisisteis	queríais
(ellos/ellas/ ustedes)	quisieron	querían

GERUND	PAST PARTICIPLE
queriendo	querido

EXAMPLE PHRASES

Lo hice sin **querer.** I didn't mean to do it.

Te **quiero.** I love you.

Quiero que vayas. I want you to go.

Tú lo **has querido.** You were asking for it.

No **quería** decírmelo. She didn't want to tell me.

Remember that subject pronouns are not used very often in Spanish.

querer

	FUTURE	CONDITIONAL
(yo)	querré	querría
(tú)	querrás	querrías
(él/ella/usted)	querrá	querría
(nosotros/as)	querremos	querríamos
(vosotros/as)	querréis	querríais
(ellos/ellas/ ustedes)	querrán	querrían

	PRESENT SUBJUNCTIVE	IMPERFECT SUBJUNCTIVE
(yo)	quiera	quisiera or quisiese
(tú)	quieras	quisieras or quisieses
(él/ella/usted)	quiera	quisiera or quisiese
(nosotros/as)	queramos	quisiéramos or quisiésemos
(vosotros/as)	queráis	quisierais or quisieseis
(ellos/ellas/ ustedes)	quieran	quisieran or quisiesen

IMPERATIVE
quiere / quered

Use the present subjunctive in all cases other than these **tú** and **vosotros** affirmative forms.

EXAMPLE PHRASES
¿**Querrá** firmarme un autógrafo? Will you give me your autograph?
Querría que no hubiera pasado nunca. I wish it had never happened.
¡Por lo que más **quieras**! ¡Cállate! For goodness' sake, shut up!
Quisiera preguntar una cosa. I'd like to ask something.

Remember that subject pronouns are not used very often in Spanish.

reducir (to reduce)

	PRESENT		PRESENT PERFECT
(yo)	reduzco		he reducido
(tú)	reduces		has reducido
(él/ella/usted)	reduce		ha reducido
(nosotros/as)	reducimos		hemos reducido
(vosotros/as)	reducís		habéis reducido
(ellos/ellas/ ustedes)	reducen		han reducido

	PRETERITE		IMPERFECT
(yo)	reduje		reducía
(tú)	redujiste		reducías
(él/ella/usted)	redujo		reducía
(nosotros/as)	redujimos		reducíamos
(vosotros/as)	redujisteis		reducíais
(ellos/ellas/ ustedes)	redujeron		reducían

GERUND	PAST PARTICIPLE
reduciendo	reducido

EXAMPLE PHRASES

Al final todo **se reduce** a eso. In the end it all comes down to that.

Le **han reducido** la pena a dos meses. His sentence has been reduced to two months.

Se ha reducido la tasa de natalidad. The birth rate has fallen.

Sus gastos **se redujeron** a la mitad. Their expenses were cut by half.

Remember that subject pronouns are not used very often in Spanish.

reducir

	FUTURE	CONDITIONAL
(yo)	reduciré	reduciría
(tú)	reducirás	reducirías
(él/ella/usted)	reducirá	reduciría
(nosotros/as)	reduciremos	reduciríamos
(vosotros/as)	reduciréis	reduciríais
(ellos/ellas/ ustedes)	reducirán	reducirían

	PRESENT SUBJUNCTIVE	IMPERFECT SUBJUNCTIVE
(yo)	reduzca	redujera or redujese
(tú)	reduzcas	redujeras or redujeses
(él/ella/usted)	reduzca	redujera or redujese
(nosotros/as)	reduzcamos	redujéramos or redujésemos
(vosotros/as)	reduzcáis	redujerais or redujeseis
(ellos/ellas/ ustedes)	reduzcan	redujeran or redujesen

IMPERATIVE
reduce / reducid

Use the present subjunctive in all cases other than these **tú** and **vosotros** affirmative forms.

EXAMPLE PHRASES
Reducirán la producción en un 20%. They'll cut production by 20%.

Reduzca la velocidad. Reduce speed.

Remember that subject pronouns are not used very often in Spanish.

rehusar (to refuse)

	PRESENT		PRESENT PERFECT
(yo)	rehúso		he rehusado
(tú)	rehúsas		has rehusado
(él/ella/usted)	rehúsa		ha rehusado
(nosotros/as)	rehusamos		hemos rehusado
(vosotros/as)	rehusáis		habéis rehusado
(ellos/ellas/ ustedes)	rehúsan		han rehusado

	PRETERITE		IMPERFECT
(yo)	rehusé		rehusaba
(tú)	rehusaste		rehusabas
(él/ella/usted)	rehusó		rehusaba
(nosotros/as)	rehusamos		rehusábamos
(vosotros/as)	rehusasteis		rehusabais
(ellos/ellas/ ustedes)	rehusaron		rehusaban

GERUND	PAST PARTICIPLE
rehusando	rehusado

EXAMPLE PHRASES

Rehúso tomar parte en esto. I refuse to take part in this.

Ha rehusado la oferta de trabajo. He declined the job offer.

Su familia **rehusó** hacer declaraciones. His family refused to comment.

Remember that subject pronouns are not used very often in Spanish.

rehusar

	FUTURE	CONDITIONAL
(yo)	rehusaré	rehusaría
(tú)	rehusarás	rehusarías
(él/ella/usted)	rehusará	rehusaría
(nosotros/as)	rehusaremos	rehusaríamos
(vosotros/as)	rehusaréis	rehusaríais
(ellos/ellas/ ustedes)	rehusarán	rehusarían

	PRESENT SUBJUNCTIVE	IMPERFECT SUBJUNCTIVE
(yo)	rehúse	rehusara or rehusase
(tú)	rehúses	rehusaras or rehusases
(él/ella/usted)	rehúse	rehusara or rehusase
(nosotros/as)	rehusemos	rehusáramos or rehusásemos
(vosotros/as)	rehuséis	rehusarais or rehusaseis
(ellos/ellas/ ustedes)	rehúsen	rehusaran or rehusasen

IMPERATIVE
rehúsa / rehusad

Use the present subjunctive in all cases other than these **tú** and **vosotros** affirmative forms.

Remember that subject pronouns are not used very often in Spanish.

reír (to laugh)

	PRESENT		PRESENT PERFECT
(yo)	río		he reído
(tú)	ríes		has reído
(él/ella/usted)	ríe		ha reído
(nosotros/as)	reímos		hemos reído
(vosotros/as)	reís		habéis reído
(ellos/ellas/ ustedes)	ríen		han reído

	PRETERITE		IMPERFECT
(yo)	reí		reía
(tú)	reíste		reías
(él/ella/usted)	rio		reía
(nosotros/as)	reímos		reíamos
(vosotros/as)	reísteis		reíais
(ellos/ellas/ ustedes)	rieron		reían

GERUND	PAST PARTICIPLE
riendo	reído

EXAMPLE PHRASES

Se echó a **reír**. She burst out laughing.

Se ríe de todo. She doesn't take anything seriously.

¿De qué **te ríes**? What are you laughing at?

Siempre **están riéndose** en clase. They're always laughing in class.

Me reía mucho con él. I always had a good laugh with him.

reír

	FUTURE	CONDITIONAL
(yo)	reiré	reiría
(tú)	reirás	reirías
(él/ella/usted)	reirá	reiría
(nosotros/as)	reiremos	reiríamos
(vosotros/as)	reiréis	reiríais
(ellos/ellas/ ustedes)	reirán	reirían

	PRESENT SUBJUNCTIVE	IMPERFECT SUBJUNCTIVE
(yo)	ría	riera or riese
(tú)	rías	rieras or rieses
(él/ella/usted)	ría	riera or riese
(nosotros/as)	riamos	riéramos or riésemos
(vosotros/as)	riais	rierais or rieseis
(ellos/ellas/ ustedes)	rían	rieran or riesen

IMPERATIVE

ríe / reíd

*Use the present subjunctive in all cases other than these **tú** and **vosotros** affirmative forms.*

EXAMPLE PHRASES

Te reirás cuando te lo cuente. You'll have a laugh when I tell you about it.

Que **se rían** lo que quieran. Let them laugh as much as they want.

No **te rías** de mí. Don't laugh at me.

¡Tú **ríete**, pero he pasado muchísimo miedo! You may laugh, but I was really frightened.

Remember that subject pronouns are not used very often in Spanish.

reñir (to scold; to quarrel)

	PRESENT		PRESENT PERFECT
(yo)	riño		he reñido
(tú)	riñes		has reñido
(él/ella/usted)	riñe		ha reñido
(nosotros/as)	reñimos		hemos reñido
(vosotros/as)	reñís		habéis reñido
(ellos/ellas/ ustedes)	riñen		han reñido

	PRETERITE		IMPERFECT
(yo)	reñí		reñía
(tú)	reñiste		reñías
(él/ella/usted)	riñó		reñía
(nosotros/as)	reñimos		reñíamos
(vosotros/as)	reñisteis		reñíais
(ellos/ellas/ ustedes)	riñeron		reñían

GERUND	PAST PARTICIPLE
riñendo	reñido

EXAMPLE PHRASES

Se pasan el día entero **riñendo**. They spend the whole day quarrelling.

Ha reñido con su novio. She has fallen out with her boyfriend.

Les **riñó** por llegar tarde a casa. She told them off for getting home late.

Nos **reñía** sin motivo. She used to tell us off for no reason.

Remember that subject pronouns are not used very often in Spanish.

reñir

	FUTURE		CONDITIONAL
(yo)	reñiré		reñiría
(tú)	reñirás		reñirías
(él/ella/usted)	reñirá		reñiría
(nosotros/as)	reñiremos		reñiríamos
(vosotros/as)	reñiréis		reñiríais
(ellos/ellas/ ustedes)	reñirán		reñirían

	PRESENT SUBJUNCTIVE	IMPERFECT SUBJUNCTIVE
(yo)	riña	riñera or riñese
(tú)	riñas	riñeras or riñeses
(él/ella/usted)	riña	riñera or riñese
(nosotros/as)	riñamos	riñéramos or riñésemos
(vosotros/as)	riñáis	riñerals or riñeseis
(ellos/ellas/ ustedes)	riñan	riñeran or riñesen

IMPERATIVE
riñe / reñid

Use the present subjunctive in all cases other than these tú and vosotros affirmative forms.

EXAMPLE PHRASES
Si se entera, te **reñirá**. He'll tell you off if he finds out.

No la **riñas**, no es culpa suya. Don't tell her off, it's not her fault.

¡Niños, no **riñáis**! Children, don't quarrel!

Remember that subject pronouns are not used very often in Spanish.

repetir (to repeat)

	PRESENT		PRESENT PERFECT
(yo)	repito		he repetido
(tú)	repites		has repetido
(él/ella/usted)	repite		ha repetido
(nosotros/as)	repetimos		hemos repetido
(vosotros/as)	repetís		habéis repetido
(ellos/ellas/ ustedes)	repiten		han repetido

	PRETERITE		IMPERFECT
(yo)	repetí		repetía
(tú)	repetiste		repetías
(él/ella/usted)	repitió		repetía
(nosotros/as)	repetimos		repetíamos
(vosotros/as)	repetisteis		repetíais
(ellos/ellas/ ustedes)	repitieron		repetían

GERUND

repitiendo

PAST PARTICIPLE

repetido

EXAMPLE PHRASES

¿Podría **repetirlo**, por favor? Could you repeat that, please?

Le **repito** que es imposible. I'm telling you again that it is impossible.

Se lo **he repetido** mil veces, pero no escucha. I've told him hundreds of times but he won't listen.

Repetía una y otra vez que era inocente. He kept repeating that he was innocent.

Remember that subject pronouns are not used very often in Spanish.

repetir

	FUTURE	CONDITIONAL
(yo)	repetiré	repetiría
(tú)	repetirás	repetirías
(él/ella/usted)	repetirá	repetiría
(nosotros/as)	repetiremos	repetiríamos
(vosotros/as)	repetiréis	repetiríais
(ellos/ellas/ ustedes)	repetirán	repetirían

	PRESENT SUBJUNCTIVE	IMPERFECT SUBJUNCTIVE
(yo)	repita	repitiera or repitiese
(tú)	repitas	repitieras or repitieses
(él/ella/usted)	repita	repitiera or repitiese
(nosotros/as)	repitamos	repitiéramos or repitiésemos
(vosotros/as)	repitáis	repitierais or repitieseis
(ellos/ellas/ ustedes)	repitan	repitieran or repitiesen

IMPERATIVE
repite / repetid

Use the present subjunctive in all cases other than these **tú** and **vosotros** affirmative forms.

EXAMPLE PHRASES

Si sigue así, **repetirá** curso. If she goes on like this, she'll end up having to repeat the year.

Espero que no **se repita**. I hope this won't happen again.

Repetid detrás de mí... Repeat after me...

Remember that subject pronouns are not used very often in Spanish.

resolver (to solve)

	PRESENT		PRESENT PERFECT
(yo)	resuelvo		he resuelto
(tú)	resuelves		has resuelto
(él/ella/usted)	resuelve		ha resuelto
(nosotros/as)	resolvemos		hemos resuelto
(vosotros/as)	resolvéis		habéis resuelto
(ellos/ellas/ ustedes)	resuelven		han resuelto

	PRETERITE		IMPERFECT
(yo)	resolví		resolvía
(tú)	resolviste		resolvías
(él/ella/usted)	resolvió		resolvía
(nosotros/as)	resolvimos		resolvíamos
(vosotros/as)	resolvisteis		resolvíais
(ellos/ellas/ ustedes)	resolvieron		resolvían

GERUND

resolviendo

PAST PARTICIPLE

resuelto

EXAMPLE PHRASES

Trataré de **resolver** tus dudas. I'll try to answer your questions.

Enfadarse no **resuelve** nada. Getting angry doesn't help at all.

No **hemos resuelto** los problemas. We haven't solved the problems.

Resolvimos el problema entre todos. We solved the problem together.

Remember that subject pronouns are not used very often in Spanish.

resolver

	FUTURE	CONDITIONAL
(yo)	resolveré	resolvería
(tú)	resolverás	resolverías
(él/ella/usted)	resolverá	resolvería
(nosotros/as)	resolveremos	resolveríamos
(vosotros/as)	resolveréis	resolveríais
(ellos/ellas/ ustedes)	resolverán	resolverían

	PRESENT SUBJUNCTIVE	IMPERFECT SUBJUNCTIVE
(yo)	resuelva	resolviera or resolviese
(tú)	resuelvas	resolvieras or resolvieses
(él/ella/usted)	resuelva	resolviera or resolviese
(nosotros/as)	resolvamos	resolviéramos or resolviésemos
(vosotros/as)	resolváis	resolvierais or resolvieseis
(ellos/ellas/ ustedes)	resuelvan	resolvieran or resolviesen

IMPERATIVE
resuelve / resolved

Use the present subjunctive in all cases other than these **tú** and **vosotros** affirmative forms.

EXAMPLE PHRASES
No te preocupes, ya lo **resolveremos**. Don't worry, we'll get it sorted.

Yo lo **resolvería** de otra forma. I'd sort it out another way.

Hasta que no lo **resuelva** no descansaré. I won't rest until I've sorted it out.

reunir (to put together; to gather)

	PRESENT		PRESENT PERFECT
(yo)	reúno		he reunido
(tú)	reúnes		has reunido
(él/ella/usted)	reúne		ha reunido
(nosotros/as)	reunimos		hemos reunido
(vosotros/as)	reunís		habéis reunido
(ellos/ellas/ ustedes)	reúnen		han reunido

	PRETERITE		IMPERFECT
(yo)	reuní		reunía
(tú)	reuniste		reunías
(él/ella/usted)	reunió		reunía
(nosotros/as)	reunimos		reuníamos
(vosotros/as)	reunisteis		reuníais
(ellos/ellas/ ustedes)	reunieron		reunían

GERUND	PAST PARTICIPLE
reuniendo	reunido

EXAMPLE PHRASES

Hemos conseguido **reunir** suficiente dinero. We've managed to raise enough money.

Hace tiempo que no **me reúno** con ellos. I haven't seen them for ages.

Reunió a todos para comunicarles la noticia. He called them all together to tell them the news.

No **reunía** los requisitos. She didn't satisfy the requirements.

Remember that subject pronouns are not used very often in Spanish.

reunir

	FUTURE	CONDITIONAL
(yo)	reuniré	reuniría
(tú)	reunirás	reunirías
(él/ella/usted)	reunirá	reuniría
(nosotros/as)	reuniremos	reuniríamos
(vosotros/as)	reuniréis	reuniríais
(ellos/ellas/ustedes)	reunirán	reunirían

	PRESENT SUBJUNCTIVE	IMPERFECT SUBJUNCTIVE
(yo)	reúna	reuniera or reuniese
(tú)	reúnas	reunieras or reunieses
(él/ella/usted)	reúna	reuniera or reuniese
(nosotros/as)	reunamos	reuniéramos or reuniésemos
(vosotros/as)	reunáis	reunierais or reunieseis
(ellos/ellas/ustedes)	reúnan	reunieran or reuniesen

IMPERATIVE
reúne / reunid

Use the present subjunctive in all cases other than these **tú** and **vosotros** affirmative forms.

EXAMPLE PHRASES

Se reunirán el viernes. They'll meet on Friday.

Necesito encontrar un local que **reúna** las condiciones. I need to find premises that will meet the requirements.

Consiguió que su familia **se reuniera** tras una larga separación. She managed to get her family back together again after a long separation.

Antes de acusarle, **reúne** las pruebas suficientes. Get enough evidence together before accusing him.

Remember that subject pronouns are not used very often in Spanish.

rogar (to beg; to pray)

	PRESENT	PRESENT PERFECT
(yo)	ruego	he rogado
(tú)	ruegas	has rogado
(él/ella/usted)	ruega	ha rogado
(nosotros/as)	rogamos	hemos rogado
(vosotros/as)	rogáis	habéis rogado
(ellos/ellas/ ustedes)	ruegan	han rogado

	PRETERITE	IMPERFECT
(yo)	rogué	rogaba
(tú)	rogaste	rogabas
(él/ella/usted)	rogó	rogaba
(nosotros/as)	rogamos	rogábamos
(vosotros/as)	rogasteis	rogabais
(ellos/ellas/ ustedes)	rogaron	rogaban

GERUND	PAST PARTICIPLE
rogando	rogado

EXAMPLE PHRASES

Les **rogamos** acepten nuestras disculpas. Please accept our apologies.

Te **ruego** que me lo devuelvas. Please give it back to me.

"**Se ruega** no fumar" "Please do not smoke"

Me **rogó** que le perdonara. He begged me to forgive him.

Le **rogaba** a Dios que se curara. I prayed to God to make him better.

Remember that subject pronouns are not used very often in Spanish.

rogar

	FUTURE	CONDITIONAL
(yo)	rogaré	rogaría
(tú)	rogarás	rogarías
(él/ella/usted)	rogará	rogaría
(nosotros/as)	rogaremos	rogaríamos
(vosotros/as)	rogaréis	rogaríais
(ellos/ellas/ ustedes)	rogarán	rogarían

	PRESENT SUBJUNCTIVE	IMPERFECT SUBJUNCTIVE
(yo)	ruegue	rogara or rogase
(tú)	ruegues	rogaras or rogases
(él/ella/usted)	ruegue	rogara or rogase
(nosotros/as)	roguemos	rogáramos or rogásemos
(vosotros/as)	roguéis	rogarais or rogaseis
(ellos/ellas/ ustedes)	rueguen	rogaran or rogasen

IMPERATIVE
ruega / rogad

Use the present subjunctive in all cases other than these **tú** and **vosotros** affirmative forms.

EXAMPLE PHRASES
Ruega por mí. Pray for me.

romper (to break)

	PRESENT		PRESENT PERFECT
(yo)	rompo		he roto
(tú)	rompes		has roto
(él/ella/usted)	rompe		ha roto
(nosotros/as)	rompemos		hemos roto
(vosotros/as)	rompéis		habéis roto
(ellos/ellas/ ustedes)	rompen		han roto

	PRETERITE		IMPERFECT
(yo)	rompí		rompía
(tú)	rompiste		rompías
(él/ella/usted)	rompió		rompía
(nosotros/as)	rompimos		rompíamos
(vosotros/as)	rompisteis		rompíais
(ellos/ellas/ ustedes)	rompieron		rompían

GERUND	PAST PARTICIPLE
rompiendo	roto

EXAMPLE PHRASES

La cuerda **se** va a **romper**. The rope is going to snap.

Siempre **están rompiendo** cosas. They're always breaking things.

Se ha roto una taza. A cup's broken.

Se rompió el jarrón. The vase broke.

Remember that subject pronouns are not used very often in Spanish.

romper

	FUTURE	CONDITIONAL
(yo)	romperé	rompería
(tú)	romperás	romperías
(él/ella/usted)	romperá	rompería
(nosotros/as)	romperemos	romperíamos
(vosotros/as)	romperéis	romperíais
(ellos/ellas/ ustedes)	romperán	romperían

	PRESENT SUBJUNCTIVE	IMPERFECT SUBJUNCTIVE
(yo)	rompa	rompiera or rompiese
(tú)	rompas	rompieras or rompieses
(él/ella/usted)	rompa	rompiera or rompiese
(nosotros/as)	rompamos	rompiéramos or rompiésemos
(vosotros/as)	rompáis	rompierais or rompieseis
(ellos/ellas/ ustedes)	rompan	rompieran or rompiesen

IMPERATIVE
rompe / romped

*Use the present subjunctive in all cases other than these **tú** and **vosotros** affirmative forms.*

EXAMPLE PHRASES
Yo nunca **rompería** una promesa. I'd never break a promise.

Si lo **rompiera**, tendría que pagarlo. If you broke it, you'd have to pay for it.

Rompe con él, si ya no le quieres. If you don't love him any more, finish
   with him.

Cuidado, no lo **rompas**. Careful you don't break it.

saber (to know)

	PRESENT		PRESENT PERFECT
(yo)	sé		he sabido
(tú)	sabes		has sabido
(él/ella/usted)	sabe		ha sabido
(nosotros/as)	sabemos		hemos sabido
(vosotros/as)	sabéis		habéis sabido
(ellos/ellas/ ustedes)	saben		han sabido

	PRETERITE		IMPERFECT
(yo)	supe		sabía
(tú)	supiste		sabías
(él/ella/usted)	supo		sabía
(nosotros/as)	supimos		sabíamos
(vosotros/as)	supisteis		sabíais
(ellos/ellas/ ustedes)	supieron		sabían

GERUND	PAST PARTICIPLE
sabiendo	sabido

EXAMPLE PHRASES

No lo **sé**. I don't know.

¿**Sabes** una cosa? Do you know what?

¿Cuándo lo **has sabido**? When did you find out?

No **supe** qué responder. I didn't know what to answer.

Pensaba que lo **sabías**. I thought you knew.

Remember that subject pronouns are not used very often in Spanish.

saber

	FUTURE	CONDITIONAL
(yo)	sabré	sabría
(tú)	sabrás	sabrías
(él/ella/usted)	sabrá	sabría
(nosotros/as)	sabremos	sabríamos
(vosotros/as)	sabréis	sabríais
(ellos/ellas/ ustedes)	sabrán	sabrían

	PRESENT SUBJUNCTIVE	IMPERFECT SUBJUNCTIVE
(yo)	sepa	supiera or supiese
(tú)	sepas	supieras or supieses
(él/ella/usted)	sepa	supiera or supiese
(nosotros/as)	sepamos	supiéramos or supiésemos
(vosotros/as)	sepáis	supierais or supieseis
(ellos/ellas/ ustedes)	sepan	supieran or supiesen

IMPERATIVE
sabe / sabed

*Use the present subjunctive in all cases other than these **tú** and **vosotros** affirmative forms.*

EXAMPLE PHRASES

Nunca se **sabrá** quién la mató. We'll never know who killed her.

Si no le tuvieras tanto miedo al agua, ya **sabrías** nadar. If you weren't so afraid of water, you'd already be able to swim.

Que yo **sepa**, vive en París. As far as I know, she lives in Paris.

¡Si **supiéramos** al menos dónde está! If only we knew where he was!

Remember that subject pronouns are not used very often in Spanish.

sacar (to take out)

	PRESENT	PRESENT PERFECT
(yo)	saco	he sacado
(tú)	sacas	has sacado
(él/ella/usted)	saca	ha sacado
(nosotros/as)	sacamos	hemos sacado
(vosotros/as)	sacáis	habéis sacado
(ellos/ellas/ustedes)	sacan	han sacado

	PRETERITE	IMPERFECT
(yo)	saqué	sacaba
(tú)	sacaste	sacabas
(él/ella/usted)	sacó	sacaba
(nosotros/as)	sacamos	sacábamos
(vosotros/as)	sacasteis	sacabais
(ellos/ellas/ustedes)	sacaron	sacaban

GERUND	PAST PARTICIPLE
sacando	sacado

EXAMPLE PHRASES

¿**Me sacas** una foto? Will you take a photo of me?

Estás sacando las cosas de quicio. You're blowing things out of all proportion.

Ya **he sacado** las entradas. I've already bought the tickets.

Saqué un 7 en el examen. I got a 7 in the exam.

¿De dónde **sacaba** tanto dinero? Where did he get so much money from?

Remember that subject pronouns are not used very often in Spanish.

sacar

	FUTURE	CONDITIONAL
(yo)	sacaré	sacaría
(tú)	sacarás	sacarías
(él/ella/usted)	sacará	sacaría
(nosotros/as)	sacaremos	sacaríamos
(vosotros/as)	sacaréis	sacaríais
(ellos/ellas/ ustedes)	sacarán	sacarían

	PRESENT SUBJUNCTIVE	IMPERFECT SUBJUNCTIVE
(yo)	saque	sacara or sacase
(tú)	saques	sacaras or sacases
(él/ella/usted)	saque	sacara or sacase
(nosotros/as)	saquemos	sacáramos or sacásemos
(vosotros/as)	saquéis	sacarais or sacaseis
(ellos/ellas/ ustedes)	saquen	sacaran or sacasen

IMPERATIVE

saca / sacad

Use the present subjunctive in all cases other than these **tú** and **vosotros** affirmative forms.

EXAMPLE PHRASES

Yo no **sacaría** todavía ninguna conclusión. I wouldn't draw any conclusions yet.

Quiero que **saques** inmediatamente esa bicicleta de casa. I want you to get that bike out of the house immediately.

Si te **sacaras** el carnet de conducir, serías mucho más independiente. You'd be much more independent if you got your driving licence.

No **saques** la cabeza por la ventanilla. Don't lean out of the window.

Remember that subject pronouns are not used very often in Spanish.

salir (to go out)

	PRESENT		PRESENT PERFECT
(yo)	salgo		he salido
(tú)	sales		has salido
(él/ella/usted)	sale		ha salido
(nosotros/as)	salimos		hemos salido
(vosotros/as)	salís		habéis salido
(ellos/ellas/ustedes)	salen		han salido

	PRETERITE		IMPERFECT
(yo)	salí		salía
(tú)	saliste		salías
(él/ella/usted)	salió		salía
(nosotros/as)	salimos		salíamos
(vosotros/as)	salisteis		salíais
(ellos/ellas/ustedes)	salieron		salían

GERUND	PAST PARTICIPLE
saliendo	salido

EXAMPLE PHRASES

Hace tiempo que no **salimos**. We haven't been out for a while.

Está saliendo con un compañero de trabajo. She's going out with a colleague from work.

Ha salido. She's gone out.

Su foto **salió** en todos los periódicos. Her picture appeared in all the newspapers.

Salía muy tarde de trabajar. He used to finish work very late.

Remember that subject pronouns are not used very often in Spanish.

salir

	FUTURE	CONDITIONAL
(yo)	saldré	saldría
(tú)	saldrás	saldrías
(él/ella/usted)	saldrá	saldría
(nosotros/as)	saldremos	saldríamos
(vosotros/as)	saldréis	saldríais
(ellos/ellas/ ustedes)	saldrán	saldrían

	PRESENT SUBJUNCTIVE	IMPERFECT SUBJUNCTIVE
(yo)	salga	saliera or saliese
(tú)	salgas	salieras or salieses
(él/ella/usted)	salga	saliera or saliese
(nosotros/as)	salgamos	saliéramos or saliésemos
(vosotros/as)	salgáis	salierais or salieseis
(ellos/ellas/ ustedes)	salgan	salieran or saliesen

IMPERATIVE
sal / salid

Use the present subjunctive in all cases other than these tú *and* vosotros *affirmative forms.*

EXAMPLE PHRASES
Te dije que **saldría** muy caro. I told you it would work out very expensive.
Espero que todo **salga** bien. I hope everything works out all right.
Si **saliera** elegido... If I were elected...
Por favor, **salgan** por la puerta de atrás. Please leave via the back door.

Remember that subject pronouns are not used very often in Spanish.

satisfacer (to satisfy)

	PRESENT		PRESENT PERFECT
(yo)	satisfago		he satisfecho
(tú)	satisfaces		has satisfecho
(él/ella/usted)	satisface		ha satisfecho
(nosotros/as)	satisfacemos		hemos satisfecho
(vosotros/as)	satisfacéis		habéis satisfecho
(ellos/ellas/ ustedes)	satisfacen		han satisfecho

	PRETERITE		IMPERFECT
(yo)	satisfice		satisfacía
(tú)	satisficiste		satisfacías
(él/ella/usted)	satisfizo		satisfacía
(nosotros/as)	satisficimos		satisfacíamos
(vosotros/as)	satisficisteis		satisfacíais
(ellos/ellas/ ustedes)	satisficieron		satisfacían

GERUND	PAST PARTICIPLE
satisfaciendo	satisfecho

EXAMPLE PHRASES

No me **satisface** nada el resultado. I'm not at all satisfied with the result.

Ha satisfecho mis expectativas. It came up to my expectations.

Eso **satisfizo** mi curiosidad. That satisfied my curiosity.

Aquella vida **satisfacía** todas mis necesidades. That lifestyle satisfied all my needs.

satisfacer

	FUTURE	CONDITIONAL
(yo)	satisfaré	satisfaría
(tú)	satisfarás	satisfarías
(él/ella/usted)	satisfará	satisfaría
(nosotros/as)	satisfaremos	satisfaríamos
(vosotros/as)	satisfaréis	satisfaríais
(ellos/ellas/ ustedes)	satisfarán	satisfarían

	PRESENT SUBJUNCTIVE	IMPERFECT SUBJUNCTIVE
(yo)	satisfaga	satisficiera or satisficiese
(tú)	satisfagas	satisficieras or satisficieses
(él/ella/usted)	satisfaga	satisficiera or satisficiese
(nosotros/as)	satisfagamos	satisficiéramos or satisficiésemos
(vosotros/as)	satisfagáis	satisficierais or satisficieseis
(ellos/ellas/ ustedes)	satisfagan	satisficieran or satisficiesen

IMPERATIVE

satisfaz or satisface / satisfaced

Use the present subjunctive in all cases other than these tú and vosotros affirmative forms.

EXAMPLE PHRASES

Le **satisfará** saber que hemos cumplido nuestros objetivos. You'll be happy to know that we have achieved our objectives.

Me **satisfaría** mucho más que estudiaras una carrera. I'd be far happier if you went to university.

Remember that subject pronouns are not used very often in Spanish.

seguir (to follow)

	PRESENT	PRESENT PERFECT
(yo)	sigo	he seguido
(tú)	sigues	has seguido
(él/ella/usted)	sigue	ha seguido
(nosotros/as)	seguimos	hemos seguido
(vosotros/as)	seguís	habéis seguido
(ellos/ellas/ ustedes)	siguen	han seguido

	PRETERITE	IMPERFECT
(yo)	seguí	seguía
(tú)	seguiste	seguías
(él/ella/usted)	siguió	seguía
(nosotros/as)	seguimos	seguíamos
(vosotros/as)	seguisteis	seguíais
(ellos/ellas/ ustedes)	siguieron	seguían

GERUND	PAST PARTICIPLE
siguiendo	seguido

EXAMPLE PHRASES

Si **sigues** así, acabarás mal. If you go on like this you'll end up badly.

¿Te **han seguido**? Have you been followed?

Siguió cantando como si nada. He went on singing as if nothing was the matter.

El ordenador **seguía** funcionando a pesar del apagón. The computer went on working in spite of the power cut.

Les **estuvimos siguiendo** mucho rato. We followed them for a long time.

Remember that subject pronouns are not used very often in Spanish.

seguir

	FUTURE		CONDITIONAL
(yo)	seguiré		seguiría
(tú)	seguirás		seguirías
(él/ella/usted)	seguirá		seguiría
(nosotros/as)	seguiremos		seguiríamos
(vosotros/as)	seguiréis		seguiríais
(ellos/ellas/ustedes)	seguirán		seguirían

	PRESENT SUBJUNCTIVE		IMPERFECT SUBJUNCTIVE
(yo)	siga		siguiera or siguiese
(tú)	sigas		siguieras or siguieses
(él/ella/usted)	siga		siguiera or siguiese
(nosotros/as)	sigamos		siguiéramos or siguiésemos
(vosotros/as)	sigáis		siguierais or siguieseis
(ellos/ellas/ustedes)	sigan		siguieran or siguiesen

IMPERATIVE
sigue / seguid

*Use the present subjunctive in all cases other than these **tú** and **vosotros** affirmative forms.*

EXAMPLE PHRASES
Nos seguiremos viendo. We will go on seeing each other.
Quiero que **sigas** estudiando. I want you to go on with your studies.
Si **siguieras** mis consejos, te iría muchísimo mejor. You'd be much better
   off if you followed my advice.
Siga por esta calle hasta el final. Go on till you get to the end of the street.

Remember that subject pronouns are not used very often in Spanish.

sentir (to feel; to be sorry)

	PRESENT		PRESENT PERFECT
(yo)	siento		he sentido
(tú)	sientes		has sentido
(él/ella/usted)	siente		ha sentido
(nosotros/as)	sentimos		hemos sentido
(vosotros/as)	sentís		habéis sentido
(ellos/ellas/ ustedes)	sienten		han sentido

	PRETERITE		IMPERFECT
(yo)	sentí		sentía
(tú)	sentiste		sentías
(él/ella/usted)	sintió		sentía
(nosotros/as)	sentimos		sentíamos
(vosotros/as)	sentisteis		sentíais
(ellos/ellas/ ustedes)	sintieron		sentían

GERUND	PAST PARTICIPLE
sintiendo	sentido

EXAMPLE PHRASES

Te vas a **sentir** sola. You'll feel lonely.

Siento mucho lo que pasó. I'm really sorry about what happened.

Ha sentido mucho la muerte de su padre. He has been greatly affected by his father's death.

Sentí un pinchazo en la pierna. I felt a sharp pain in my leg.

Me sentía muy mal. I didn't feel well at all.

Remember that subject pronouns are not used very often in Spanish.

sentir

	FUTURE		CONDITIONAL
(yo)	sentiré		sentiría
(tú)	sentirás		sentirías
(él/ella/usted)	sentirá		sentiría
(nosotros/as)	sentiremos		sentiríamos
(vosotros/as)	sentiréis		sentiríais
(ellos/ellas/ ustedes)	sentirán		sentirían

	PRESENT SUBJUNCTIVE		IMPERFECT SUBJUNCTIVE
(yo)	sienta		sintiera or sintiese
(tú)	sientas		sintieras or sintieses
(él/ella/usted)	sienta		sintiera or sintiese
(nosotros/as)	sintamos		sintiéramos or sintiésemos
(vosotros/as)	sintáis		sintierais or sintieseis
(ellos/ellas/ ustedes)	sientan		sintieran or sintiesen

IMPERATIVE
siente / sentid

Use the present subjunctive in all cases other than these **tú** and **vosotros** affirmative forms.

EXAMPLE PHRASES

Al principio **te sentirás** un poco raro. You'll feel a bit strange at first.

Yo **sentiría** mucho que se fuera de la empresa. I'd be really sorry if you left the firm.

No creo que lo **sienta**. I don't think she's sorry.

Sería mucho más preocupante si no **sintiera** la pierna. It would be much more worrying if he couldn't feel his leg.

Remember that subject pronouns are not used very often in Spanish.

ser (to be)

	PRESENT	PRESENT PERFECT
(yo)	soy	he sido
(tú)	eres	has sido
(él/ella/usted)	es	ha sido
(nosotros/as)	somos	hemos sido
(vosotros/as)	sois	habéis sido
(ellos/ellas/ ustedes)	son	han sido

	PRETERITE	IMPERFECT
(yo)	fui	era
(tú)	fuiste	eras
(él/ella/usted)	fue	era
(nosotros/as)	fuimos	éramos
(vosotros/as)	fuisteis	erais
(ellos/ellas/ ustedes)	fueron	eran

GERUND	PAST PARTICIPLE
siendo	sido

EXAMPLE PHRASES

Soy español. I'm Spanish.

Estás siendo muy paciente con él. You're being very patient with him.

Ha sido un duro golpe. It was a major blow.

¿**Fuiste** tú el que llamó? Was it you who phoned?

Era de noche. It was dark.

Remember that subject pronouns are not used very often in Spanish.

ser

	FUTURE	CONDITIONAL
(yo)	seré	sería
(tú)	serás	serías
(él/ella/usted)	será	sería
(nosotros/as)	seremos	seríamos
(vosotros/as)	seréis	seríais
(ellos/ellas/ ustedes)	serán	serían

	PRESENT SUBJUNCTIVE	IMPERFECT SUBJUNCTIVE
(yo)	sea	fuera or fuese
(tú)	seas	fueras or fueses
(él/ella/usted)	sea	fuera or fuese
(nosotros/as)	seamos	fuéramos or fuésemos
(vosotros/as)	seáis	fuerais or fueseis
(ellos/ellas/ ustedes)	sean	fueran or fuesen

IMPERATIVE
sé / sed

Use the present subjunctive in all cases other than these **tú** and **vosotros** affirmative forms.

EXAMPLE PHRASES
Será de Joaquín. It must be Joaquin's.
Eso **sería** estupendo. That would be great.
O **sea**, que no vienes. So you're not coming.
No **seas** tan perfeccionista. Don't be such a perfectionist.
¡**Sed** buenos! Behave yourselves!

Remember that subject pronouns are not used very often in Spanish.

soler (to be in the habit of; to be accustomed to)

	PRESENT	PRESENT PERFECT
(yo)	suelo	*not used*
(tú)	sueles	
(él/ella/usted)	suele	
(nosotros/as)	solemos	
(vosotros/as)	soléis	
(ellos/ellas/ ustedes)	suelen	

	PRETERITE	IMPERFECT
(yo)	*not used*	solía
(tú)		solías
(él/ella/usted)		solía
(nosotros/as)		solíamos
(vosotros/as)		solíais
(ellos/ellas/ ustedes)		solían

GERUND	PAST PARTICIPLE
soliendo	*not used*

EXAMPLE PHRASES

Suele salir a las ocho. He usually goes out at eight.

Solíamos ir todos los años a la playa. We used to go to the beach every year.

Remember that subject pronouns are not used very often in Spanish.

soler

	FUTURE	CONDITIONAL
(yo)	*not used*	*not used*
(tú)		
(él/ella/usted)		
(nosotros/as)		
(vosotros/as)		
(ellos/ellas/ ustedes)		

	PRESENT SUBJUNCTIVE	IMPERFECT SUBJUNCTIVE
(yo)	suela	soliera *or* soliese
(tú)	suelas	solieras *or* solieses
(él/ella/usted)	suela	soliera *or* soliese
(nosotros/as)	solamos	soliéramos *or* soliésemos
(vosotros/as)	soláis	solierais *or* solieseis
(ellos/ellas/ ustedes)	suelan	solieran *or* soliesen

IMPERATIVE

not used

Remember that subject pronouns are not used very often in Spanish.

soltar (to let go of; to release)

	PRESENT	PRESENT PERFECT
(yo)	suelto	he soltado
(tú)	sueltas	has soltado
(él/ella/usted)	suelta	ha soltado
(nosotros/as)	soltamos	hemos soltado
(vosotros/as)	soltáis	habéis soltado
(ellos/ellas/ ustedes)	sueltan	han soltado

	PRETERITE	IMPERFECT
(yo)	solté	soltaba
(tú)	soltaste	soltabas
(él/ella/usted)	soltó	soltaba
(nosotros/as)	soltamos	soltábamos
(vosotros/as)	soltasteis	soltabais
(ellos/ellas/ ustedes)	soltaron	soltaban

GERUND	PAST PARTICIPLE
soltando	soltado

EXAMPLE PHRASES

Al final logró **soltarse**. Eventually she managed to break free.

No para de **soltar** tacos. He swears all the time.

¿Por qué no **te sueltas** el pelo? Why don't you have your hair loose?

Han soltado a los rehenes. They've released the hostages.

Soltó una carcajada. He burst out laughing.

Remember that subject pronouns are not used very often in Spanish.

soltar

	FUTURE	CONDITIONAL
(yo)	soltaré	soltaría
(tú)	soltarás	soltarías
(él/ella/usted)	soltará	soltaría
(nosotros/as)	soltaremos	soltaríamos
(vosotros/as)	soltaréis	soltaríais
(ellos/ellas/ ustedes)	soltarán	soltarían

	PRESENT SUBJUNCTIVE	IMPERFECT SUBJUNCTIVE
(yo)	suelte	soltara or soltase
(tú)	sueltes	soltaras or soltases
(él/ella/usted)	suelte	soltara or soltase
(nosotros/as)	soltemos	soltáramos or soltásemos
(vosotros/as)	soltéis	soltarais or soltaseis
(ellos/ellas/ ustedes)	suelten	soltaran or soltasen

IMPERATIVE

suelta / soltad

*Use the present subjunctive in all cases other than these **tú** and **vosotros** affirmative forms.*

EXAMPLE PHRASES

Te **soltaré** el brazo si me dices dónde está. I'll let go of your arm if you tell me where he is.

Te dije que lo **soltaras**. I told you to let it go.

No **sueltes** la cuerda. Don't let go of the rope.

¡**Suéltame**! Let me go!

Remember that subject pronouns are not used very often in Spanish.

sonar (to sound; to ring)

	PRESENT		PRESENT PERFECT
(yo)	sueno		he sonado
(tú)	suenas		has sonado
(él/ella/usted)	suena		ha sonado
(nosotros/as)	sonamos		hemos sonado
(vosotros/as)	sonáis		habéis sonado
(ellos/ellas/ ustedes)	suenan		han sonado

	PRETERITE		IMPERFECT
(yo)	soné		sonaba
(tú)	sonaste		sonabas
(él/ella/usted)	sonó		sonaba
(nosotros/as)	sonamos		sonábamos
(vosotros/as)	sonasteis		sonabais
(ellos/ellas/ ustedes)	sonaron		sonaban

GERUND	PAST PARTICIPLE
sonando	sonado

EXAMPLE PHRASES

¿**Te suena** su nombre? Does her name sound familiar?

Ha sonado tu móvil. Your mobile rang.

Justo en ese momento **sonó** el timbre. Just then the bell rang.

Sonabas un poco triste por teléfono. You sounded a bit sad on the phone.

Estaba sonando el teléfono. The phone was ringing.

Remember that subject pronouns are not used very often in Spanish.

sonar

	FUTURE	CONDITIONAL
(yo)	sonaré	sonaría
(tú)	sonarás	sonarías
(él/ella/usted)	sonará	sonaría
(nosotros/as)	sonaremos	sonaríamos
(vosotros/as)	sonaréis	sonaríais
(ellos/ellas/ ustedes)	sonarán	sonarían

	PRESENT SUBJUNCTIVE	IMPERFECT SUBJUNCTIVE
(yo)	suene	sonara or sonase
(tú)	suenes	sonaras or sonases
(él/ella/usted)	suene	sonara or sonase
(nosotros/as)	sonemos	sonáramos or sonásemos
(vosotros/as)	sonéis	sonarais or sonaseis
(ellos/ellas/ ustedes)	suenen	sonaran or sonasen

IMPERATIVE
suena / sonad

Use the present subjunctive in all cases other than these **tú** and **vosotros** affirmative forms.

EXAMPLE PHRASES
Hay que esperar a que **suene** un pitido. We have to wait until we hear a beep.
¡**Suénate** la nariz! Blow your nose!

temer (to be afraid)

	PRESENT		PRESENT PERFECT
(yo)	temo		he temido
(tú)	temes		has temido
(él/ella/usted)	teme		ha temido
(nosotros/as)	tememos		hemos temido
(vosotros/as)	teméis		habéis temido
(ellos/ellas/ ustedes)	temen		han temido

	PRETERITE		IMPERFECT
(yo)	temí		temía
(tú)	temiste		temías
(él/ella/usted)	temío		temía
(nosotros/as)	temimos		temíamos
(vosotros/as)	temisteis		temíais
(ellos/ellas/ ustedes)	temieron		temían

GERUND	PAST PARTICIPLE
temiendo	temido

EXAMPLE PHRASES

Me temo que no. I'm afraid not.

Se temen lo peor. They fear the worst.

–Ha empezado a llover. –**Me** lo **temía**. "It's started raining." – "I was afraid it would."

Temí ofenderles. I was afraid of offending them.

Temían por su seguridad. They feared for their security.

Remember that subject pronouns are not used very often in Spanish.

temer

	FUTURE	CONDITIONAL
(yo)	temeré	temería
(tú)	temerás	temerías
(él/ella/usted)	temerá	temería
(nosotros/as)	temeremos	temeríamos
(vosotros/as)	temeréis	temeríais
(ellos/ellas/ ustedes)	temerán	temerían

	PRESENT SUBJUNCTIVE	IMPERFECT SUBJUNCTIVE
(yo)	tema	temiera or temiese
(tú)	temas	temieras or temieses
(él/ella/usted)	tema	temiera or temiese
(nosotros/as)	temamos	temiéramos or temiésemos
(vosotros/as)	temáis	temierais or temieseis
(ellos/ellas/ ustedes)	teman	temieran or temiesen

IMPERATIVE

teme / temed

Use the present subjunctive in all cases other than these **tú** and **vosotros** affirmative forms.

EXAMPLE PHRASES

No **temas.** Don't be afraid.

Remember that subject pronouns are not used very often in Spanish.

tener (to have)

	PRESENT	PRESENT PERFECT
(yo)	tengo	he tenido
(tú)	tienes	has tenido
(él/ella/usted)	tiene	ha tenido
(nosotros/as)	tenemos	hemos tenido
(vosotros/as)	tenéis	habéis tenido
(ellos/ellas/ ustedes)	tienen	ha tenido

	PRETERITE	IMPERFECT
(yo)	tuve	tenía
(tú)	tuviste	tenías
(él/ella/usted)	tuvo	tenía
(nosotros/as)	tuvimos	teníamos
(vosotros/as)	tuvisteis	teníais
(ellos/ellas/ ustedes)	tuvieron	tenían

GERUND	PAST PARTICIPLE
teniendo	tenido

EXAMPLE PHRASES

Tengo sed. I'm thirsty.

Están teniendo muchos problemas con el coche. They're having a lot
of trouble with the car.

Ha tenido una gripe muy fuerte. She's had very bad flu.

Tuvimos que irnos. We had to leave.

No **tenía** suficiente dinero. She didn't have enough money.

Remember that subject pronouns are not used very often in Spanish.

tener

	FUTURE	CONDITIONAL
(yo)	tendré	tendría
(tú)	tendrás	tendrías
(él/ella/usted)	tendrá	tendría
(nosotros/as)	tendremos	tendríamos
(vosotros/as)	tendréis	tendríais
(ellos/ellas/ ustedes)	tendrán	tendrían

	PRESENT SUBJUNCTIVE	IMPERFECT SUBJUNCTIVE
(yo)	tenga	tuviera or tuviese
(tú)	tengas	tuvieras or tuvieses
(él/ella/usted)	tenga	tuviera or tuviese
(nosotros/as)	tengamos	tuviéramos or tuviésemos
(vosotros/as)	tengáis	tuvierais or tuvieseis
(ellos/ellas/ ustedes)	tengan	tuvieran or tuviesen

IMPERATIVE
ten / tened

Use the present subjunctive in all cases other than these tú and vosotros affirmative forms.

EXAMPLE PHRASES

Tendrás que pagarlo tú. You'll have to pay for it yourself.

Tendrías que comer más. You should eat more.

No creo que **tenga** suficiente dinero. I don't think I've got enough money.

Si **tuviera** tiempo, haría un curso de catalán. If I had time, I'd do a Catalan course.

Ten cuidado. Be careful.

No **tengas** miedo. Don't be afraid.

Remember that subject pronouns are not used very often in Spanish.

tocar (to touch; to play)

	PRESENT		PRESENT PERFECT
(yo)	toco		he tocado
(tú)	tocas		has tocado
(él/ella/usted)	toca		ha tocado
(nosotros/as)	tocamos		hemos tocado
(vosotros/as)	tocáis		habéis tocado
(ellos/ellas/ ustedes)	tocan		han tocado

	PRETERITE		IMPERFECT
(yo)	toqué		tocaba
(tú)	tocaste		tocabas
(él/ella/usted)	tocó		tocaba
(nosotros/as)	tocamos		tocábamos
(vosotros/as)	tocasteis		tocabais
(ellos/ellas/ ustedes)	tocaron		tocaban

GERUND	PAST PARTICIPLE
tocando	tocado

EXAMPLE PHRASES

Toca el violín. He plays the violin.

Te **toca** fregar los platos. It's your turn to do the dishes.

Me **ha tocado** el peor asiento. I've ended up with the worst seat.

Le **tocó** la lotería. He won the lottery.

Me **tocaba** tirar a mí. It was my turn.

Remember that subject pronouns are not used very often in Spanish.

tocar

	FUTURE	CONDITIONAL
(yo)	tocaré	tocaría
(tú)	tocarás	tocarías
(él/ella/usted)	tocará	tocaría
(nosotros/as)	tocaremos	tocaríamos
(vosotros/as)	tocaréis	tocaríais
(ellos/ellas/ustedes)	tocarán	tocarían

	PRESENT SUBJUNCTIVE	IMPERFECT SUBJUNCTIVE
(yo)	toque	tocara or tocase
(tú)	toques	tocaras or tocases
(él/ella/usted)	toque	tocara or tocase
(nosotros/as)	toquemos	tocáramos or tocásemos
(vosotros/as)	toquéis	tocarais or tocaseis
(ellos/ellas/ustedes)	toquen	tocaran or tocasen

IMPERATIVE
toca / tocad

Use the present subjunctive in all cases other than these **tú** and **vosotros** affirmative forms.

EXAMPLE PHRASES
Sabía que me **tocaría** ir a mí. I knew I'd be the one to have to go.

No lo **toques**. Don't touch it.

Tócalo, verás que suave. Touch it and see how soft it is.

Remember that subject pronouns are not used very often in Spanish.

torcer (to twist)

	PRESENT		PRESENT PERFECT
(yo)	tuerzo		he torcido
(tú)	tuerces		has torcido
(él/ella/usted)	tuerce		ha torcido
(nosotros/as)	torcemos		hemos torcido
(vosotros/as)	torcéis		habéis torcido
(ellos/ellas/ ustedes)	tuercen		han torcido

	PRETERITE		IMPERFECT
(yo)	torcí		torcía
(tú)	torciste		torcías
(él/ella/usted)	torció		torcía
(nosotros/as)	torcimos		torcíamos
(vosotros/as)	torcisteis		torcíais
(ellos/ellas/ ustedes)	torcieron		torcían

GERUND	PAST PARTICIPLE
torciendo	torcido

EXAMPLE PHRASES

Acaba de **torcer** la esquina. She has just turned the corner.

El sendero **tuerce** luego a la derecha. Later on the path bends round to the right.

Se le **ha torcido** la muñeca. She's sprained her wrist.

Se me **torció** el tobillo. I twisted my ankle.

torcer

	FUTURE	CONDITIONAL
(yo)	torceré	torcería
(tú)	torcerás	torcerías
(él/ella/usted)	torcerá	torcería
(nosotros/as)	torceremos	torceríamos
(vosotros/as)	torceréis	torceríais
(ellos/ellas/ ustedes)	torcerán	torcerían

	PRESENT SUBJUNCTIVE	IMPERFECT SUBJUNCTIVE
(yo)	tuerza	torciera or torciese
(tú)	tuerzas	torcieras or torcieses
(él/ella/usted)	tuerza	torciera or torciese
(nosotros/as)	torzamos	torciéramos or torciésemos
(vosotros/as)	torzáis	torcierais or torcieseis
(ellos/ellas/ ustedes)	tuerzan	torcieran or torciesen

IMPERATIVE
tuerce / torced

Use the present subjunctive in all cases other than these **tú** and **vosotros** affirmative forms.

EXAMPLE PHRASES
Tuerza a la izquierda. Turn left.
Tuércelo un poco más. Twist it a little more.

traer (to bring)

	PRESENT		PRESENT PERFECT
(yo)	traigo		he traído
(tú)	traes		has traído
(él/ella/usted)	trae		ha traído
(nosotros/as)	traemos		hemos traído
(vosotros/as)	traéis		habéis traído
(ellos/ellas/ ustedes)	traen		han traído

	PRETERITE		IMPERFECT
(yo)	traje		traía
(tú)	trajiste		traías
(él/ella/usted)	trajo		traía
(nosotros/as)	trajimos		traíamos
(vosotros/as)	trajisteis		traíais
(ellos/ellas/ ustedes)	trajeron		traían

GERUND	PAST PARTICIPLE
trayendo	traído

EXAMPLE PHRASES

¿Me puedes **traer** una toalla? Can you bring me a towel?

Nos **está trayendo** muchos problemas. It's causing us a lot of trouble.

¿**Has traído** lo que te pedí? Have you brought what I asked for?

Traía un vestido nuevo. She was wearing a new dress.

No **trajo** el dinero. He didn't bring the money.

Remember that subject pronouns are not used very often in Spanish.

traer

	FUTURE	CONDITIONAL
(yo)	traeré	traería
(tú)	traerás	traerías
(él/ella/usted)	traerá	traería
(nosotros/as)	traeremos	traeríamos
(vosotros/as)	traeréis	traeríais
(ellos/ellas/ ustedes)	traerán	traerían

	PRESENT SUBJUNCTIVE	IMPERFECT SUBJUNCTIVE
(yo)	traiga	trajera *or* trajese
(tú)	traigas	trajeras *or* trajeses
(él/ella/usted)	tralga	trajera *or* trajese
(nosotros/as)	traigamos	trajéramos *or* trajésemos
(vosotros/as)	traigáis	trajerais *or* trajeseis
(ellos/ellas/ ustedes)	traigan	trajeran *or* trajesen

IMPERATIVE

trae / traed

Use the present subjunctive in all cases other than these **tú** *and* **vosotros** *affirmative forms.*

EXAMPLE PHRASES

Me pregunto qué **se traerán** entre manos. I wonder what they're up to.

Se lo **traería** de África. He must have brought it over from Africa.

Dile que **traiga** a algún amigo. Tell him to bring a friend with him.

Trae eso. Give that here.

Remember that subject pronouns are not used very often in Spanish.

valer (to be worth)

	PRESENT	PRESENT PERFECT
(yo)	valgo	he valido
(tú)	vales	has valido
(él/ella/usted)	vale	ha valido
(nosotros/as)	valemos	hemos valido
(vosotros/as)	valéis	habéis valido
(ellos/ellas/ ustedes)	valen	han valido

	PRETERITE	IMPERFECT
(yo)	valí	valía
(tú)	valiste	valías
(él/ella/usted)	valió	valía
(nosotros/as)	valimos	valíamos
(vosotros/as)	valisteis	valíais
(ellos/ellas/ ustedes)	valieron	valían

GERUND	PAST PARTICIPLE
valiendo	valido

EXAMPLE PHRASES

No puede **valerse** por sí mismo. He can't look after himself.

¿Cuánto **vale** eso? How much is that?

¿**Vale**? OK?

No le **valió** de nada suplicar. Begging got her nowhere.

No **valía** la pena. It wasn't worth it.

Remember that subject pronouns are not used very often in Spanish.

valer

	FUTURE	CONDITIONAL
(yo)	valdré	valdría
(tú)	valdrás	valdrías
(él/ella/usted)	valdrá	valdría
(nosotros/as)	valdremos	valdríamos
(vosotros/as)	valdréis	valdríais
(ellos/ellas/ ustedes)	valdrán	valdrían

	PRESENT SUBJUNCTIVE	IMPERFECT SUBJUNCTIVE
(yo)	valga	valiera *or* valiese
(tú)	valgas	valieras *or* valieses
(él/ella/usted)	valga	valiera *or* valiese
(nosotros/as)	valgamos	valiéramos *or* valiésemos
(vosotros/as)	valgáis	valierais *or* valieseis
(ellos/ellas/ ustedes)	valgan	valieran *or* valiesen

IMPERATIVE
vale / valed

Use the present subjunctive in all cases other than these **tú** and **vosotros** affirmative forms.

EXAMPLE PHRASES
Valdrá unos 500 euros. It must cost around 500 euros.
Yo no **valdría** para enfermera. I'd make a hopeless nurse.
Valga lo que **valga**, lo compro. I'll buy it, no matter how much it costs.

Remember that subject pronouns are not used very often in Spanish.

vencer (to win; to beat)

	PRESENT		PRESENT PERFECT
(yo)	venzo		he vencido
(tú)	vences		has vencido
(él/ella/usted)	vence		ha vencido
(nosotros/as)	vencemos		hemos vencido
(vosotros/as)	vencéis		habéis vencido
(ellos/ellas/ ustedes)	vencen		han vencido

	PRETERITE		IMPERFECT
(yo)	vencí		vencía
(tú)	venciste		vencías
(él/ella/usted)	venció		vencía
(nosotros/as)	vencimos		vencíamos
(vosotros/as)	vencisteis		vencíais
(ellos/ellas/ ustedes)	vencieron		vencían

GERUND

venciendo

PAST PARTICIPLE

vencido

EXAMPLE PHRASES

Tienes que **vencer** el miedo. You must overcome your fear.

El plazo de matrícula **vence** mañana. Tomorrow is the last day for registration.

Finalmente le **ha vencido** el sueño. At last, he was overcome by sleep.

Vencimos por dos a uno. We won two-one.

Le **vencía** la curiosidad. His curiosity got the better of him.

Remember that subject pronouns are not used very often in Spanish.

vencer

	FUTURE	CONDITIONAL
(yo)	venceré	vencería
(tú)	vencerás	vencerías
(él/ella/usted)	vencerá	vencería
(nosotros/as)	venceremos	venceríamos
(vosotros/as)	venceréis	venceríais
(ellos/ellas/ ustedes)	vencerán	vencerían

	PRESENT SUBJUNCTIVE	IMPERFECT SUBJUNCTIVE
(yo)	venza	venciera or venciese
(tú)	venzas	vencieras or vencieses
(él/ella/usted)	venza	venclera or venciese
(nosotros/as)	venzamos	venciéramos or venciésemos
(vosotros/as)	venzáis	vencierais or vencieseis
(ellos/ellas/ ustedes)	venzan	vencieran or venciesen

IMPERATIVE
vence / venced

Use the present subjunctive in all cases other than these **tú** and **vosotros** affirmative forms.

EXAMPLE PHRASES
Nuestro ejército **vencerá**. Our army will be victorious.

No dejes que te **venza** la impaciencia. Don't let your impatience get the better of you.

venir (to come)

	PRESENT	PRESENT PERFECT
(yo)	vengo	he venido
(tú)	vienes	has venido
(él/ella/usted)	viene	ha venido
(nosotros/as)	venimos	hemos venido
(vosotros/as)	venís	habéis venido
(ellos/ellas/ustedes)	vienen	han venido

	PRETERITE	IMPERFECT
(yo)	vine	venía
(tú)	viniste	venías
(él/ella/usted)	vino	venía
(nosotros/as)	vinimos	veníamos
(vosotros/as)	vinisteis	veníais
(ellos/ellas/ustedes)	vinieron	venían

GERUND	PAST PARTICIPLE
viniendo	venido

EXAMPLE PHRASES

Vengo andando desde la playa. I've walked all the way from the beach.

La casa **se está viniendo** abajo. The house is falling apart.

Ha venido en taxi. He came by taxi.

Vinieron a verme al hospital. They came to see me in hospital.

La noticia **venía** en el periódico. The news was in the paper.

Remember that subject pronouns are not used very often in Spanish.

venir

	FUTURE	CONDITIONAL
(yo)	vendré	vendría
(tú)	vendrás	vendrías
(él/ella/usted)	vendrá	vendría
(nosotros/as)	vendremos	vendríamos
(vosotros/as)	vendréis	vendríais
(ellos/ellas/ ustedes)	vendrán	vendrían

	PRESENT SUBJUNCTIVE	IMPERFECT SUBJUNCTIVE
(yo)	venga	viniera or viniese
(tú)	vengas	vinieras or vinieses
(él/ella/usted)	venga	vinlera or viniese
(nosotros/as)	vengamos	viniéramos or viniésemos
(vosotros/as)	vengáis	vinierais or vinieseis
(ellos/ellas/ ustedes)	vengan	vinieran or viniesen

IMPERATIVE
ven / venid

*Use the present subjunctive in all cases other than these **tú** and **vosotros** affirmative forms.*

EXAMPLE PHRASES
¿**Vendrás** conmigo al cine? Will you come to the cinema with me?

A mí me **vendría** mejor el sábado. Saturday would be better for me.

¡**Venga**, vámonos! Come on, let's go!

No **vengas** si no quieres. Don't come if you don't want to.

¡**Ven** aquí! Come here!

Remember that subject pronouns are not used very often in Spanish.

ver (to see)

	PRESENT		PRESENT PERFECT
(yo)	veo		he visto
(tú)	ves		has visto
(él/ella/usted)	ve		ha visto
(nosotros/as)	vemos		hemos visto
(vosotros/as)	veis		habéis visto
(ellos/ellas/ ustedes)	ven		han visto

	PRETERITE		IMPERFECT
(yo)	vi		veía
(tú)	viste		veías
(él/ella/usted)	vio		veía
(nosotros/as)	vimos		veíamos
(vosotros/as)	visteis		veíais
(ellos/ellas/ ustedes)	vieron		veían

GERUND

viendo

PAST PARTICIPLE

visto

EXAMPLE PHRASES

No **veo** muy bien. I can't see very well.

Están viendo la televisión. They're watching television.

No **he visto** esa película. I haven't seen that film.

¿**Viste** lo que pasó? Did you see what happened?

Los **veía** a todos desde la ventana. I could see them all from the window.

Remember that subject pronouns are not used very often in Spanish.

ver

	FUTURE	CONDITIONAL
(yo)	veré	vería
(tú)	verás	verías
(él/ella/usted)	verá	vería
(nosotros/as)	veremos	veríamos
(vosotros/as)	veréis	veríais
(ellos/ellas/ ustedes)	verán	verían

	PRESENT SUBJUNCTIVE	IMPERFECT SUBJUNCTIVE
(yo)	vea	viera or viese
(tú)	veas	vieras or vieses
(él/ella/usted)	vea	viera or viese
(nosotros/as)	veamos	viéramos or viésemos
(vosotros/as)	veáis	vierais or vieseis
(ellos/ellas/ ustedes)	vean	vieran or viesen

IMPERATIVE

ve / ved

*Use the present subjunctive in all cases other than these **tú** and **vosotros** affirmative forms.*

EXAMPLE PHRASES

Eso ya se **verá**. We'll see.

No **veas** cómo se puso. He got incredibly worked up.

¡Si **vieras** cómo ha cambiado todo aquello! If you could see how everything has changed.

Veamos, ¿qué le pasa? Let's see now, what's the matter?

Remember that subject pronouns are not used very often in Spanish.

verter (to pour)

	PRESENT	PRESENT PERFECT
(yo)	vierto	he vertido
(tú)	viertes	has vertido
(él/ella/usted)	vierte	ha vertido
(nosotros/as)	vertemos	hemos vertido
(vosotros/as)	vertéis	habéis vertido
(ellos/ellas/ ustedes)	vierten	han vertido

	PRETERITE	IMPERFECT
(yo)	vertí	vertía
(tú)	vertiste	vertías
(él/ella/usted)	vertió	vertía
(nosotros/as)	vertimos	vertíamos
(vosotros/as)	vertisteis	vertíais
(ellos/ellas/ ustedes)	vertieron	vertían

GERUND	PAST PARTICIPLE
vertiendo	vertido

EXAMPLE PHRASES

Primero **viertes** el contenido del sobre en un recipiente. First you empty out the contents of the packet into a container.

Me **has vertido** agua encima. You've spilt water on me.

Vertió un poco de leche en el cazo. He poured some milk into the saucepan.

Se vertían muchos residuos radioactivos en el mar. A lot of nuclear waste was dumped in the sea.

Remember that subject pronouns are not used very often in Spanish.

verter

	FUTURE	CONDITIONAL
(yo)	verteré	vertería
(tú)	verterás	verterías
(él/ella/usted)	verterá	vertería
(nosotros/as)	verteremos	verteríamos
(vosotros/as)	verteréis	verteríais
(ellos/ellas/ustedes)	verterán	verterían

	PRESENT SUBJUNCTIVE	IMPERFECT SUBJUNCTIVE
(yo)	vierta	vertiera or vertiese
(tú)	viertas	vertieras or vertieses
(él/ella/usted)	vierta	vertiera or vertiese
(nosotros/as)	vertamos	vertiéramos or vertiésemos
(vosotros/as)	vertáis	vertierais or vertieseis
(ellos/ellas/ustedes)	viertan	vertieran or vertiesen

IMPERATIVE

vierte / verted

Use the present subjunctive in all cases other than these tú and vosotros affirmative forms.

EXAMPLE PHRASES

Se vertirán muchas lágrimas por esto. A lot of tears will be shed over this.

Ten cuidado no **viertas** el café. Be careful you don't knock over the coffee.

Por favor, **vierta** el contenido del bolso sobre la mesa. Please empty out your bag on the table.

Remember that subject pronouns are not used very often in Spanish.

vestir (to dress)

	PRESENT		PRESENT PERFECT
(yo)	visto		he vestido
(tú)	vistes		has vestido
(él/ella/usted)	viste		ha vestido
(nosotros/as)	vestimos		hemos vestido
(vosotros/as)	vestís		habéis vestido
(ellos/ellas/ ustedes)	visten		han vestido

	PRETERITE		IMPERFECT
(yo)	vestí		vestía
(tú)	vestiste		vestías
(él/ella/usted)	vistió		vestía
(nosotros/as)	vestimos		vestíamos
(vosotros/as)	vestisteis		vestíais
(ellos/ellas/ ustedes)	vistieron		vestían

GERUND	PAST PARTICIPLE
vistiendo	vestido

EXAMPLE PHRASES

Tengo una familia que **vestir** y que alimentar. I have a family to feed and clothe.

Viste bien. She's a smart dresser.

Estaba vistiendo a los niños. I was dressing the children.

Me he vestido en cinco minutos. It took me five minutes to get dressed.

Remember that subject pronouns are not used very often in Spanish.

vestir

	FUTURE	CONDITIONAL
(yo)	vestiré	vestiría
(tú)	vestirás	vestirías
(él/ella/usted)	vestirá	vestiría
(nosotros/as)	vestiremos	vestiríamos
(vosotros/as)	vestiréis	vestiríais
(ellos/ellas/ ustedes)	vestirán	vestirían

	PRESENT SUBJUNCTIVE	IMPERFECT SUBJUNCTIVE
(yo)	vista	vistiera or vistiese
(tú)	vistas	vistieras or vistieses
(él/ella/usted)	vista	vistiera or vistiese
(nosotros/as)	vistamos	vistiéramos or vistiésemos
(vosotros/as)	vistáis	vistierais or vistieseis
(ellos/ellas/ ustedes)	vistan	vistieran or vistiesen

IMPERATIVE
viste / vestid

Use the present subjunctive in all cases other than these **tú** and **vosotros** affirmative forms.

EXAMPLE PHRASES
Se vistió de princesa. She dressed up as a princess.
Vestía pantalones vaqueros y una camiseta. He was wearing jeans and a T-shirt.
Su padre **vestirá** de uniforme. Her father will wear a uniform.
¡**Vístete** de una vez! For the last time, go and get dressed!

Remember that subject pronouns are not used very often in Spanish.

vivir (to live)

	PRESENT		PRESENT PERFECT
(yo)	vivo		he vivido
(tú)	vives		has vivido
(él/ella/usted)	vive		ha vivido
(nosotros/as)	vivimos		hemos vivido
(vosotros/as)	vivís		habéis vivido
(ellos/ellas/ ustedes)	viven		han vivido

	PRETERITE		IMPERFECT
(yo)	viví		vivía
(tú)	viviste		vivías
(él/ella/usted)	vivió		vivía
(nosotros/as)	vivimos		vivíamos
(vosotros/as)	vivisteis		vivíais
(ellos/ellas/ ustedes)	vivieron		vivían

GERUND	PAST PARTICIPLE
viviendo	vivido

EXAMPLE PHRASES

Me gusta **vivir** sola. I like living on my own.

¿Dónde **vives**? Where do you live?

Siempre **han vivido** muy bien. They've always had a very comfortable life.

Vivían de su pensión. They lived on his pension.

Remember that subject pronouns are not used very often in Spanish.

vivir

	FUTURE	CONDITIONAL
(yo)	viviré	viviría
(tú)	vivirás	vivirías
(él/ella/usted)	vivirá	viviría
(nosotros/as)	viviremos	viviríamos
(vosotros/as)	viviréis	viviríais
(ellos/ellas/ ustedes)	vivirán	vivirían

	PRESENT SUBJUNCTIVE	IMPERFECT SUBJUNCTIVE
(yo)	viva	viviera or viviese
(tú)	vivas	vivieras or vivieses
(él/ella/usted)	viva	viviera or vivlese
(nosotros/as)	vivamos	viviéramos or viviésemos
(vosotros/as)	viváis	vivierais or vivieseis
(ellos/ellas/ ustedes)	vivan	vivieran or viviesen

IMPERATIVE

vive / vivid

Use the present subjunctive in all cases other than these **tú** and **vosotros** affirmative forms.

EXAMPLE PHRASES

Viviremos en el centro de la ciudad. We'll live in the city centre.

Si pudiéramos, **viviríamos** en el campo. We'd live in the country if we could.

Si **vivierais** más cerca, nos veríamos más a menudo. We'd see each other more often if you lived nearer.

¡**Viva**! Hurray!

Remember that subject pronouns are not used very often in Spanish.

volcar (to overturn)

	PRESENT	PRESENT PERFECT
(yo)	vuelco	he volcado
(tú)	vuelcas	has volcado
(él/ella/usted)	vuelca	ha volcado
(nosotros/as)	volcamos	hemos volcado
(vosotros/as)	volcáis	habéis volcado
(ellos/ellas/ ustedes)	vuelcan	han volcado

	PRETERITE	IMPERFECT
(yo)	volqué	volcaba
(tú)	volcaste	volcabas
(él/ella/usted)	volcó	volcaba
(nosotros/as)	volcamos	volcábamos
(vosotros/as)	volcasteis	volcabais
(ellos/ellas/ ustedes)	volcaron	volcaban

GERUND	PAST PARTICIPLE
volcando	volcado

EXAMPLE PHRASES

Se vuelca en su trabajo. She throws herself into her work.

Se han volcado con nosotros. They've been very kind to us.

El camión **volcó**. The lorry overturned.

Remember that subject pronouns are not used very often in Spanish.

volcar

	FUTURE	CONDITIONAL
(yo)	volcaré	volcaría
(tú)	volcarás	volcarías
(él/ella/usted)	volcará	volcaría
(nosotros/as)	volcaremos	volcaríamos
(vosotros/as)	volcaréis	volcaríais
(ellos/ellas/ ustedes)	volcarán	volcarían

	PRESENT SUBJUNCTIVE	IMPERFECT SUBJUNCTIVE
(yo)	vuelque	volcara or volcase
(tú)	vuelques	volcaras or volcases
(él/ella/usted)	vuelque	volcara or volcase
(nosotros/as)	volquemos	volcáramos or volcásemos
(vosotros/as)	volquéis	volcarais or volcaseis
(ellos/ellas/ ustedes)	vuelquen	volcaran or volcasen

IMPERATIVE
vuelca / volcad

Use the present subjunctive in all cases other than these tú and vosotros affirmative forms.

EXAMPLE PHRASES
Si sigues moviéndote, harás que **vuelque** el bote. If you keep on moving like that, you'll make the boat capsize.

Ten cuidado, no **vuelques** el vaso. Be careful not to knock over the glass.

Vuelca el contenido sobre la cama. Empty the contents onto the bed.

Remember that subject pronouns are not used very often in Spanish.

volver (to return)

	PRESENT		PRESENT PERFECT
(yo)	vuelvo		he vuelto
(tú)	vuelves		has vuelto
(él/ella/usted)	vuelve		ha vuelto
(nosotros/as)	volvemos		hemos vuelto
(vosotros/as)	volvéis		habéis vuelto
(ellos/ellas/ ustedes)	vuelven		han vuelto

	PRETERITE		IMPERFECT
(yo)	volví		volvía
(tú)	volviste		volvías
(él/ella/usted)	volvió		volvía
(nosotros/as)	volvimos		volvíamos
(vosotros/as)	volvisteis		volvíais
(ellos/ellas/ ustedes)	volvieron		volvían

GERUND

volviendo

PAST PARTICIPLE

vuelto

EXAMPLE PHRASES

Mi padre **vuelve** mañana. My father's coming back tomorrow.

Se **está volviendo** muy pesado. He's becoming a real pain in the neck.

Ha vuelto a casa. He's gone back home.

Me volví para ver quién era. I turned round to see who it was.

Volvía agotado de trabajar. I used to come back exhausted from work.

Remember that subject pronouns are not used very often in Spanish.

volver

	FUTURE	CONDITIONAL
(yo)	volveré	volvería
(tú)	volverás	volverías
(él/ella/usted)	volverá	volvería
(nosotros/as)	volveremos	volveríamos
(vosotros/as)	volveréis	volveríais
(ellos/ellas/ ustedes)	volverán	volverían

	PRESENT SUBJUNCTIVE	IMPERFECT SUBJUNCTIVE
(yo)	vuelva	volviera or volviese
(tú)	vuelvas	volvieras or volvieses
(él/ella/usted)	vuelva	volviera or volviese
(nosotros/as)	volvamos	volviéramos or volviésemos
(vosotros/as)	volváis	volvierais or volvieseis
(ellos/ellas/ ustedes)	vuelvan	volvieran or volviesen

IMPERATIVE
vuelve / volved

Use the present subjunctive in all cases other than these tú and vosotros affirmative forms.

EXAMPLE PHRASES
Todo **volverá** a la normalidad. Everything will go back to normal.

Yo **volvería** a intentarlo. I'd try again.

No quiero que **vuelvas** a las andadas. I don't want you to go back to your old ways.

No **vuelvas** por aquí. Don't come back here.

¡**Vuelve** a la cama! Go back to bed!

Remember that subject pronouns are not used very often in Spanish.

zurcir (to darn)

	PRESENT	PRESENT PERFECT
(yo)	zurzo	he zurcido
(tú)	zurces	has zurcido
(él/ella/usted)	zurce	ha zurcido
(nosotros/as)	zurcimos	hemos zurcido
(vosotros/as)	zurcís	habéis zurcido
(ellos/ellas/ustedes)	zurcen	han zurcido

	PRETERITE	IMPERFECT
(yo)	zurcí	zurcía
(tú)	zurciste	zurcías
(él/ella/usted)	zurció	zurcía
(nosotros/as)	zurcimos	zurcíamos
(vosotros/as)	zurcisteis	zurcíais
(ellos/ellas/ustedes)	zurcieron	zurcían

GERUND	PAST PARTICIPLE
zurciendo	zurcido

EXAMPLE PHRASES

¿Quién le **zurce** las camisas? Who darns his shirts?

Se pasa el día **zurciéndole** la ropa. She spends the whole day darning his clothes.

Remember that subject pronouns are not used very often in Spanish.

zurcir

	FUTURE	CONDITIONAL
(yo)	zurciré	zurciría
(tú)	zurcirás	zurcirías
(él/ella/usted)	zurcirá	zurciría
(nosotros/as)	zurciremos	zurciríamos
(vosotros/as)	zurciréis	zurciríais
(ellos/ellas/ ustedes)	zurcirán	zurcirían

	PRESENT SUBJUNCTIVE	IMPERFECT SUBJUNCTIVE
(yo)	zurza	zurciera or zurciese
(tú)	zurzas	zurcieras or zurcieses
(él/ella/usted)	zurza	zurciera or zurciese
(nosotros/as)	zurzamos	zurciéramos or zurciésemos
(vosotros/as)	zurzáis	zurcierais or zurcieseis
(ellos/ellas/ ustedes)	zurzan	zurcieran or zurciesen

IMPERATIVE
zurce / zurcid

Use the present subjunctive in all cases other than these tú and vosotros affirmative forms.

EXAMPLE PHRASES
¡Que te **zurzan**! Get lost!

How to use the Verb Index

The verbs in bold are the model verbs which you will find in the Verb Tables. All the other verbs follow one of these patterns, so the number next to each verb indicates which pattern fits this particular verb. For example, **acampar** (*to camp*) follows the same pattern as **hablar** (number 118 in the Verb Tables).

All the verbs are in alphabetical order. Superior numbers (¹ etc) refer you to notes on page 247. These notes explain any differences between verbs and their model.

Verb index 245

Notes

[1] The verbs **anochecer, atardecer, granizar, helar, llover, nevar, nublarse** and **tronar** are used almost exclusively in the infinitive and third person singular forms.

[2] The **past participle** of the verb **pudrir** is **podrido**.

Collins

easy learning Spanish

Easy Learning Spanish Dictionary
978-0-00-753094-6 £9.99

Easy Learning Spanish Conversation
[Second edition] 978-0-00-811197-7 £7.99

Easy Learning Spanish Grammar
978-0-00-814201-8 £7.99

Easy Learning Spanish Verbs
978-0-00-815843-9 £7.99

Easy Learning Spanish Vocabulary
978-0-00-748393-8 £7.99

Easy Learning Spanish Idioms
978-0-00-733736-1 £9.99

Easy Learning Complete Spanish Grammar, Verbs and Vocabulary
(3 books in 1) 978-0-00-814173-8 £12.99

Easy Learning Spanish Grammar & Practice
978-0-00-814164-6 £9.99

Easy Learning Spanish Verbs & Practice
978-0-00-814209-4 £10.99

Available to buy from all good booksellers and online.
Many titles are also available as ebooks.
www.collins.co.uk/languagesupport

facebook.com/collinsdictionary

@collinsdict